DISCOVER

The Prismatic Product System™

A three-phased system for transforming customer insight into successful products.

Book 1: DISCOVER

Defining a market, understanding customer needs and building a living customer insight system

Book 2: STRATEGIZE

Translating insight into a winning market position supported by clear product strategy

Book 3: EXECUTE

Guiding product teams to execute a product strategy to design and develop products engineered to succeed in the market.

Book 1 of The Prismatic Product System

DISCOVER

From Customer Noise to Product Signal

A Jobs-to-be-Done Guide to Customer Interviews and Product Insight

W. Scott Burleson

DISCOVER

This book is a work of nonfiction. Any references to real individuals, organizations, or products are used for illustrative purposes only.

First edition.
PAPERBACK
ISBN: 978-1-972240-05-2

Cover design by Palustris Publishing
Interior design by Palustris Publishing

Published by Palustris Publishing
North Carolina, USA

For more information, visit:
www.WScottBurleson.com

Dedication

To Elizabeth, Katie and Noelle

It is a mistake to look too far ahead. The chain of destiny can only be grasped one link at a time.

Winston S. Churchill

TABLE OF CONTENTS

How to Use This Book ix

Introduction xi

I. FOUNDATIONS OF DISCOVERY 1

Chapter 1: Problem Space vs. Solution Space 3

Chapter 2: Divergence and Convergence 17

Chapter 3: Job Success Criteria 27

Chapter 4: The Jobs-to-be-Done Pyramid™ 37

Chapter 5: The Discovery Engine 53

II. STEP 1: UNCOVER CUSTOMER NEEDS 67

Chapter 6: Task 1, Define the Market Lens 71

Chapter 7: Task 2, Map the Job 83

Chapter 8: Task 3, Generate Initial Job Success Criteria 97

Chapter 9: Task 4, Prepare for Customer Interviews — Getting Started 117

Chapter 10: Task 4, Prepare for Customer Interviews — The Moderator's Mindset 131

Chapter 11: Task 4, Prepare for Customer Interviews — Sampling 145

Chapter 12: Task 4, Prepare for Customer Interviews — Discussion Guides 163

Chapter 13: Task 5, Conduct Customer Interviews — The 3D Probing Model 191

Chapter 14: Task 5, Conduct Customer Interviews — Probing Identity and Emotion 227

Chapter 15: Task 5, Conduct Customer Interviews — Bringing It All Together 241

Chapter 16: Task 6, Refine Job Success Criteria 257

III. STEP 2: RANK OPPORTUNITIES 273

Chapter 17: Task 7, Design the Survey 275

Chapter 18: Task 8, Field the Survey 295

Chapter 19: Task 9, Identify Opportunities 317

IV. STEP 3: SYNTHESIZE INSIGHTS 335

Chapter 20: Task 10, Scan for Signals 337

Chapter 21: Task 11, Build the Signal Translator 347

Chapter 22: Task 12, Maintain the Signal Translator 361

V. EPILOGUE: From Needs to Product Strategy — A Preview of STRATEGIZE 377

About the Author 383

How to Use This Book

DISCOVER IS WRITTEN FOR A RANGE OF READERS, from hands-on practitioners to executives responsible for guiding product and innovation strategy. You do not need to become a full-time practitioner of the methods in this book to benefit from it. But you do need to understand how customer insight is built, and how it should inform decisions.

If you are a practitioner, such as a product manager, researcher, or marketer, this book provides the detail required to put the DISCOVER process into practice. You will find step-by-step guidance on defining a Market Lens, preparing and conducting interviews, translating problems into Job Success Criteria, designing and fielding surveys, and identifying high-value opportunities. The methods are specific and structured so that you can apply them directly in your own work.

If you are a leader or executive, your role is different, but critical. You may not conduct interviews or build surveys yourself, but you are responsible for ensuring that your organization develops a knowledge base of customer needs. Focus on how the system works as a whole. As you meet the Big Sky Outdoors team in the ongoing case, note how discovery unfolds in real conditions: messy, iterative, and often uncertain. The case is designed to help you see what good looks like, and where your own organization may fall short.

Regardless of your role, you may also find value in using this book to strengthen a specific skill. Whether you are looking to improve how you interview customers, evaluate research, or interpret survey results, the structure of DISCOVER allows you to focus on individual components without losing sight of the broader system.

At its core, DISCOVER is about building something most organizations lack: a living system of insight. Not merely a one-time study, not a collection of disconnected findings, but a continuously maintained system. It becomes the foundation for the countless decisions across strategy, product, marketing, and even sales.

You can read this book from start to finish to follow the full process, or return to specific sections as needed. But the greatest value comes from seeing how the pieces connect. Each step builds on the last, and together they form a practice designed to replace uncertainty with confidence.

Introduction

Your Mission: Build a Market-Winning Backpacking Tent

THE ASSIGNMENT ARRIVED ON TUESDAY MORNING.

Shelton, product manager for backpacking tents at Big Sky Outdoors, had been summoned to meet with the CEO. The conversation was brief and direct. Big Sky had built a solid reputation among serious backpackers for dependable, thoughtfully engineered gear. But growth had stalled. Newer brands were gaining ground with the most passionate segment of the market: experienced hikers willing to pay premium prices for equipment they trusted in demanding conditions.

Leadership had decided that it was time to build the next-generation backpacking tent. One that wins.

Shelton walked back to his desk, understanding exactly what was expected. The new tent had to outperform the competition, attract serious backpackers, command a premium price, and restore Big Sky's momentum. Engineering needed direction. Marketing needed a story. Sales needed a product customers would seek out by name.

The pressure was immediate, and the clock was ticking.

What Shelton did not yet have was an in-focus picture of the market. Something beyond opinions, assumptions, or the loudest voices from last quarter's sales calls. A real picture: structured, verified, and confident enough to build on.

By the end of this process, he would.

The Real Challenge

At first glance, the assignment sounds straightforward. Build a better tent.

But anyone who has worked in product development knows how quickly that simple sentence begins to break apart. Better for whom? Better in what situation? Better by what standard?

These questions sit at the heart of every serious innovation effort. Teams are routinely asked to build the next generation of a product. Or they are asked to just build a better one. But they lack a disciplined way to define what 'better' means to the customer.

The result is often a product built on internal assumptions, competitive imitation, or the loudest requests, rather than an understanding of what customers are truly trying to accomplish.

That is where Shelton and his team found themselves. They had a mandate. What they did not yet have was a method for turning that mandate into insight. Nor did they know how to translate that insight into a product strategy.

This book is about what they did and the method they used.

What This Book Is About

DISCOVER teaches a disciplined approach to understanding customer needs, not through guesswork, mere brainstorming, or scattered feedback. Instead, it delivers a structured process that produces clear, measurable, and actionable insight.

The method is grounded in Jobs-to-be-Done philosophy, the idea that customers do not simply buy products. They hire products to accomplish a job. Understanding that job and how customers measure success is the foundation of progress.

The framework used throughout this book is **The Prismatic Product System™**, which organizes innovation work into three connected phases: DISCOVER, STRATEGIZE, and EXECUTE.

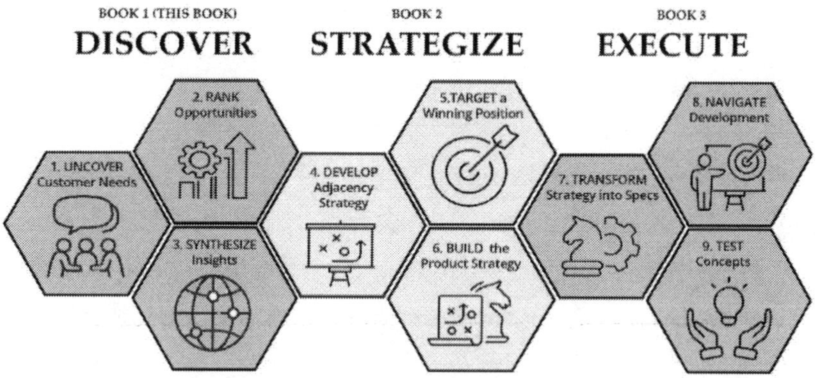

The full name of the system is also its acronym: PRISM, which stands for Problem Research Into Signals Methodology. Throughout this book, we'll refer to it simply as Prism.

Book 1 (This book): DISCOVER

This book focuses entirely on the first phase, DISCOVER. It answers three fundamental questions:

- What are customers trying to accomplish? (Step 1)
- What are their priorities? (Step 2)
- How confident are we in what we know? (Step 3)

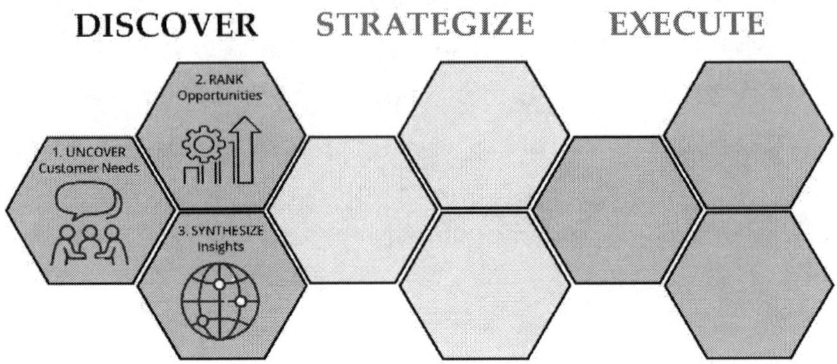

Answering those questions with rigor and structure produces something concrete. The result is The Signal Translator™, an artifact that makes customer insight operational. It is a living synthesis framework that converts fragmented signals from multiple sources into a single, cross-validated picture of what customers need and what the market will reward. By the time Shelton's team reaches the end of this process, they will have built one.

The deeper promise is not just a better research deliverable. It is a different way for a team to see the market together. Instead of scattered observations living in separate conversations, slide decks, support logs, sales notes, and executive opinions, the team begins to work from a shared picture of customer need. The Prism does not eliminate judgment, but it gives judgment a stronger foundation. It helps the organization move from disconnected signals to defined, actionable insight.

DISCOVER is the first phase of Prism, but it is not the whole system. The work begun here continues through two additional phases: STRATEGIZE and EXECUTE.

Book 2 (Next in the series): STRATEGIZE

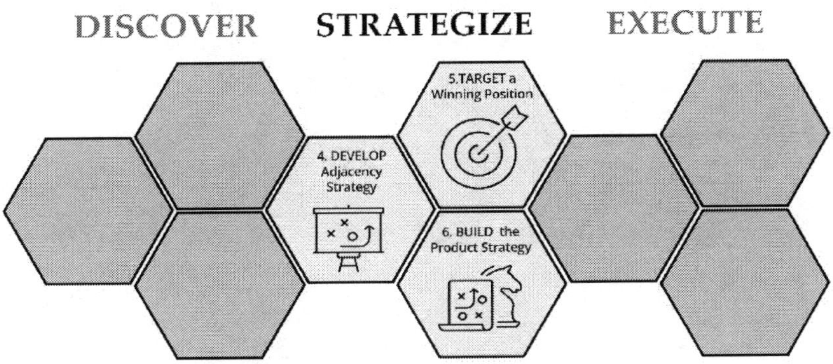

STRATEGIZE is the second phase and is the topic of the next book in this series. Using the insight generated during discovery, teams make decisions about which opportunities to pursue, how to position their offering relative to the competitive landscape, and where to invest innovation effort for maximum impact. A strategy that is not grounded in discovery is guesswork. Discovery that never informs strategy is an academic exercise.

Book 3 (Final book in the series): EXECUTE

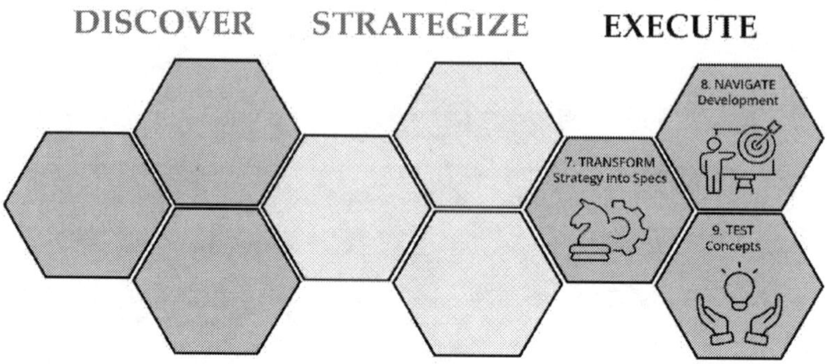

EXECUTE is the third phase and is the final book in this series. With a clear strategic direction established, teams design and deliver the solution. They can translate insight and intent into something that can be built, shipped, and experienced by customers.

DISCOVER is where the foundation is laid. Everything in STRATEGIZE and EXECUTE depends on the quality of the work done here. Together, the three phases form a complete path from customer understanding to market-winning innovation.

How This Book Is Structured

The book follows a progression from concepts to method to synthesis, organized into three acts.

We begin with the conceptual foundations of discovery. Before Shelton's team conducts a single interview or analyzes a single data point, they need to understand how to think about customer needs. That is, they must consider why innovation must begin in the problem space rather than the solution space, how disciplined discovery moves through cycles of exploration and focus, and how customers judge whether a product performs well.

Next, we shift from principles to practice. This is where the book becomes method-driven. Working step by step through the Discovery Engine, the structured workflow that powers the DISCOVER phase, the reader follows the Big Sky team as they define their market, map the customer's job, generate and refine Job Success Criteria, conduct interviews, and ultimately identify the strongest opportunities for innovation.

In the final act, the work synthesizes into something durable. The team takes everything gathered across all prior steps and then builds the Signal Translator™: a structured framework that maps each customer need against multiple independent signal sources, normalizes them with a shared scale, and produces cross-validated confidence in what matters most. A Signal Translator built well does not become obsolete when the study ends. Maintained over time, it becomes the team's ongoing market intelligence system.

Throughout all three acts, the Big Sky case serves as the running example. The team's work is shown in realistic detail, including the assumptions they start with, the surprises they encounter, and the moments when the market reveals something they did not expect.

A Word on Expectations

When done correctly, Discovery does not produce product specifications or feature lists. It produces something far more valuable first: understanding of what customers are trying to accomplish, how they judge success, and where current solutions fall short.

That knowledge becomes the platform for strategy. Teams that enter strategy and execution with discovery behind them make sharper choices, argue from evidence rather than opinion, and build with greater confidence that they are solving the right problem.

This work takes time. Many executives would rather skip past it. Some of what discovery reveals will be uncomfortable. Assumptions will be challenged. Priorities will shift. But the teams willing to follow the evidence are the ones most likely to build something special.

A Note on the Word "Product"

Throughout this book, and throughout Prism, the word *product* is used broadly. It does not refer only to a physical object sitting on a shelf or in a warehouse. It refers to any solution a company offers to help a customer accomplish a job.

That includes services. A checking account is a product. So is a home insurance policy, a consulting engagement, a software subscription, or a logistics contract. In each case, a customer is hiring that offering to accomplish something, and the provider's job is to make sure it performs well.

This matters because the discovery methods in this book apply equally across all of these contexts. Job maps, Job Success Criteria, and the Discovery Engine were not designed for manufacturers alone. They work wherever a customer has a job-to-be-done and a solution is being offered to help them do it. Whether that solution is made of fabric and aluminum or delivered over a phone call makes no difference to the underlying logic.

So, whenever you see the word *product* in these pages, read it as *solution*. The principles hold regardless of what form that solution takes.

Where the Journey Begins

You've met Shelton. Soon you will meet the rest of the Big Sky team and accompany them through the earliest stages of discovery. Like most product teams, they begin where thinking naturally starts: with products, features, and competitive comparisons.

The journey ahead moves them somewhere different. Not because that starting point is wrong, but because building something the market wants requires *learning what customers are trying to do before deciding what to build.* That shift in perspective is where this book begins.

Where We Begin

We begin with Part I: Foundations of Discovery. There, we meet the Big Sky Outdoors team and explore the principles that separate disciplined discovery from guesswork.

I. FOUNDATIONS OF DISCOVERY

We begin with the Foundations of Discovery, spanning five chapters.

Chapter 1 establishes the distinction between problem space and solution space, and introduces Jobs-to-be-Done as the philosophical framework that defines the relationship between customers and the products they hire to perform a job.

Chapter 2 explores the cadence of divergence and convergence, and why managing their distinct purposes is the heart of rigorous discovery work.

Chapter 3 introduces Job Success Criteria: what they are, why they exist, the compression problem they solve, and the precision they enable.

Chapter 4 presents the Jobs-to-be-Done Pyramid, the structural model that organizes customer motivation across multiple levels of abstraction.

Chapter 5 introduces the Discovery Engine, the end-to-end process that runs through the remainder of the book. It is the mechanism that transforms customer conversations, survey data, and organizational intelligence into a Signal Translator: a living insight system capable of grounding product strategy for years beyond the initial study.

The journey begins with the Big Sky Outdoors team gathered for their first product meeting.

Chapter 1: Problem Space vs. Solution Space

Ideas, Ideas, and More Ideas.

SHELTON STOOD AT THE FRONT OF THE CONFERENCE ROOM holding a marker. The rest of the team had already started talking.

Luis leaned forward in his chair. "If we can shave 200 grams off the frame without losing strength, we'll immediately stand out. Weight was everything last year at the Appalachian Trail's 'Trail Days' event."

Jenna nodded. "Sure. Weight matters, but setup speed might matter even more. People hate complicated tents. I know that I do."

Tom, who spent half his time visiting retailers and hiking trails, jumped in next. "I hear people complain about condensation all the time. Waking up to water dripping on their face. Ventilation could be a huge selling point. That new Outdoor Owls company just released a so-called 'no-condensation' tent. If we let them get too far ahead, we'll never catch up. Those guys are always innovating."

Jenna jumped back in, "That matters more in the east than the west, though. Nobody talks about that in Glacier, or along the PCT. Or not as much, anyway."

Tom rolled his eyes and exhaled a slow breath.

Shelton began writing on the whiteboard as the ideas came faster.

Lighter materials. Faster setup. Better ventilation. Stronger poles. Larger vestibules. Improved weather protection.

Within minutes, the board was full.

Luis stepped back and smiled. *"Not bad for a first meeting."*

Shelton stared at the board for a moment. Something was bothering him. He appreciated the input, but something was not right. The list looked productive. The conversation had been good, if not a bit stressful from some disagreements. Everyone in the room knew backpacking gear, and the ideas seemed reasonable.

He uncapped the marker again and held it over the whiteboard. Then he asked a simple question.

"How do we know these are the *right improvements*?"

The room went quiet.

Tom broke the silence. "Well... customers ask for them. These are things we hear about. And most of us have been in this game a long time."

Shelton nodded slowly. "Fair enough. They do ask for them... but do we always know for what reason? Like, why do they want stronger poles? What are they trying to do with those larger vestibules? And do we really understand the conditions driving the need for ventilation? The east vs. west thing is part of it. But is it all of it?"

No one answered.

They had plenty of ideas. But even more questions. What they certainly did not have was an understanding of the problems.

The Solution-Space Trap

What happened in that conference room is not unusual. It happens in product organizations everywhere, across every category and industry. Teams sit down to innovate and begin, almost instinctively, by listing their ideas. *Their solutions.*

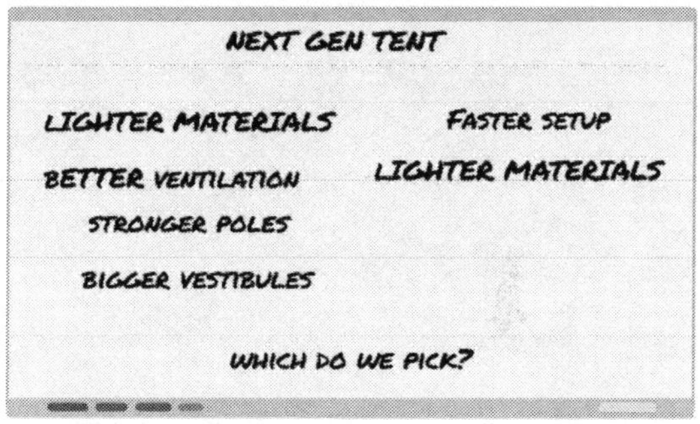

They brainstorm features. They talk about competitors. They recite customer requests. In cycles, new technologies are described as amazing or useless. This feels productive because it creates output quickly, such as lists, sketches, concepts, and debate.

But there's a problem. When teams begin in solution space, they're tempted to make decisions before they've earned the right to make them. The ideas on the whiteboard might be good. They may even be things customers have asked for. But without first understanding the customer's underlying issue, there's no way to know whether those ideas address anything that actually matters.

If the team were to push forward, the result would likely be innovation built on opinions rather than market data. Features get prioritized based on what engineers find interesting, what marketing believes will resonate, or what the competition appears to be doing. This can work on occasion, but not reliably. More often, it produces something technically impressive that fails to move the needle.

Shelton's team was not on the verge of an unusual mistake. They were doing what product teams are rewarded for: moving fast and chasing momentum. The problem was not effort. It was the lack of exploration into the customer's world.

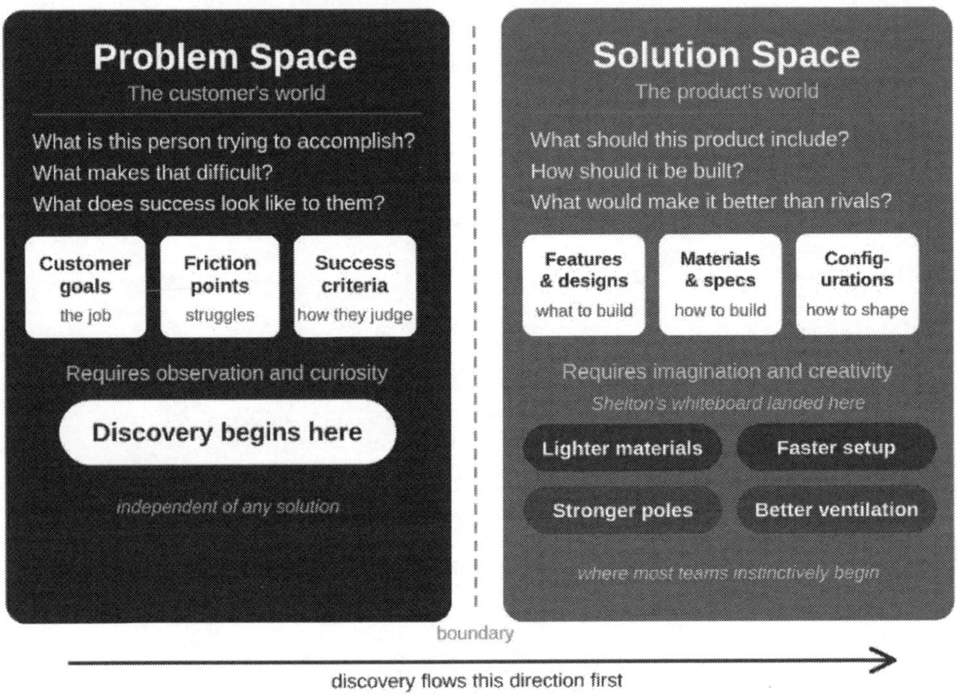

Two Different Realms

The problem begins when teams fail to distinguish between two fundamentally different modes of thinking.

Solution space is the world of products: features, materials, technologies, and design choices. Questions in solution space sound like: What should this product include? What should the interface be? What features should it have? What should it look like? This is where engineering creativity happens, where design decisions are made, and where product conversations naturally drift. It is a necessary and valuable mode of thinking, but it is only half the picture.

Problem space is an entirely different territory. It is the realm of the customer's aspirations, their goals, their struggles, the conditions they work in, and the standards they use to judge whether something is working. Questions in problem space sound like: What is this person trying to do? What makes that difficult? What does success look like? Problem space is a parallel universe. It is about the customer's situation, independent of any means.

The distinction matters. Designing a solution requires imagination and creativity. Defining a problem requires observation and curiosity. Teams that skip directly to solution thinking in order to make quick decisions are guessing. They are designing for a problem they have assumed rather than one they have fully diagnosed. And this assumption often goes unstated, with multiple team members having different mental models of what that problem is.

Designing a solution requires imagination and creativity. Defining a problem requires observation and curiosity.

When Shelton looked at his whiteboard full of ideas, every item on it lived in solution space. Lighter materials. Better ventilation. Stronger poles. These were answers to questions the team had not yet asked.

The Next Generation Tent Project

Let's look at the Big Sky whiteboard more closely.

The team's ideas were solution-space thinking: lighter poles, stronger fabric, a redesigned vestibule, and improved ventilation. Each one describes something the product might become.

But underneath those ideas, the real customer challenges might look quite different. A backpacker arriving at camp after a long day, racing to pitch a tent before a storm rolls in, is not thinking about pole weight. They are trying to get shelter up fast before the rain starts. A hiker struggling to stake a tent into rocky alpine ground is not thinking about metal alloys. They're frustrated that the tent will not anchor properly and are worried about overnight stability.

These are problem-space realities. They describe what customers are experiencing: the frustration, the uncertainty, the moments where the job becomes difficult. The solution ideas on the whiteboard may or may not address these realities. Without understanding the problem first, there's no way to know.

A team that designs a lighter tent *has resolved an engineering challenge.* A team that designs a tent that goes up reliably in deteriorating conditions *has solved a customer problem.* Those are not the same thing, and the market rewards the latter far more than the former.

You've Got to Keep Them Separated

Beginning in the problem space does not mean avoiding solutions. In time, of course, the point is to build something. But the sequence matters.

When teams understand the customer's problem before designing the solution, they are in a stronger position. They know what they are optimizing for. They can evaluate design choices against a clear standard: Does this decision help customers accomplish the job more successfully? They can identify which improvements will be valued and which will be ignored.

When teams skip problem space and move directly to solutions, they lose this orientation. Design decisions get made against internal, often disjointed, criteria rather than customer criteria. The resulting product may be well-built, but it's built for an assumed market rather than an actual one.

The discipline of starting in problem space is not instinctive for most product teams. It requires resisting the pull toward action, toward generating, building and shipping. It requires sitting with uncertainty long enough to understand the customer's experience before reaching for answers. That is difficult in companies that reward speed and visible progress.

But the teams willing to invest in that discipline consistently make better decisions downstream. Discovery done well does not slow innovation; it redirects it toward problems worth solving. This concept of the customer's goals, objectives, and problems to be solved is so profound that the innovation world has created a term for it, **the customer's job-to-be-done**.

Jobs-to-be-Done: The Structure of Market Problems

Once a team commits to starting in problem space, a new question immediately arises: What are we trying to understand?

The customer's world is complex. People buy products for overlapping reasons, and their needs are frequently obscured by the language they use to describe them. When customers are asked what they want, they tend to answer with solution attributes: "make it lighter," "make it stronger." Or they ask for vague benefits such as "Make it easier to use." Neither response reveals the underlying structure of the problem, not because customers cannot state their needs, but because the questions are asking customers to do something they are not well-positioned to do: design a solution.

It's important to establish what customers can, and cannot, reliably tell us. A simple rule helps: ask for the pain and the past, not the prescription.

Customers are reliable sources of information about two things:

1. **Their problems** — what is difficult, frustrating, risky, slow, confusing, or inadequate.
2. **Their experiences** — what they have actually done, seen, felt, tried, avoided, or struggled through.

In other words, customers are experts in their own lived reality.

But customers are much less reliable when asked for three other kinds of information:

1. **The best solution** — what product, feature, design, or technology would work best.
2. **The imagined future** — how they would respond to things they have not experienced.
3. **The irrelevant or unnoticed** — aspects of a product or situation they do not understand, notice, or care about.

A patient walking into a doctor's office may not know what medication they need, but they usually know what prompted them to make the appointment. They can describe the pain and the past. The diagnosis and treatment are the doctor's role.

It would be poor practice for a doctor to ask the patient for a list of desired medications. And yet, that is often what product teams do when they ask customers what products or features they want.

This is where Jobs-to-be-Done becomes useful. It gives teams a structure for listening to customers without asking them to design the answer.

Jobs-to-be-Done is a methodology to operationalize this thinking. By keeping problem space and solution space separate, the framework preserves the distinction between the types of information customers can reliably provide and the types they cannot.

The idea is this: A customer hires a product to accomplish a job. This reinforces the core principle: customers are the authority on their job-to-be-done and on what makes it difficult. The product team's role is to design the solution. Problems arise when those roles are mixed, when customers are asked to define features, or when teams assume they already understand the problem without properly uncovering it through disciplined questioning.

Customers do not simply purchase products. *They hire them to accomplish something.* A job-to-be-done is a customer's goal, objective, or problem to be solved. It's the progress they seek. The product is just the means.

Jobs-to-be-Done is a core principle of Prism and everything we'll discuss in this book and beyond.

For the backpacking tent market, the job is not "own a tent." Nobody buys a tent for the joy of owning it. The job is something more fundamental, such as *staying protected from the elements while traveling through demanding terrain*. That is what customers are hiring a tent to help them to do. The tent is merely one solution to that job. Future materials, shelter systems, and technologies not yet invented will be other ways to serve the same job. But the job itself will not change significantly with the passage of time.

A Job-to-be-Done is Stable Over Time

Products evolve. Technologies change. Customer preferences shift in response to new options. But the underlying job, the fundamental goal the customer is trying to accomplish, persists. Teams that understand the job are pursuing something durable. Teams that study only current products and current preferences are studying something that may look quite different in a few short years.

For Shelton's team, framing the work around the job reoriented everything. They were no longer going to ask how to build a better tent. They were going to explore how to help backpackers stay protected from the elements. Their investigation must reveal what stands in the way of that goal.

How to Write a Job Statement

Understanding what a job-to-be-done is raises an immediate practical question: how does a team actually express a job in a way that is useful? In practice, teams struggle with this more than they expect. A job statement is a statement of action. It begins with a verb.

Consider the kinds of statements that typically emerge in product discussions:

Lightweight tent. Better ventilation. Faster setup. Stronger poles.

These are not jobs. They describe desired attributes, or what a product might become. Now compare them to JTBD statements written as actions:

- Carry shelter during a backpacking trip.
- Set up shelter at a campsite.

- Maintain a protected sleeping environment overnight.
- Secure shelter to the ground.

Each begins with a verb. Each describes something the customer is trying to accomplish. And none of them assume how that result should be achieved. When a team writes "better ventilation," they have already decided how to solve the problem. Conversely, when they write "maintain a dry sleeping environment," they are focused on the problem itself. However, the job does not yet define how success is measured; that comes later.

Job statements can also be written at different levels of scope. At a broad level:

Stay protected from the elements while traveling through demanding terrain.

This captures the overarching goal, the reason the product category exists at all. At a narrower level, the same reality breaks into its component actions:

Select a location to set up shelter. Assemble the shelter structure. Anchor the shelter to the ground. Enter and exit the shelter. Pack the shelter for transport.

These are not competing jobs. They are different views into the same objective. The broader statement defines the aim; the narrower statements describe what accomplishing it actually requires.

Context can also be added without invalidating a job statement. It simply narrows the scope. *Set up shelter* is broad. *Set up shelter on uneven ground* directs attention to a specific situation. Both are valid, depending on what the team is trying to understand.

One final note: the right level of job to focus on is not an abstract question. It's a practical one. The job a team chooses to anchor their discovery work shapes everything that follows, such as the questions asked in interviews, the criteria defined later, and the opportunities identified. That is why it matters to write job statements with care. A team that frames its work around *carry shelter for a backpacking trip* will explore a very different terrain than one that frames it around *pitch a tent.* In chapter 4, The Jobs-to-be-Done Pyramid, the Big Sky team will learn the nuances of this framing.

A Key Principle of Discovery

The lesson from that first Big Sky meeting was not that the team's ideas were wrong. Some of them likely were good ones. The lesson was that while ideas generated before the problem may be valid, they might not be big issues. They are hypotheses at best, mere guesses.

We all have ideas, often born from industry experience, or even our thoughts as customers ourselves. There's nothing wrong with that. However, in Discovery, we should set those aside for a season. Not forever, but long enough to understand the customer's experience first. Design decisions can wait. What cannot wait is the work of learning what customers are trying to accomplish and where current options are failing them.

Shelton wiped the whiteboard clean.

The team understood something now that they had not understood before. They needed to see the customer's world through their eyes. To do so, they must first study the customer's job-to-be-done before they can design anything worth building. The ideas would eventually come back, but better ideas, more grounded ones, informed by reality.

What Comes Next

With the first principle established, a practical question surfaces. If discovery must begin in problem space, how should a team explore that space? The customer's world is large and complex. There are many possible problems, frustrations, and dimensions of the job that might matter.

Should a team immediately try to identify the most important problem and focus there? Or should they explore broadly first?

The answer to that question introduces the rhythm that governs effective discovery work. This rhythm has expansion and focus, exploration and clarity. It is the cadence of divergence and convergence.

Key Takeaways

- Solution space is the world of features, designs, and product ideas. Problem space is the world of customer goals, struggles, and performance standards.
- Discovery begins in problem space. Otherwise, innovation is based upon likely-flawed assumptions.
- Customers are reliable authorities on their own experience. They know what is difficult, what fails, and what they wish worked better. They are not reliable sources about desired products and product attributes.
- A Job-to-be-Done is a customer's goal, objective, or problem to be solved. Jobs are more stable over time than the technologies and products designed to accomplish them. Teams that anchor discovery to the job are studying something enduring, and a worthy basis for a durable product strategy.

Chapter 2: Divergence and Convergence

We've Got Problems

A WEEK AFTER THEIR FIRST MEETING, the Big Sky team gathered again.

Shelton had spent the past few days talking to retailers and reading customer reviews. When the meeting began, he projected a list on the screen.

Jenna said, "Problems this time, right?"

Shelton nodded. "Yep. Here are some of the issues backpackers mention," he said.

The list was long.

Tents that take too long to pitch. Lost stakes. Instability on hillsides. Rain blowing in from under the doors. And the drip, drip, drip drops come the condensation plops in the night. Stretch cords in the pole sets losing their stretchy personalities. Zippers breaking. Cord locks slipping. Vestibule doors flapping in the wind.

Luis whistled quietly. "That's a lot of issues."

Tom leaned back in his chair. "And that's just what people talk about online."

Jenna frowned slightly. "Quite a bunch. Which ones matter?"

Shelton shook his head. "That's exactly the problem. We don't know yet."

Moving from products to problems, the team's thinking was better. But one challenge had been postponed, and another had taken its place. The problem space was not remotely empty; it was, in fact, crowded. There were too many possible directions, too many complaints, too many dimensions of the job that might turn out to be important. *Or so it seemed*.

They needed a way to explore without jumping to conclusions. What they needed, though they did not yet have a name for it, was a thinking rhythm. A cadence. A disciplined path forward.

The Temptation to Converge Too Early

When a team encounters a long list of problems, the instinct is to grab one and focus there. Pick a direction and go.

That's a natural instinct. Companies reward decisiveness. Meetings that end with clear priorities feel more productive than meetings that end with more questions. Leaders who narrow the field quickly appear confident and in control.

But in discovery, premature convergence is not the path to greatness. The problem is not that focusing is wrong. Eventually, focus is exactly what discovery must produce. The problem is making decisions before the landscape is understood.

When teams converge too early, they tend to lock onto the most visible problem, the loudest complaint, the pet project of an executive, or the most interesting challenge. Often, a team converges because a competitor has launched a new product, and there's a rush to copy them.

In all these cases, they have not yet done the work of exploring what else might be there. They have not navigated the edges of the problem space, surfaced the less obvious frustrations, or examined how the job-to-be-done breaks down across different contexts and conditions.

The result is a conclusion built on an incomplete picture. The team feels aligned, but they are circling a partial understanding. Downstream decisions, design choices, positioning, and feature priorities all follow from that incomplete knowledge, compounding the original error.

Effective discovery requires patience with an environment of uncertainty. The surest path is to explore broadly first, to reserve judgment and ensure that all the possibilities have been considered.

That discipline is captured within the distinct phases of divergence and convergence.

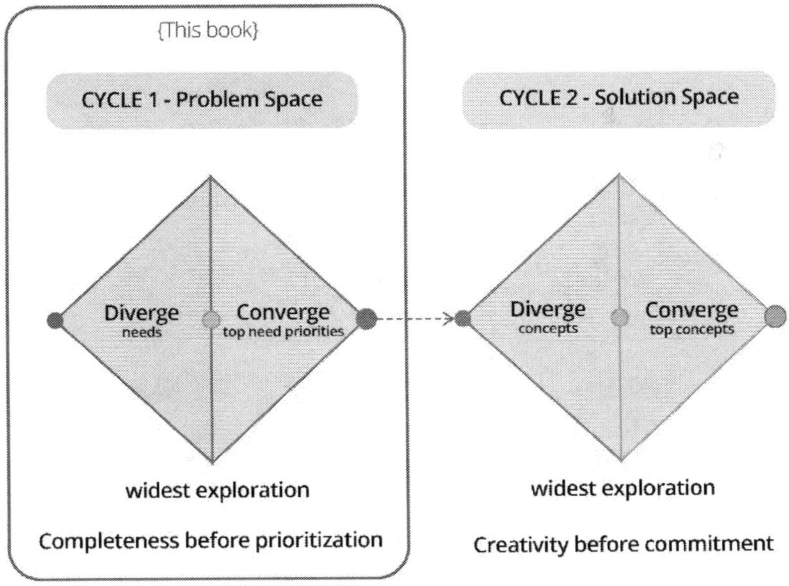

Two Modes of Thinking

Divergence and convergence are different cognitive modes, and effective discovery requires both in sequence.

Divergence expands. During this phase, judgment is suspended. The goal is not to evaluate possibilities but to surface them. We begin by asking what problems customers might face, what patterns appear across their experiences, and what dimensions of their job-to-be-done have not yet been considered.

Success during divergence is judged by completeness. The focus is not on which problems matter most, but whether the list of problems is complete enough that the right answer is somewhere within.

A restaurant menu is a useful analogy. When you sit down and open a menu for the first time, you first scan the options before narrowing down to a choice. That scanning is not wasted energy. It would be strange to order the first thing you see. It's unlikely to be the best option.

Divergence works the same way. It is the discipline of expanding options before committing.

Divergence is the discipline of expanding options before committing.

Convergence begins only after the problem space has been explored with sufficient breadth. Judgment is reengaged as the question shifts from what possibilities exist to which matter most. Convergence narrows the field toward a clear set of priorities that can guide action.

Neither mode works well without the other. Divergence without convergence produces an ever-growing pile of needs. Convergence without divergence produces confident priorities from a small dataset. The pattern of moving through both expanding and focusing is what allows discovery to be both thorough and accurate.

It Takes Two (Cycles)

As a practitioner of Design Thinking will recognize, this thinking pattern cycles twice within the innovation process.

The first cycle is in problem space. Teams diverge to uncover the full landscape of customer needs: every dimension of the customer's job-to-be-done, every point of friction, every standard customers use to judge success. Then they converge to identify which needs represent the strongest opportunities: the ones that matter most and are least well served by existing solutions. The output of this first cycle is not a product concept. It is a prioritized list of unmet market needs.

The second cycle is in solution space. With a clear problem to solve, teams (again) diverge to generate a wide range of possible approaches. What are all the different design directions, different technologies, different solutions? Our first idea is unlikely to be our best. Then they converge to select the most promising concept and develop it into something buildable.

This distinction matters because the two cycles require different inputs and produce different outputs. The first cycle requires customer research. The second requires strategy and design.

This book focuses on the first cycle. Understanding how to execute the problem-space cycle well is the foundation of everything that follows in DISCOVER. The next phases of Prism, STRATEGIZE and EXECUTE, operate within the second cycle.

A Common Misstep: Build it, and they will come

Understanding the divergence-convergence cadence also helps explain a persistent failure mode in product development: solution justification.

This happens when a team begins with a concept and then conducts research to confirm it. The sequence has been reversed: instead of understanding the problem and then designing the solution, they design the solution and then look for evidence that the problem exists. The research is not discovery. It is an attempt to rationalize the previously made decision.

This is common practice and often invisible to the teams caught in it. It tends to emerge when a strong internal voice, such as an executive, a founder, or a passionate engineer, champions an idea. It gains momentum. Resources are allocated. A roadmap takes shape. By the time research begins, the organization has already committed, at least implicitly, to the answer. The research is framed not as exploration but as confirmation. With each day and dollar spent, it becomes increasingly difficult to change course. It becomes a freight train.

The process becomes corrupted. Interviews are conducted with leading questions. Survey results are interpreted generously. Contradictory evidence gets rationalized or set aside. The team ends up with a product built on corrupted data and a market that responds with indifference.

The divergence-convergence framework is a corrective to this pattern. It insists that exploration precede conclusion, that the full range of possibilities be examined before priorities are set. That judgment should be applied only after the problem space has been genuinely understood. It does not eliminate the role of strong intuition or decisive leadership. But it ensures that intuition is tested rather than assumed.

Playing the Rhythm at Big Sky

Shelton explained the idea to the team using the list still projected on the screen.

"Right now, we're in divergence. Our job is to expand this list, not shrink it."

Jenna's eyes widened. She said, "What! There's too much here already."

Shelton replied with a smile, "Yes, there's a lot, isn't there! It feels overwhelming, and that's to be expected. We're trying to understand everything backpackers struggle with. Not just the obvious things, but the things that don't show up until you're nine miles in and the weather is turning. *Everything*."

Jenna repeated, "Everything?"

Shelton confirmed with a nod.

Luis spoke slowly. "So, we shouldn't try to pick the most important problem yet."

"Exactly, that's it," Shelton said. "We need to understand the full landscape first. Let's get a handle on that. Make sure we haven't missed anything. That's our goal for now. Then we'll sort through which needs matter most. Later."

Tom looked at the list. "All of these stay on the board for now?"

"All of them," Shelton confirmed. "The ones that seem obvious. The ones that seem minor. The ones that seem crazy. We don't know yet which ones matter, and we won't know until we've done the work. We withhold judgment for now."

Jenna leaned back in her chair. “Does that mean that we want more? That more ideas are better?”

Shelton replied. “More ideas are better.”

“And then convergence tells us where to focus?”

Shelton smiled. “Convergence is focusing.”

The team turned back to the screen. The list that had felt overwhelming a few minutes earlier now felt different, less like an urgent decision to make, and more like a mystery to explore.

That shift in orientation, from anxiety about too many choices to curiosity about what those possibilities might reveal, is what disciplined divergence makes possible.

What Comes Next

The Big Sky team now had a mental frame for how to approach the problem space: explore broadly before narrowing, expand before focusing, resist the pull toward premature conclusions.

But a new challenge emerged.

As the team began talking to retailers, reading reviews, gathering impressions from the field, etc., they noticed something frustrating. Customers used vague language. They wanted the tent to be tough. They wanted the setup to be easier. They wanted better performance in bad weather.

Tough. Easier. Better.

There was certainly a truth within each of these statements. But it was obscured by casual and imprecise language. What did they mean by “tough,” “easier,” or “better performance?”

Understanding what customers are trying to accomplish and translating their language into something precise and actionable is the challenge the next chapter addresses. It introduces a powerful concept in the DISCOVER framework: Job Success Criteria.

Key Takeaways

- Discovery requires two distinct cognitive modes in sequence. Divergence expands the problem space by suspending judgment and surfacing possibilities. Convergence applies judgment to identify patterns, priorities, and the strongest opportunities. Neither mode works without the other.
- Premature convergence produces weak insight. When teams lock onto the most visible problem before understanding the full landscape, they make decisions based on a partial map, and every downstream choice compounds the original error.
- Success during divergence is measured by completeness. The question is not which problems matter most, but whether the full range of problems is somewhere on the list before prioritization begins.
- The divergence-convergence rhythm applies twice in innovation: once in problem space, to identify the strongest opportunities, and once in solution space, to develop the best response.
- Flipping these cycles, generating solutions before the problem is understood, or researching after the design is chosen, undermines both.
- Solution justification is the failure mode where research is conducted to confirm a decision already made. It is common, often invisible to the teams caught in it, and consistently produces products that the market does not reward. The divergence-convergence framework is a structural corrective.

Chapter 3: Job Success Criteria

"Make It Better"

A FEW DAYS AFTER THE KICKOFF MEETING, Shelton gathered the team again.

Tom had just returned from visiting several outdoor retailers and hiking groups. He dropped a stack of notes on the conference table.

"You guys wanted divergence. Well, I've got a bunch of customer feedback," he said.

Luis leaned forward immediately. "Great. What are people asking for?"

Tom scanned the top page. "Pretty much what you'd expect."

He started reading. "People want the tent to be faster to pack."

Luis nodded. "Yep."

Tom continued. "They say pitching the tent should be easier."

Jenna wrote that down. "And ventilation needs to be better. Apparently, condensation is a big complaint."

Shelton began writing the phrases on the whiteboard.

Faster. Easier. Better ventilation. More durable.

The list looked promising until Luis pointed to the first item.

"Alright," he said. "What did they mean by 'easier'?"

Tom shrugged. "I'm not sure."

Jenna looked up from her notes. "I'm pretty sure that 'easier' means 'without any experience.' You know, so that anyone can do it."

Shelton scratched his chin. "Yeah, maybe. Or does it mean fewer steps? Or less physical effort?"

Tom flipped through the pages again as if searching for something that he remembered seeing, but had apparently vanished. "No one really explained."

Shelton stared at the board. The words had sounded helpful when Tom read them aloud. But the more the team examined them, the less useful they became.

"Faster," Shelton said slowly, tapping the marker against the board. "When does it start? When does it end? What exactly are we measuring?"

Luis crossed his arms. "And 'durable' could mean ten different things depending on the situation."

Jenna nodded. "This is somewhat helpful. But it's not enough, is it?"

The team had customer feedback. What they did not have was conviction about a customer's definition of success.

They had finally relaxed into the task of writing as many problems as possible. But now, there were more questions.

The Problem with the Word "Better"

Customer feedback is usually packaged in the same form. People say they want something lighter, easier, faster, more reliable, or better. These statements feel informative because they point toward something real. Hidden within is a genuine frustration, a desire for improvement. But when a product team tries to translate them into design decisions, the language is inadequate.

What does faster actually mean? Ten percent less time? Less bulk to push into the stuff sack? Each interpretation points toward a different engineering priority. What does easier mean? Faster setup time? Fewer components to manage? Less physical effort when the hiker is already exhausted? These are not the same problem, and solving one does not necessarily solve the others.

The work of discovery is to surface the specific standard underneath the vague request, and that requires understanding how customers judge performance.

How Customers Judge Performance

Recall from Chapter 1 that a customer hires a product to accomplish a job-to-be-done.

Underneath every vague request for improvement, there is a more specific standard that relates to how well a customer can accomplish their job-to-be-done. Customers apply criteria, consciously or not, when they evaluate whether a product is performing well.

When a backpacker says the tent should be lighter, they may be measuring pack weight at the trailhead, or fatigue accumulated over miles of elevation gain, or the ease of fitting gear into a limited stuff sack. *Or it could be all of those.*

When they say setup should be easier, they may be measuring time from arrival at camp to shelter established, or the number of errors made when assembling poles in fading light, or the physical effort required after a long day of hiking. One phrase may compress several distinct performance dimensions, each of which represents a separate way the job can succeed or fail.

These underlying standards are what customers use to judge products. Not the vague language they reach for when asked to describe their preferences, but the specific criteria they apply when deciding whether something worked well enough.

A tent that goes up in four minutes feels easier than one that takes 12. That same 12 minutes felt "easier" when done in the backyard than it did after a 14-mile hike. A shelter that stays dry during a storm feels more reliable than one that lets rain in at a corner seam. These judgments are precise, even when the language used to express them is not.

The work of discovery is to move from the vague to the specific, from the symptom to the customer's actual criteria.

The work of discovery is to surface those underlying standards and move from the vague to the specific, from the symptom to the criterion, from "easier" to a statement precise enough to actually guide a design decision.

Tony Ulwick's Outcome-Driven Innovation

The concept of capturing customer needs as precise, measurable performance standards was essentially created by Tony Ulwick through his work on Outcome-Driven Innovation, which established a practical research methodology for applying Jobs-to-be-Done. His book, *What Customers Want*, is required reading for anyone in product strategy.

Ulwick recognized that customers evaluate products not by features or attributes, but by "outcomes," which are specific metrics tied to the job they are trying to accomplish. His framework for capturing and measuring those outcomes transformed Jobs-to-be-Done from a compelling theory into a rigorous research discipline.

Ulwick's term for these performance standards is the *Desired Outcome*. It is a precise and well-defined concept, and his body of work around it is substantial. Throughout this book, we use the term *Job Success Criteria* to describe the same underlying idea. We have found this language tends to be immediately intuitive for practitioners and product teams, as the phrase orients people quickly toward a simple question: what criteria does the customer use to judge whether the job was done successfully?

The concept itself remains Ulwick's. The shift in terminology is intended to improve accessibility and usability in modern product teams, not to replace or reinterpret the original thinking. In adopting the phrase *success criteria*, we also want to explicitly acknowledge the work of Jim Kalbach, whose book *The Jobs to Be Done Playbook* helped popularize this language within the broader jobs-to-be-done community. While the terminology emerges from a different source, it maps directly and faithfully to Ulwick's original concept of Desired Outcomes.

Whatever term is used, the insight is the same: customer needs can be expressed as measurable standards of performance, and those standards, not feature requests, not vague preferences, not competitive benchmarks, are the most reliable foundation for strategy and innovation decisions. But going forward, we will use the term *Job Success Criteria*, sometimes abbreviated as *JSC* or informally shortened to Kalbach's convention of *Success Criteria*.

What Job Success Criteria Are

A Job Success Criterion is a measurable standard that a customer uses to evaluate how well they can perform their job-to-be-done. It is solution-agnostic. It describes what successful performance *is without specifying how that performance should be achieved*.

Just like a job-to-be-done, it is stable over time. The criterion persists even as the products designed to meet it evolve. And it is precise enough to be actionable. A team that understands the criterion knows what it is trying to improve and can evaluate design choices against a clear standard.

Strong Job Success Criteria follow a consistent structure: a direction of improvement, a performance metric, and, when helpful, a context.

For example:

- Minimize the time to pitch a tent in adverse weather conditions.
- Minimize the likelihood of setup errors when assembling poles in low light.
- Minimize the amount of water exposure inside the tent when setting up in the rain.

Each of these is precise, measurable, and independent of any product design. A tent with a freestanding structure addresses them differently than one with a trekking pole system. Future shelter technologies not yet invented will address them differently still. But the criteria themselves remain valid regardless of how the solution evolves.

Compare these to the language Tom brought back from the field. “Make it easier to pitch” could mean any of the three criteria above, or all of them, or none of them, depending on the customer and the situation. The criterion makes explicit what the vague request had left hidden.

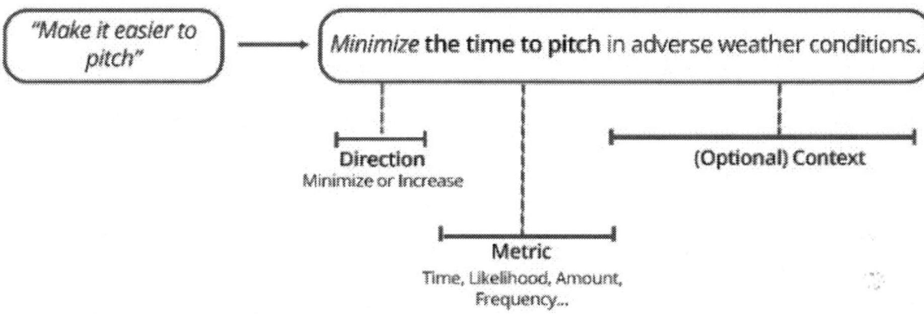

KEY PRINCIPLE
Frame criteria around what can go wrong
"Minimize the time...." is better than "Increase pitching speed" because it names the failure condition customers experience

One Phrase, Many Criteria

One practical implication of this framework is that customer feedback is almost always more compressed than it appears. A single request for improvement frequently contains multiple Job Success Criteria, each representing a separate element of performance.

When the Big Sky team unpacked Tom’s field notes, they found that “make it easier to pitch” contained at least five separate criteria: setup time, physical effort, likelihood of assembly errors, performance under adverse weather, and cognitive effort when fatigued. Each one is a legitimate and distinct standard. Improving on one does not automatically improve the others. A freestanding design might reduce assembly errors without reducing physical effort. A simplified pole system might reduce setup time in good conditions, but perform poorly in the wind.

This compression matters during discovery because collapsing multiple criteria into a single vague category can mask important distinctions. A product that performs well on setup speed but poorly on adverse-weather reliability may satisfy some customers and frustrate others, depending on what they value most. Discovery that exposes the individual criteria, rather than accepting the compressed version, gives the product team a more precise map of where improvement is needed.

Hundreds of criteria can be used as performance metrics for a single job-to-be-done. Further, it takes a comprehensive set to fully understand a customer's true definition of success.

The End of the Beginning

Shelton looked at the whiteboard again. The words were still there: *lighter, easier, better ventilation, more durable*. They had not changed. But the team's relationship with them had.

These were no longer the answer. They were the initial clues: what specifically does each mean, in the customer's experience, in the moments that matter most?

That question, asked with discipline and precision across the full range of the customer's job-to-be-done, is what transforms scattered customer feedback into something a product team can use.

Shelton began to write:

- Minimize the time to pitch the tent
- Minimize the likelihood of water ingress

- Minimize the time to secure the tent's stakes

He paused before continuing.

- Minimize the physical effort to secure the tent's stakes
- Minimize the time to find a suitable campsite

Jenna approached the whiteboard and said, "What does *suitable* mean?"

After a moment of silence, the room rumbled with laughter.

What Comes Next

The team now understood what they were looking for: precise, measurable standards customers use to judge success when performing their job-to-be-done. But understanding the concept and surfacing those criteria from real customer conversations are two different challenges.

Before Big Sky's team could talk to customers effectively, they needed to understand something that complicates the picture a bit. Customers do not make product decisions based on functional performance alone. *The team was still missing some criteria.*

Understanding why that happens, and what it means for discovery, is revealed within the Jobs-to-be-Done Pyramid, the topic of the next chapter.

Key Takeaways

- Customer feedback almost always arrives compressed and vague. "Lighter," "easier," and "better" point toward real frustrations but are not precise enough to guide design decisions. The product team's job is to translate that language into specific, measurable performance standards.
- A Job Success Criterion is a measurable standard a customer uses to evaluate how well a job is being performed. It is as solution-independent as possible, stable over time, and precise enough to be actionable. A team that understands the criterion knows what they are optimizing for and can evaluate design choices against a clear standard.
- A single customer request typically contains multiple distinct Job Success Criteria. "Make it easier to pitch" may compress setup time, physical effort, assembly error rate, and adverse-weather performance: each a separate dimension, each requiring its own criterion. Accepting the compressed version masks distinctions that matter.
- A comprehensive criteria set, well over 200 statements for a complex job, is not a problem. It is the point. Completeness at this stage is what makes prioritization meaningful later.

Chapter 4: The Jobs-to-be-Done Pyramid™

The Spreadsheet Problem

A WEEK LATER, SHELTON SAT IN THE CONFERENCE ROOM STARING AT HIS LAPTOP.

On the screen was a spreadsheet Luis had helped assemble, comparing the most popular backpacking tents. The columns listed the most obvious performance criteria: weight, condensation performance, weather resistance, interior space, packed volume, and price.

Shelton scrolled down the list. One model kept standing out, the EchoMid. It was lighter than most competitors. It had excellent condensation ratings. It could handle some of the highest winds. Its price was competitive.

"According to this," Shelton said, turning the laptop toward the rest of the team, "this tent should be dominating the market."

Luis nodded. "That's right. On paper, the EchoMid is really one of the best."

Tom leaned forward and studied the screen. "Funny thing," he said. "We spent a week hiking in Glacier last summer. And the whole time, I cannot remember seeing that tent on the trail. Not one."

Shelton looked up. "You didn't?"

Tom shrugged. "I didn't. But that's not all. When I'm talking to backpackers or visiting retailers, people usually buy this one instead, the Wolf-X." He pointed to another row on the spreadsheet.

Luis frowned. The Wolf-X was a bit heavier and slightly more expensive.

Shelton leaned back in his chair. "Why are they buying that? What do you think about the EchoMid?"

Tom thought for a second, "I'm not sure. Hey, Jenna, didn't you just buy a Wolf-X?"

Jenna's eyes widened, "I did! I remember watching the mailbox for days, couldn't wait to open it up. When it arrived, I set it up in the yard and lay down inside. I couldn't wait to get it out on the trail."

Shelton answered, "Did you think about the EchoMid?"

Jenna replied, "I did. I really did. In fact, I had them both in my cart for a bit. I was going to buy both and then return one. But I knew that I really didn't want the EchoMid."

Shelton asked, "Could you tell me why?"

Jenna started to speak and then stopped before continuing, "I don't know. I was just more excited about the Wolf-X."

Shelton turned to Tom. "What do you think about this?"

Tom smiled. "Well, we should probably consider that real backpackers don't choose gear the way spreadsheets do."

The Limits of Functional Thinking

Product teams encounter this puzzle regularly. A competitor that wins despite appearing inferior on the metrics that are supposed to matter, or a product that loses despite being objectively better on every dimension the team thought was important.

The standard response is to question the metrics. Maybe weight matters less than we thought. Maybe setup time is not as important as the ease of learning. Maybe there is something we missed. These adjustments may be warranted. But they often fail to resolve the riddle, because the explanation is not hiding in a different functional metric. It is operating at a different level of motivation entirely.

When Tom said that backpackers do not choose gear the way spreadsheets do, he was pointing at something that experienced marketers sense. Functional performance, how well a product accomplishes the core task, is genuinely important. *But it is not the only thing customers evaluate.* Customers bring a more complex set of motivations to their decisions than any functional analysis can capture, and discovery that ignores those will assemble an incomplete picture of the market.

The Jobs-to-be-Done Pyramid is the framework that brings those motivations into focus.

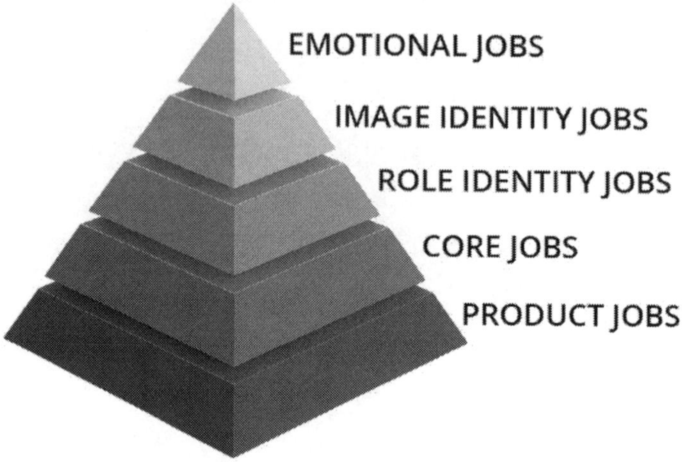

Introducing the Jobs-to-be-Done Pyramid

The Jobs-to-be-Done Pyramid helps product teams see the full range of customer motivation. It organizes those motivations across five levels, from the practical work customers are trying to accomplish to the identity and emotional meaning attached to the experience.

When customers hire a product to do a job, they are not just trying to complete a functional task. They may also be expressing something about who they are, managing how they are perceived, and shaping how they want to feel.

Understanding these layers does not replace functional analysis. It completes it. A product team that understands only the functional dimensions of the job is working with an incomplete map. The Jobs-to-be-Done Pyramid fills in the rest.

Functional performance matters, but it does not explain the full structure of customer choice.

It's not only a classification scheme for organizing customer motivations into neat categories. *It is also a listening framework.* It's a structure that helps product teams hear what would otherwise be missed in customer interviews. When an interviewer understands the Jobs-to-be-Done Pyramid, they recognize an identity signal when it appears. They know how to probe an emotional reaction. They understand why a customer's stated reason for a product choice might not be the complete explanation. The Jobs-to-be-Done Pyramid changes what teams listen for, and therefore what they learn. For simplicity, the five levels can be understood in three broad groups: what customers are trying to do, who customers are trying to be, and how customers want to feel.

The Functional Domain: What Customers Are Trying to Do

The base of the Pyramid covers functional motivation. That's the practical work customers are trying to accomplish. This domain contains two levels, and the distinction between them matters for how discovery is scoped.

The first level represents Product Jobs: the specific interactions a customer has with a product across its lifecycle. For readers familiar with Jobs-to-be-Done theory, this is the same concept that others have called "Consumption Jobs."

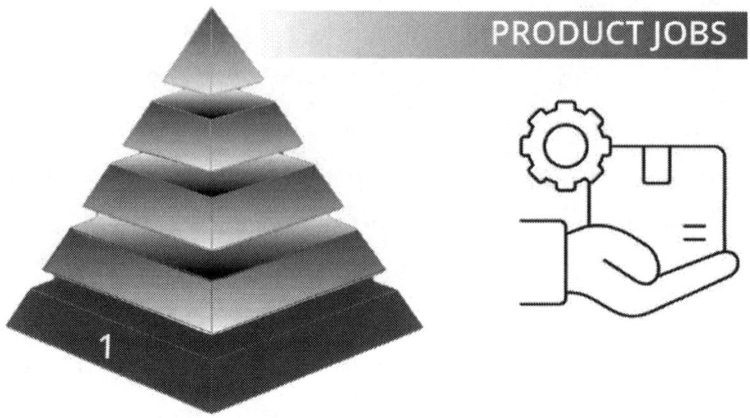

For a backpacking tent, Product Jobs include purchasing the tent, learning to pitch it, packing it into a backpack, setting it up at camp, adjusting it for changing conditions, and eventually storing, repairing, or replacing it. These are the concrete, observable actions that define the customer's interactions with the product. Product Jobs are organized into five categories: Acquisition, Preparation, Usage, Maintenance, and Disposal.

Product Jobs are important because they reveal troubles at a granular level. A customer who struggles to fold the tent back into its stuff sack after a wet night is experiencing a Product Job failure, not a failure of the core shelter function, but a real source of frustration that affects their overall experience. Discovery that attends only to the core task will miss these moments entirely.

Note that nobody buys a tent for a Product Job. That is, they don't buy a tent merely for the fun of buying it, of learning to use it, or for the joy of maintaining it. What is the reason they purchase? It's the next level of the Pyramid, it's Level 2, *the Core Job.*

The second level represents the Core Job: the fundamental, solution-agnostic goal the customer is trying to accomplish. For Big Sky's target customer, the Core Job is staying protected from the elements while backpacking through difficult terrain. This is the job that exists independent of any particular tent design, any current technology, or any specific product category. It is the reason the tent exists at all.

The distinction between Product Jobs and Core Jobs is important. A team studying Product Jobs is asking how customers interact with their product, which is essential for improving the customer journey, from acquisition to disposal. It will include the critical elements of usability. A team studying the Core Job is asking what customers are ultimately trying to accomplish, which is essential for identifying where broader innovation opportunities exist. It will help them to see how to build a strategy that's untethered from the current product. Both perspectives are valuable, and the best discovery work attends to both.

The Identity Domain: Who Customers Are Trying to Be

Above the functional levels, the Jobs-to-be-Done Pyramid introduces an element that specifications cannot easily represent: identity.

Customers do not experience products in a social vacuum. They use gear in the presence of others and in contexts loaded with personal meaning. The choices they make, what they buy, how they use it, and how they talk about it are often bound up with how they see themselves and how they want to be seen.

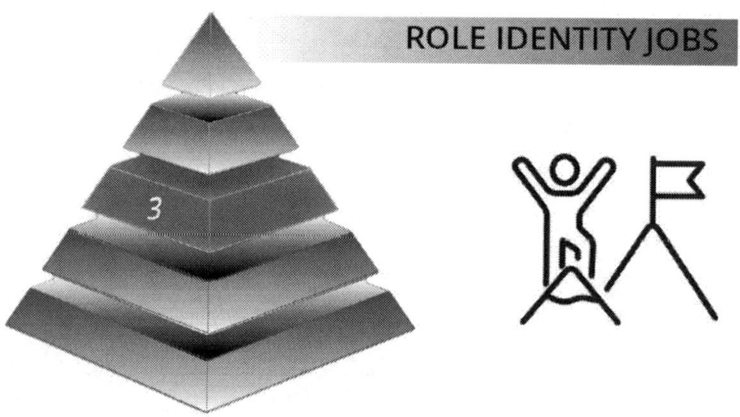

The third level of the Jobs-to-be-Done Pyramid represents Role Identity Jobs: the roles customers are trying to live into through their actions. With every purchase that a person makes, the decision, whether big or small, helps them to become who they seek to become.

A backpacker who describes themselves as someone who handles backcountry conditions competently is describing an identity they are actively maintaining. Every trip, every gear choice, every moment at camp is an opportunity to either reinforce or undermine that self-concept. Products that support the role feel right. Products that threaten it by being difficult to use or by signaling inexperience frustrate and confound customers.

The fourth level represents Image Identity Jobs: the way customers want to be perceived by others. This is subtly different from role identity. Role identity is about who a person wants to be in their own understanding. Image identity is about the impression they project outward.

A backpacker who cares about being seen as experienced and self-sufficient by their hiking companions is managing an image, not just a self-concept. The gear they choose, and how smoothly they use it, contributes to that image in ways that are real and consequential.

Tom had seen this dynamic play out on the trail more times than he could count. Experienced hikers paid attention to each other's gear. Certain brands carried reputational weight. The tent that signaled seriousness and competence was not always the tent that performed best on a weight-to-weather-resistance ratio. *It was the tent that said something about its owner.*

We see this principle play out in marketing all the time, when we see a celebrity or professional athlete using a product. The message is that if you purchase this product, then you reinforce your own identity with the celebrity's.

The Emotional Domain: How Customers Want to Feel

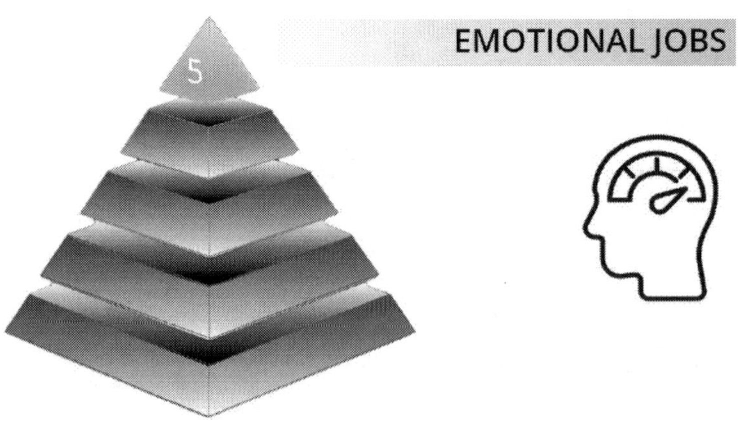

At the top of the Pyramid sits the emotional domain, the lived experience when performing a job-to-be-done.

Emotional Jobs describe how customers want to feel during the experience: confident, calm, safe, capable, free. These are not peripheral to the product's value. In many cases, they are central to it. A backpacker who sets up their tent quickly and cleanly before a storm rolls in does not just have shelter. They also feel comfortable, safe and at peace. A backpacker who struggles with the setup while rain begins to fall does not just have a wet tent. They feel anxious and concerned. The functional result and the emotional experience are intertwined, and a product that delivers on the function but fails to support the emotional experience has not fully succeeded.

Emotional Jobs may be the hardest to surface directly. Customers rarely describe their emotional motivations in abstract terms. They do not *say, "I don't want to feel fearful when sleeping in my tent."* Instead, they say, *"I like being able to close the tent doors at night."* The emotional content is real and present. It is just embedded in the story rather than stated directly. This is one reason the Jobs-to-be-Done Pyramid is a listening framework. The cues are there. The researcher has to know what to listen for.

Seeing the Pyramid in a Single Moment

Tom described a scene from a recent trip that brought all five levels into focus at once.

A group of hikers arrived at camp late in the afternoon. One of them, clearly less experienced than the rest, struggled to get his tent up while the others finished their setups and began sitting in their chairs and enjoying the evening. They were laughing. Opening snacks. Reflecting on the adventure of the day. Our struggling camper eventually got it done, but not before making several visible mistakes with the pole assembly, having to begin again more than once.

Later, he laughed it off. "I didn't want to look like it was my first trip. I hate being the last guy setting up. Everyone else has moved on, and it makes the tiredness you already feel, to *feel even worse*."

In that one remark, the Jobs-to-be-Done Pyramid was present in its entirety.

At the functional level, he had performed a Product Job, pitching the tent, with difficulty and delay. At the Core Job level, he had eventually accomplished the fundamental goal: shelter was established. But above the functional layer, other things were happening. He wanted to be someone who handles backcountry situations competently, a Role Identity Job. He was aware of how his struggle appeared to the group, an Image Identity Job. And underneath the joke, there was genuine discomfort, an Emotional Job, the desire to feel capable rather than exposed.

A product team focused only on functional performance might have seen a setup time problem and designed a faster-pitching tent. A team listening through the lens of the full Jobs-to-be-Done Pyramid would see something richer: that for this customer, in this context, the tent is not just shelter equipment. It is a means of expressing and maintaining a certain kind of identity, and a source of confidence or anxiety depending on how the moment goes.

To be fair, it's probably the correct call to address the functional challenges in setting up the tent. However, by understanding the downstream identity and emotional jobs, the team will better appreciate the full weight of the improvement.

What Each Level of the Pyramid Produces

The Jobs-to-be-Done Pyramid reveals different kinds of customer motivation at each level, but not every level is handled the same way in discovery.

At the functional levels, Product Jobs and Core Jobs, the team defines success using Job Success Criteria, as described in the previous chapter. At the identity and emotional levels, the work is different. The team listens for these cues, captures them, and documents them carefully. They inform how a product is positioned, how marketing speaks to the customer, and how the experience is designed to make the customer feel.

Job Success Criteria are not developed for identity or emotional jobs. They can be measured in a survey, but they do not need to be broken down into more specific criteria, the way functional jobs do. The identity and emotional levels are surfaced, captured, and measured as they are.

What The Jobs-to-be-Done Pyramid Changes

Returning to Shelton's spreadsheet, the puzzle of the heavier, more expensive tent that nonetheless dominated the trail becomes easier to understand.

The tent that should have won, according to the functional metrics, was genuinely better on weight and condensation performance. But the tent that actually won had something the spreadsheet could not measure. *It carried a reputation among serious backpackers*. It signaled competence and experience. *It was cool*. Owning it said something. For customers operating at the identity and emotional levels of the Jobs-to-be-Done Pyramid, which is most customers, most of the time, that signal was worth the weight penalty and the price premium.

This is not an argument for ignoring function and focusing on brand. It is an argument for understanding the full structure of what customers value. To understand all the reasons they buy, and how their product choices contribute to who they want to become. It's about understanding the dimensions that drive their choices. To see them as fully human, individual, unique, and with more mystery than can be condensed into purely functional requirements.

What Comes Next

Shelton closed the laptop. *The spreadsheet was still useful*. It captured real performance data, and that data would matter. But it was not the complete picture.

The team now had the conceptual tools they needed: a clear distinction between problem space and solution space, a cadence for moving through discovery with discipline, a method for translating vague customer language into precise performance criteria, and a framework for understanding the full range of customer motivation.

What they did not yet have was a system for structured research that could drive strategic decisions. *They didn't know what to do next.*

That is what the next chapter introduces: *The Discovery Engine.*

The Discovery Engine is the process that produces the Signal Translator: the artifact that converts everything the team learns into a structured, cross-validated picture of what the market needs. Every task from here forward is building toward it.

Key Takeaways

- Functional performance, how well a product accomplishes the core task, is necessary but not sufficient to explain customer choices.
- The Jobs-to-be-Done Pyramid organizes customer motivation across five levels, helping teams understand what customers are trying to do, who they are trying to be, how they want to be seen, and how they want to feel.
- Product Jobs, functional jobs on Level 1, are the tasks a customer performs while interacting with a product. They are segmented into five categories: acquisition, preparation, usage, maintenance, and disposal.
- Core Jobs, functional jobs on Level 2, are the solution-independent jobs that customers hired the product to accomplish.
- Products that win on functional performance alone are more vulnerable than they appear. One competitor improvement can neutralize the advantage. Products that also resonate at the identity and emotional levels are far harder to displace because what they offer cannot be fully captured in a specification.

DISCOVER

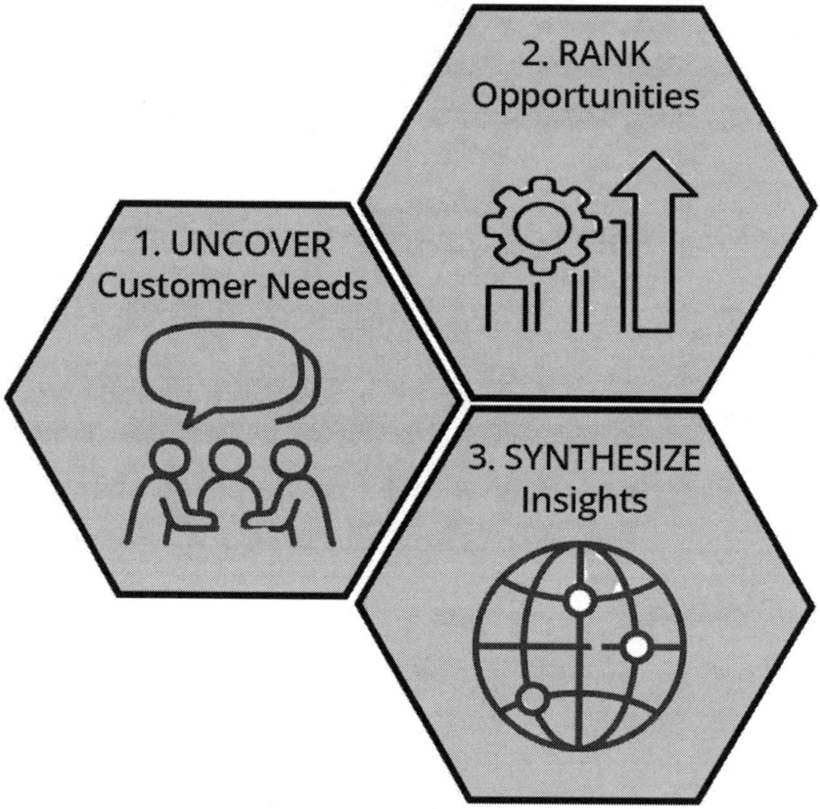
2. RANK
Opportunities
1. UNCOVER
Customer Needs
3. SYNTHESIZE
Insights

Chapter 5: The Discovery Engine

"But What Do We Do?"

BY THE TIME THE BIG SKY TEAM GATHERED for their next meeting, something had changed.

A few weeks earlier, they had been arguing about tent features. Now they were talking about customer jobs-to-be-done. They were speculating about what backpackers were trying to accomplish, not only imagining what the product should include. They were thinking about Job Success Criteria instead of specifications, and they were speculating about motivations in customer stories, beyond the numbers.

And yet, as Shelton looked around the conference room that morning, he could feel a new fog of uncertainty settling in.

Luis broke the silence. "This all makes sense," he said. *"But what do we do?"*

Shelton looked at him.

"I mean," Luis continued, "we know we should start in the problem space. And we know customers buy products based on how well they help them to accomplish their job-to-be-done."

Tom broke in, "But how do we actually run this research? Where do we begin?"

Luis continued, "I don't know, but we need to get started. We need some activity, or the leaders will wonder what we've been doing."

Jenna nodded. "Interviews? Store visits? Surveys? Online reviews? All of the above?"

Tom leaned back in his chair. "For sure, if we just start talking to people, we'll get plenty of stories. Plenty. But then what?"

That landed heavily in the room. Everyone had seen it before. Long interviews, thick reports, pages of observations. Research that never gets read. Work that dissolved into ambiguity once the team tried to make decisions. The servers were full of customer interviews, call reports, and presentations that were never read. Most of it, nearly all of it, was research that produced interesting conversations but no clear direction.

Shelton studied the whiteboard. Knowing *what to look for* is not the same as knowing *what to do*.

"We need to plug into a system," he said. *"A process."*

The Gap Between Knowledge and Action

The previous chapters covered the conceptual foundations of discovery: why teams must begin in problem space, how divergence and convergence govern the work, what Job Success Criteria are and how they are written, and how The Jobs-to-be-Done Pyramid reveals the full structure of customer motivation. *But those foundations do not tell a team what to do on Monday morning.*

Conceptual clarity does not automatically become operational clarity. Teams that understand the principles but lack process slip back into familiar patterns: scheduling a few interviews, collecting feedback through existing channels, generating observations that feel like progress but never cohere into priorities that guide decisions.

That failure is both predictable and relatable. Most teams conducting discovery are genuinely trying to understand their customers. Without a repeatable process, discovery becomes a series of somewhat disconnected activities rather than a system. Activities without structure produce information without direction.

A team can have conceptual clarity but still not know what to do next.

Why Discovery So Often Fails

Three failure patterns appear consistently: **The first is fragmentation.** Organizations are rarely short on customer data (support tickets, survey results, sales notes, product reviews), but the signals never get synthesized into a coherent picture. Each source illuminates something. But the pieces never connect. *(This failure point will be addressed in detail in Step 3 at the end of the book.)*

The second is studying the wrong thing: Teams begin discovery in solution space, asking customers to evaluate product concepts or compare features. The research feels rigorous, but the output reflects the team's assumptions rather than illuminating the market.

The third is misusing research types: Qualitative interviews are treated as sufficient for prioritization, or large surveys are fielded before the team knows what to measure. Each method has a distinct role, and using them out of sequence produces insight that is either too thin to trust or too broad to act on.

All three failures share the same root cause: the absence of a structured process. A clear sequence that defines what kind of work happens at each stage, what it is designed to produce, and how it connects to what comes before and after. That structure is what the Discovery Engine provides.

Introducing the Discovery Engine

Within the DISCOVER phase, the structured workflow used to conduct discovery is called the Discovery Engine. It is the operational core of this book: the step-by-step process that transforms raw customer experience into structured insight. The chapters that follow work through every task in that process in detail. However, before diving in, let's zoom out to see the full picture.

The Discovery Engine unfolds in three steps, each answering a fundamental question about the market.

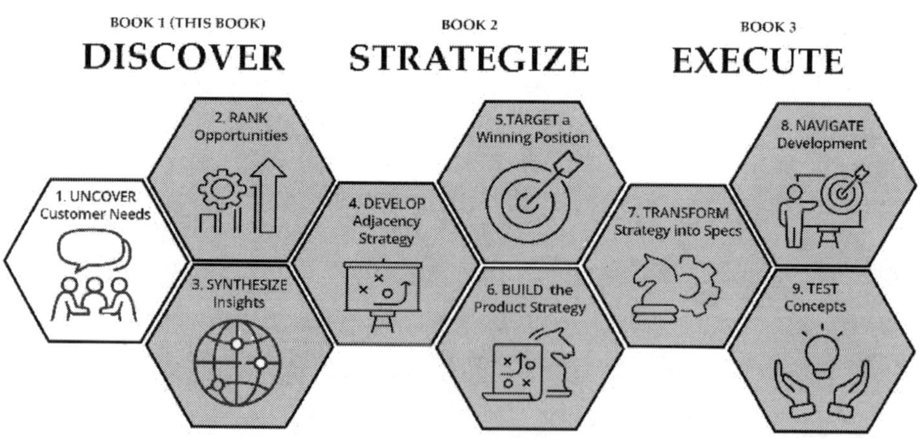

In Step 1, we ask: What are customers trying to accomplish, and how do they measure success? This step focuses on uncovering the full landscape of customer needs. Every dimension of the job, every point of friction, every standard customers use to evaluate whether the job was done well. It is deliberately expansive. The goal is completeness before prioritization.

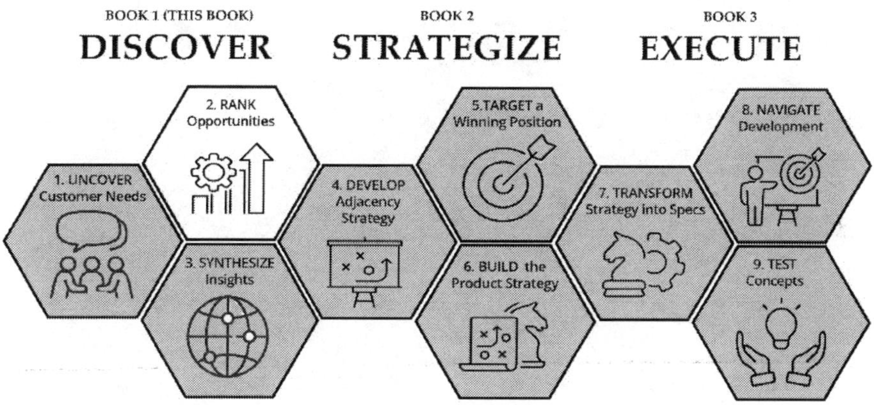

In Step 2, we ask: Which of those needs matter most, and where do existing solutions fall short? This uses quantitative research to move from a complete picture of customer needs to a ranked map of innovation opportunities. It answers the question that qualitative research alone cannot: not just what customers struggle with, but how widely those struggles are shared and how urgently they need to be addressed.

In Step 3, we ask: How do we synthesize what we've learned into insight we can trust and sustain? This step uses triangulation, comparing signals across multiple sources to build confidence in the patterns that have emerged, and establishing the organizational practices needed to keep discovery current as markets evolve.

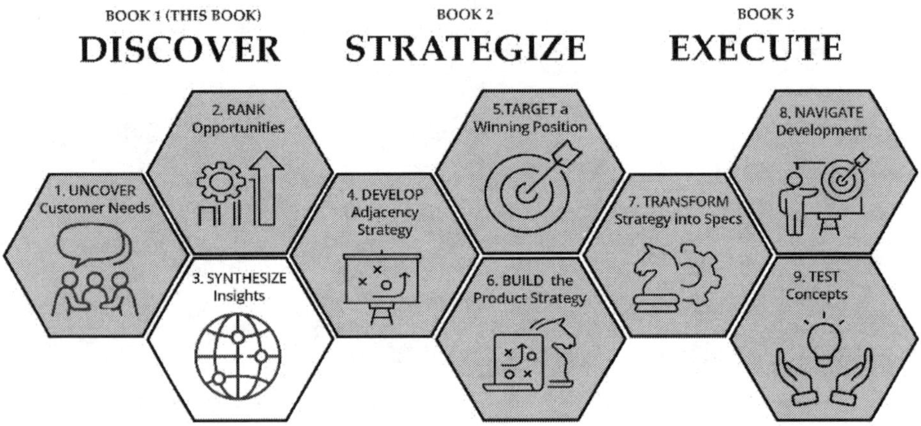

Together, these three steps move a team from a vague product mandate to structured market understanding. They also organize the rest of this book: Step 1 spans Chapters 6–16, Step 2 spans Chapters 17–19, and Step 3 spans Chapters 20–22. The twelve tasks are described briefly here and explored in full in the chapters that follow.

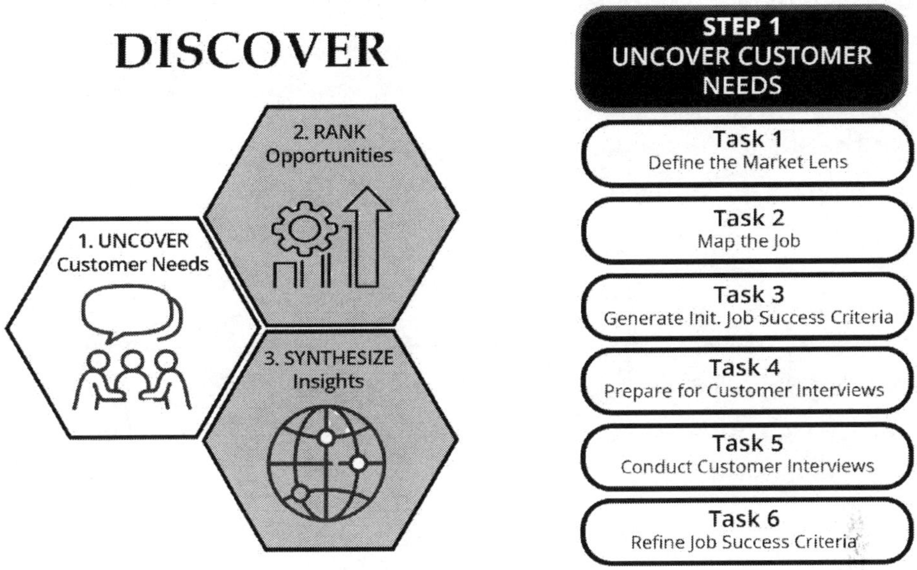

STEP 1: UNCOVER CUSTOMER NEEDS

Step 1 contains six tasks. Together, they constitute the qualitative phase of discovery. This is the work of understanding the customer's JTBD and generating a structured set of needs that can later be measured and prioritized. Most tasks in this step occupy a single chapter. Tasks 4 and 5 are exceptions, as there's just more to cover for the preparation and execution of customer interviews.

Task 1: Define the Market Lens. The Market Lens is the clear, specific frame that anchors the entire discovery effort. Before research begins, the team must establish whose world they are studying, in what context, and toward what goal. Without this clarity, discovery becomes unfocused, resulting in different team members studying different customers in varied situations and producing insights that cannot be compared or synthesized.

Task 2: Map the Job. The Job Map is the sequence of steps the customer follows when performing a JTBD. A job map reveals the structure of the customer's work, not just the obvious central action, but the preparation that precedes it, the monitoring that accompanies it, and the wrap-up that follows. Many of the most significant friction points live in these surrounding steps, invisible to teams that focus only on the execution step.

Task 3: Generate Initial Job Success Criteria. This is the initial attempt at developing a set of standards that customers use to judge how well the JTBD is performed. At this stage, the list is provisional. It is a starting hypothesis informed by the job map and available secondary sources. Direct customer research will later fully develop this list.

Task 4: Prepare for Customer Interviews. This is where the team defines the sample, designs the discussion guide, and establishes the team roles and protocols that will govern the research. Preparation determines the quality of discovery. A poorly designed sample or a leading discussion guide will undermine the entire effort regardless of how many interviews are conducted.

Task 5: Conduct Customer Interviews. Interviews are structured conversations designed to surface how the JTBD unfolds in real conditions, where problems appear, and how customers judge success. This is the work that replaces assumptions with evidence. Because conducting discovery interviews well is both technically demanding and easy to get wrong, this task also spans multiple chapters: three in total, each addressing a dimension of the work.

Task 6: Refine the Job Success Criteria: This is where all the previous work is translated into a survey-ready set of Job Success Criteria. This translation work, in which we move from scattered but comprehensive observations to organized insight, is where qualitative discovery produces its tangible output.

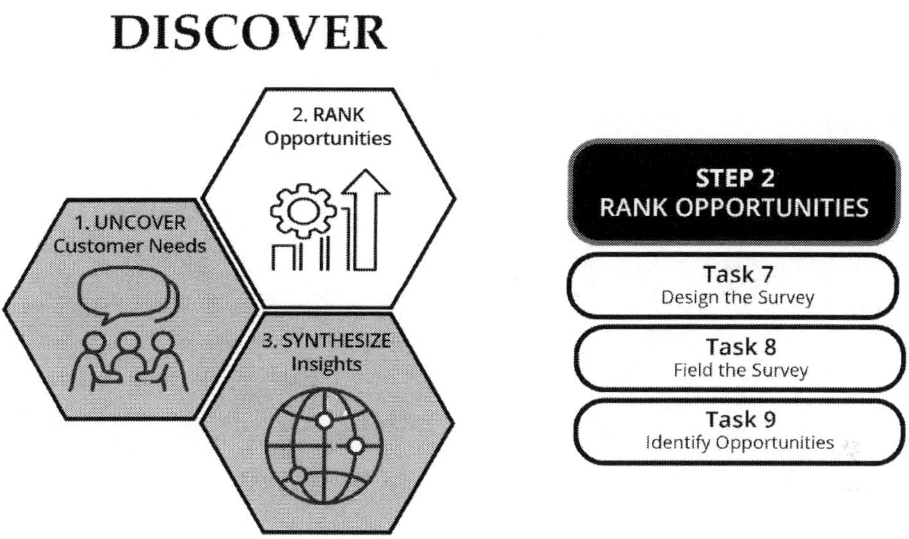

STEP 2: RANK OPPORTUNITIES

Step 2 spans Chapters 17 through 19 and contains three tasks. Together, they constitute the quantitative phase of discovery. This is the work of measuring which customer needs matter most and are least well served by existing solutions.

Task 7: Design the Survey. Here, the team translates the refined Job Success Criteria into a structured questionnaire that measures importance and satisfaction for the criteria across the target market.

Task 8: Field the Survey. The team collects responses from a representative sample of the target customer population. The quality of this data depends heavily on the rigor of the sampling approach. The survey can only reveal patterns that are present in the respondents it reaches.

Task 9: Identify Opportunities. The team analyzes the survey results to produce a ranked map of customer needs, organized by the gap between importance and satisfaction. This analysis surfaces the criteria that matter most and are least well addressed, surfacing the zones of greatest innovation opportunity.

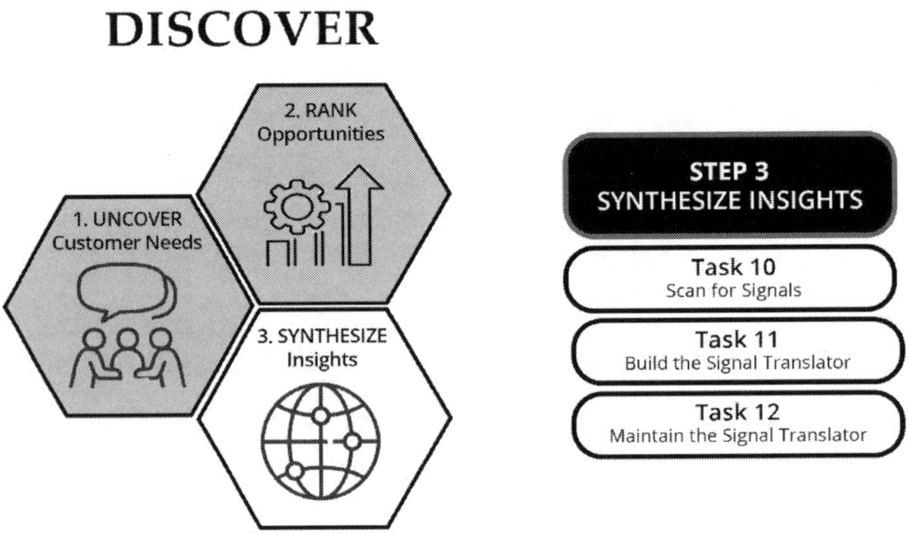

STEP 3: SYNTHESIZE INSIGHTS

Step 3 spans Chapters 20 through 22 and contains three tasks. Together, they constitute the synthesis phase of discovery. This is the work of building credibility and confidence, while establishing the organizational capability to sustain that understanding over time.

Task 10: Scan for Signals. This is the process of finding other available evidence: support data, sales observations, product reviews and competitive intelligence. These will be used in the next task to widen the analysis with additional independent sources.

Task 11: Build the Signal Translator. This is a practical synthesis framework that normalizes signals from multiple sources onto a common scale, making it possible to compare evidence of different types side by side and identify the needs that surface most consistently across all available data.

Task 12: Maintain the Signal Translator. This is the ongoing practice that keeps discovery current as markets evolve, thus ensuring that the knowledge generated by this effort does not decay into a static artifact but continues to develop as new evidence accumulates.

The Path to Actionable Results

Shelton looked at the whiteboard where the twelve tasks were now mapped out in sequence.

For the first time since the project began, the path forward was visible. Not just the desired destination, but the route to determining what weekend backpackers needed from their shelter equipment. It contained the specific steps. The order in which they would be taken. The type of work each step required and what it would produce.

Luis studied the board. "So, the interviews aren't the whole thing."

"They're in Step 1," Shelton said. "But without the job map before them and the synthesis work after them, they're just conversations and notes."

Tom nodded slowly. "And the survey comes after the interviews. It must. I see that now."

"Right," Shelton said. "Because until we know what to measure, we don't know what to ask."

Jenna looked at the sequence. "This is going to take longer than I thought."

Shelton smiled. *"It's going to take exactly as long as it needs to."* He capped the marker. "But it's also going to produce something we can actually use. With confidence. For many years to come."

Jenna repeated in a whisper, "For many years to come..."

What Comes Next

Every step in the Discovery Engine is oriented around the same frame, a clear definition of whose world the team is studying and in what context.

Before the Big Sky team could interview a single backpacker, map a single job, or generate a single success criterion, they needed to answer one deceptively simple question:

Who exactly are we building this for?

That question is what the next chapter addresses. It introduces the first task of the Discovery Engine, defining the Market Lens, and explains why the focus it provides is the foundation on which everything else depends.

Key Takeaways

- Understanding the concepts of discovery (Jobs-to-be-Done, problem space, Job Success Criteria, The Jobs-to-be-Done Pyramid, etc.) does not automatically translate into knowing how to execute discovery. Conceptual clarity and operational clarity are different things, and the gap between them is where most discovery efforts stall.
- The three most common discovery failures are: fragmenting signals without synthesizing them, studying customer reactions to solutions rather than understanding the problem, and confusing the roles of qualitative and quantitative research. All three share a common cause: the absence of a structured process.
- The Discovery Engine organizes discovery into three steps and twelve tasks. Step 1 uncovers the full landscape of customer needs through qualitative research. Step 2 measures and ranks those needs through quantitative survey work. Step 3 synthesizes the findings across multiple signal sources to build confidence and sustain understanding over time.
- Sequence matters. Qualitative work must precede quantitative work because you cannot measure what you have not yet identified. Each task in the Discovery Engine produces specific output that the next task depends on. Skipping or reordering steps does not accelerate discovery; it undermines it.
- The Prismatic Product System™ has three phases: DISCOVER, STRATEGIZE, and EXECUTE. This book covers DISCOVER entirely. The quality of everything in STRATEGIZE and EXECUTE depends on the rigor of the work done here. Discovery is not a step on the way to the real work. It is the foundation upon which everything else is built.

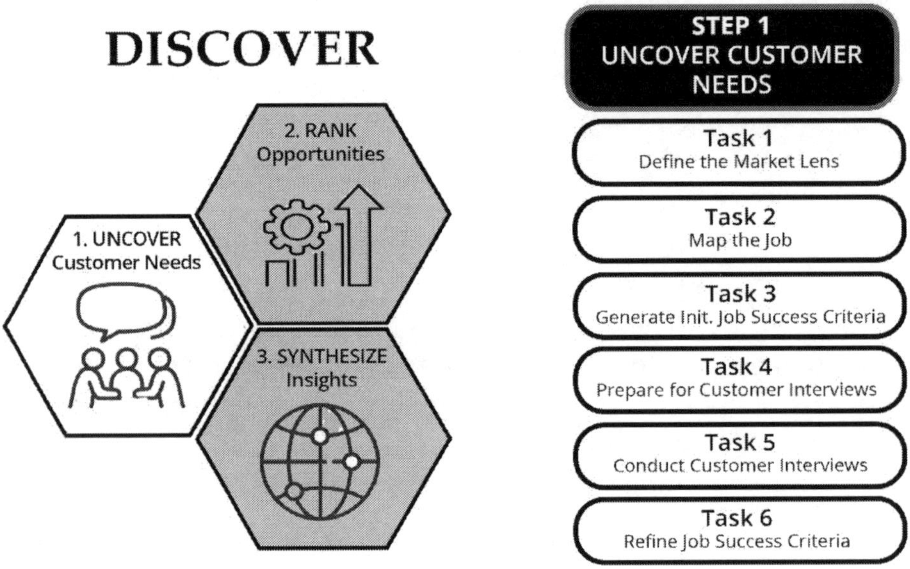
DISCOVER
1. UNCOVER
Customer Needs
2. RANK
Opportunities
3. SYNTHESIZE
Insights
STEP 1
UNCOVER CUSTOMER NEEDS
Task 1
Define the Market Lens
Task 2
Map the Job
Task 3
Generate Init. Job Success Criteria
Task 4
Prepare for Customer Interviews
Task 5
Conduct Customer Interviews
Task 6
Refine Job Success Criteria

II. STEP 1: UNCOVER CUSTOMER NEEDS

SHELTON NOTICED A NEW EMAIL from Mark Reynolds, CEO of Big Sky Outdoors:

Shelton,

I'm looking forward to the great work from you and your team on the next-generation tent project. Feel free to let me know if you anticipate any problems. This is an important project!

Thx,

MR

Shelton sighed and nodded. It was time to get to work.

The previous chapters covered the fundamentals that underpin The Discovery Engine. We followed the team from Big Sky Outdoors as they learned these basics they'll apply to their tent initiative.

This book now transitions from its grounding in core principles to Step 1 of DISCOVER, "Uncover Customer Needs," which walks through six tasks:

Task 1: Define the Market Lens

Task 2: Map the Job

Task 3: Generate Initial Job Success Criteria

Task 4: Prepare for Customer Interviews

Task 5: Conduct Customer Interviews

Task 6: Refine Job Success Criteria

Where We Are in DISCOVER

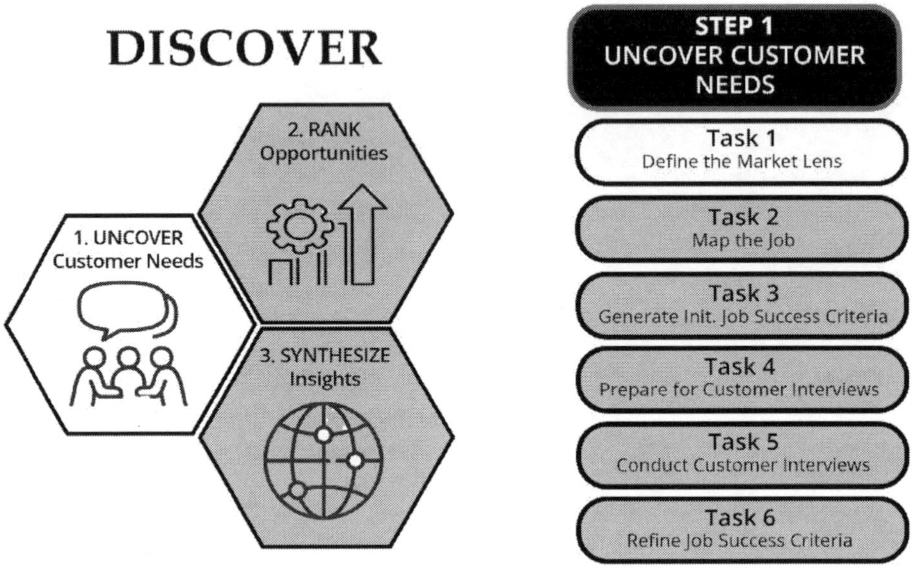

Step 1, Task 1: Define the Market Lens

What this chapter helps you do

Define the market, customer, use context, and Core Job Anchor that will guide the discovery effort.

What you will have by the end

A clear Market Lens that keeps the rest of the DISCOVER process focused.

Coming next

Task 2: Map the Job

Chapter 6: Task 1, Define the Market Lens

Who Are We Building This For?

SHELTON SET HIS NOTEBOOK ON THE CONFERENCE TABLE. Jenna was already in the room, taking notes in a weathered spiral-bound notebook, as the rest of the team filed into the room. A moment of silence hovered in the space.

"Alright," Shelton began. "Mark Reynolds, yes, our CEO, actually just sent me a direct email. He let me know that he's expecting good things from our work. I've heard that he's calling it the next-generation tent project now. Expect to hear that name in the notes from the executives' meetings."

Tom said, "Honestly, I understand where he's coming from. The company needs a winner. Did you know that REI just cut its forecast for next year?"

Shelton said, "That pressure shifts to us now, doesn't it?"

Luis replied, "It sure does."

Jenna asked, "What should we do first? Where do we start?"

Luis answered immediately. "I know that we're supposed to start this new process and all, but Mr. Reynolds wants to go fast. He's made that clear enough. We don't need to be professors here. Don't we know the key spec already? It's weight. If we cut a few hundred grams without sacrificing strength, we'll have something to talk about. There are some promising new fabrics out there. Really interesting stuff coming out of..."

Shelton interrupted, "Guys, we've already talked about the issues when we begin with the product specs. But, I tell you what: let's go with this line of thinking for a minute. Tell me more about tent weight as an issue for backpackers. Tom, you've been around longer than most of us. What do you think?"

Tom leaned back in his chair. "Weight? Well, ok, yeah, for some, but it depends on *which backpackers* you're talking about."

Luis frowned. "What do you mean? We said 'backpackers', isn't that enough?"

Tom shook his head. "Not exactly. I spend a lot of time talking to people in stores and on the trail. You're talking about weight, right? The ultralight crowd is loud, sure. They make all the YouTube videos, but they're not the majority. Not even close. We know that there are 100 times more folks doing weekend trips, three or four days. They want gear that works without fuss."

Jenna jumped in. "You're both sort of right and wrong. Some groups don't all care about the same things. Some worry about weight. Some worry about weather. Some worry about being cold. Some just want something easy to set up. It depends on whether they're hiking alone, with friends, or with families. If we're being real here, 'Backpackers' is just too broad a term."

The conversation bounced around the room. Ultralight thru-hikers. Weekend warriors. Alpine trips. Car campers who occasionally venture further in. Each team member was drawing from a different mental picture of the customer, and the discussion kept bouncing around without landing.

Shelton let it run for a while. Then he stood and walked to the whiteboard.

He wrote one word at the top: *Backpackers*.

"This is our problem," he said, underlining it twice. "We're talking about everyone. Which means we're talking about no one in particular."

He wrote a question underneath: *Who are we building this for?*

The room went quiet.

Jenna said, "Remember Arthur? The senior product manager who retired last year. Before every project, he used to ask something similar. He'd say, "Who are we innovating for? I never fully understood what he meant. But I understand now."

Tom leaned forward. "I think I do too. And I think I have a part of the answer: weekend backpackers," he said. "That's what the research says is the biggest group, and many aren't that concerned about cost. Three to five-day trips. Mixed terrain. Not ultralight obsessives. People who want gear that performs without requiring a PhD to set up. They don't want to have to practice in their yard."

Jenna added, "And they have money to spend."

Luis nodded slowly. "That changes the engineering priorities. Ultralight hikers will tolerate a good bit of trouble if they save weight. Weekend backpackers usually just want things to work."

"Especially," Tom added, "when they're tired, and it's getting dark, and the weather is turning. But that's just one idea. There really are lots of folks. But look at Shelton's question. *Who are we building this for?"*

Luis added, "Or *who should we* be building this for?"

Shelton spoke up, "We don't have the answer yet, but you guys are asking the right question."

Luis laughed, "Technically, it was your question."

Shelton smiled.

He wrote five headings down the board, and the team spent the next 60 minutes discussing, referencing other research, debating, and finally filling them in.

When they stepped back and looked at what they had written, what formerly felt like pressure now felt like energy. There was a path forward. The conversation that had been scattered across the full landscape of backpacking was suddenly pointed at a specific person, in a specific situation, trying to accomplish a specific goal.

For the first time, they knew who they were trying to help.

Why Discovery Begins with a Lens

Before a team interviews a single customer, maps a single job step, or generates success criteria, they must answer one deceptively simple question: Whose world are we trying to understand? Who do we want to innovate for?

The simplicity of the question betrays its significance.

When the scope of a discovery effort is not clearly defined, team members bring assumptions about who the customer is and what context matters. Interviews end up covering different scenarios. Job Success Criteria reflect different jobs. Survey results describe different populations. Contexts are all over the place. The research produces a collection of observations that cannot be compared or synthesized because they were never studying the same thing.

The Market Lens solves this problem. It is a concise, explicit definition of the specific customer, situation, and goal that the discovery effort will focus on. Think of it as the anchor for the entire research effort. It's the frame that ensures every job statement, every interview question, every Job Success Criterion, and every insight generated in the study refers to the same scenario.

Without proper planning, discovery becomes blurry. With a lens, the customer's world comes into focus.

The Five Elements

The Market Lens is composed of five elements. Together, they create a complete picture of the customer situation that the discovery effort will study.

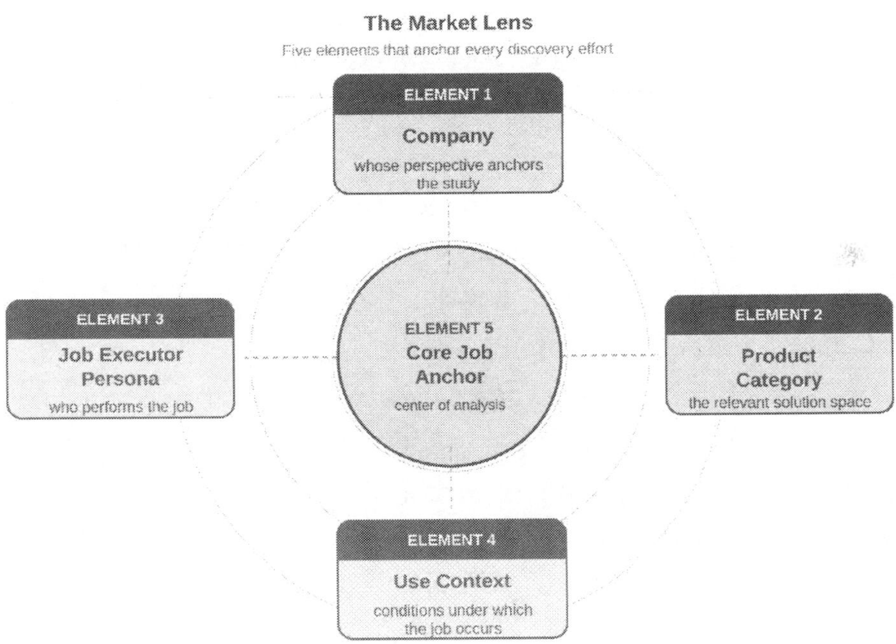

The first element is the *Company* that wants to build the strategy. This establishes whose perspective the study is taken from, which matters later when evaluating how well the company's current offering performs against customer needs. It also inherently shapes how close or far from current offerings the company wants to explore. Generally, it's lower risk to stay closer to a firm's capabilities. For Big Sky, this is straightforward: Big Sky Outdoors, a manufacturer of backpacking equipment with specific capabilities, constraints, and competitive pressures that will eventually shape how opportunities are interpreted.

The second element is the *Product Category*. Rather than naming a specific product model, the category defines the solution space in the way customers naturally think about it. For Big Sky, the category is *backpacking tents*. This boundary keeps the study focused on the relevant solution space while remaining broad enough to capture the full range of how customers interact with and evaluate tents. Defining the category matters because it determines which Product Jobs are in scope. That is, the specific interactions a customer has with a tent across its lifecycle, from purchase through disposal. As a reminder, a product is a generic term for any solution, including services.

The third element is the *Job Executor Persona*: the specific person performing the job. It is a realistic composite of the human being responsible for getting the job done. For Big Sky, the job executor is the weekend backpacker, not the thru-hiker optimizing every ounce, and not the casual camper who drives to a site. The weekend backpacker takes multi-day trips into genuine backcountry, carries everything they need, and typically arrives at camp tired after a full day of hiking. That specificity matters. The same tent category serves very different executors, and the needs of one group are not reliably predictive of the needs of another.

The fourth element is the *Use Context*: the specific conditions under which the job occurs. Context has a profound effect on what customers need and how they evaluate performance. A tent used in a backyard is a very different product than a tent used nine miles into alpine wilderness as an afternoon storm builds along the ridge. For Big Sky, the use context is three-to-five-day trips in moderate terrain with variable weather. These conditions introduce specific pressures around setup speed, weather protection, and the physical demands of tired hikers working in imperfect environments.

The fifth element is the *Core Job Anchor*: the fundamental, solution-agnostic goal the customer is trying to accomplish. This is the center point of the analysis. It is the job-to-be-done that exists independent of any particular tent design or technology. For Big Sky, the Core Job Anchor is *staying protected from the elements while backpacking*. Every Product Job, every success criterion, and every insight generated in the study ultimately connects back to improving performance against this goal. To get to the Core Job Anchor, return to the Product Category, and ask about the purpose, such as, "What does a backpacker use a tent for?" And the answer is, "To stay protected from the elements while backpacking."

The Big Sky Market Lens

When Shelton's team finished their conversation, the Market Lens for the Big Sky discovery effort looked like this:

Company: Big Sky Outdoors

Product Category: Backpacking tents

Job Executor Persona: Weekend backpackers

Use Context: Three-to-five-day trips in moderate terrain with variable weather

Core Job Anchor: Stay protected from the elements while backpacking

Written out plainly, it appears almost self-evident. But the team had spent over an hour arriving at it, working through disagreements about who the target customer actually was, what context defined their experience, and what goal anchored the analysis.

That conversation was the most important alignment the team would achieve before research began. Every subsequent decision, who to interview, what to ask, and how to interpret what they heard, would be made in reference to this lens.

The Lens as a Filter

One of the most common errors in discovery is attempting to study too many scenarios at once. Teams try to include multiple customer roles, multiple product categories, and multiple use contexts within a single research effort.

The instinct is understandable. Executives in particular resist narrowing scope, reasoning that a wider net means broader appeal. In practice, it means less differentiated appeal.

When a discovery effort tries to understand the needs of ultralight thru-hikers and weekend backpackers simultaneously, neither group is studied with sufficient depth. The cost of breadth is depth.

Focus may create a constraint, but it's also what makes discovery reliable

And what isn't apparent early in the process is that to get valid survey results, a broader net also means a dramatically higher sample size. Otherwise, with the sample too small, the survey results will describe a population that does not actually exist, an averaged customer whose needs reflect no one's experience precisely.

The Market Lens is a filter, not just a frame. It determines what is inside the scope of the study and what belongs in a different analysis entirely. When a potential customer profile, use context, or job-to-be-done surfaces during research, the useful question is: would this person, in this situation, pursuing this goal, find this relevant? If the answer is no, it belongs in a different lens. For a different study, for a different team, at a different time.

Focus may create a constraint, but it's also what makes discovery reliable.

How the Lens Shapes Everything That Follows

Once the Market Lens is defined, it becomes the reference point for every subsequent task in the Discovery Engine.

Job mapping becomes more coherent because the job being mapped is clearly tied to a specific person in a specific context. The steps *that matter* for a weekend backpacker setting up camp after a long day may not be the same as the steps *that matter* for someone pitching a tent in their backyard for a fun night with the kids. The lens determines which version of the job the map should capture.

Customer interview sampling becomes more precise because the lens defines who qualifies as a relevant participant. Interviews conducted with people who match the Market Lens produce insight that is directly applicable to the discovery questions. Interviews conducted with people outside the lens produce interesting but noisy information.

Success criteria become more meaningful because they are interpreted in light of a specific context. "Minimize setup time" carries different weight for a rested hiker at a well-maintained campsite than for an exhausted one on rocky alpine ground in deteriorating weather. The lens keeps that context visible.

What Comes Next

With the Market Lens established, the Big Sky team knows what customers they will study, what they want to accomplish, and in what circumstances.

They know the "who." (weekend backpackers) They know the "what" they want to do. (Stay protected from the elements while backpacking) They know the context: three-to-five-day trips. And they're rooted in the world of tents.

The next step in the Discovery Engine is to look more closely at the steps they must take when using a tent to *stay protected from the elements while backpacking.* That requires more than knowing who the customer is. It requires mapping what they do.

Job mapping is the subject of the next chapter, and it is where the structure of the customer's work first becomes visible in a form that discovery can act on.

Key Takeaways

- Before any interview, job map, or success criterion can be produced, the team must establish whose world they are studying. Without a clearly defined scope, different team members bring different assumptions to the work, producing insights that cannot be compared or synthesized.
- The Market Lens is composed of five elements: the company conducting the study, the product category, the job executor persona, the use context, and the Core Job Anchor. Together, they create a complete picture of the specific customer situation that the discovery effort will focus on.
- The Market Lens is a filter, not just a frame. It determines what belongs in the current study and what belongs in a different one. Broadening the scope carries a cost. The cost of breadth is depth.
- Focus is what makes discovery reliable. A discovery effort that tries to study too many customer types, contexts, or jobs simultaneously produces an averaged picture of a customer who does not actually exist.
- Every subsequent step in the Discovery Engine, job mapping, sampling, discussion guide design, criteria generation, and survey construction is anchored in the Market Lens. Getting it right is the most important alignment the team will achieve before research begins.

Where We Are in DISCOVER

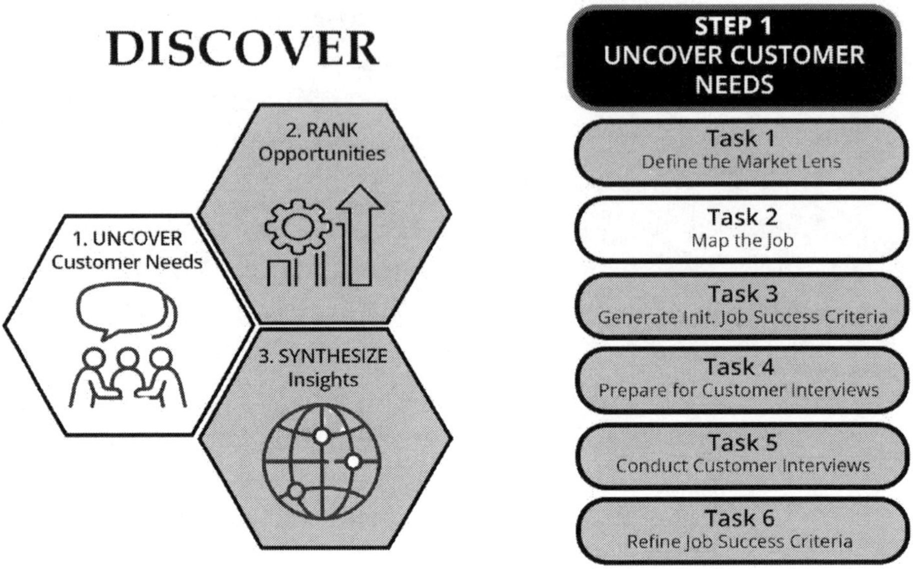

Step 1, Task 2: Map the Job

What this chapter helps you do

Build a job map that shows the major steps customers go through as they try to accomplish the job-to-be-done.

What you will have by the end

A structured view of the customer's job that helps organize interviews, identify gaps, and generate stronger Job Success Criteria.

Coming next

Task 3: Generate Initial Job Success Criteria

Chapter 7: Task 2, Map the Job

Step by Step

SHELTON STUDIED THE MARKET LENS ON THE WHITEBOARD. It looked back at him.

Big Sky Outdoors. Backpacking tents. Weekend backpackers. Three-to-five-day trips in mixed weather. Core Job: Stay protected from the elements while backpacking.

"Alright," he said, turning back to the group. "We know who we're studying. We know what they want to do. Now we need to understand what actually happens there."

Luis nodded. "So, we start designing the tent."

Shelton raised his eyebrows.

Luis, fighting back a laugh, smiled and said, "Just kidding."

The tension in the room evaporated as a laugh rumbled through the room.

Shelton shook his head slightly. "You got me on that one! Right. Not yet." He drew a long horizontal line across the whiteboard. "Before we design anything, we need to understand what the backpacker is actually trying to do. Step by step."

Tom leaned forward. "You mean pitching the tent?"

"Partly," Shelton said. "But think about the broader experience. How does this begin? Or even better, when does this begin?"

Tom spoke up, "When they arrive at camp?"

Shelton nodded and said, "There are multiple points we could select. But for this project, we're not as interested in purchase and preparation, so yes, that's the trigger, and *all jobs have a trigger*."

He wrote at the far left of the line: Arrive at camp. Picture a backpacker finishing a long day. They drop their pack. Now what happens?"

Tom started listing. "They look for a place to pitch. Sometimes it's rocky. Sometimes it's sloped. They have to figure out which direction to face."

Luis picked up the thread. "Then they unpack the tent. Separate the components. Assemble the poles."

"Stake the corners," Tom added. "Attach the rainfly."

"Adjust the tension," Luis said. "Check that it's stable."

"And all of that," Jenna said quietly, watching the list grow, "while surely they are tired. They're weekenders, not athletes. They might be extremely tired."

The ideas kept coming. Steps were added, deleted, and moved around.

Shelton stepped back and looked at what the team had produced in 30 minutes. A sequence. A structure. The job made visible as a series of connected steps.

He wrote across the top of the timeline: Establish shelter at camp.

"To be clear," he began, "we need to refine this process and the wording with our weekend warriors, our actual customers, but this is a start. This is what we need to understand before we design anything. Not the tent. Or at least, not just the tent. *The job-to-be-done.*"

The Value of Seeing the Structure

Customer interviews produce stories. Stories are valuable. They carry context, emotion, and the kind of specific detail that reveals how a job-to-be-done unfolds in practice. But stories arrive out of order. They emphasize dramatic moments and skip routine ones. Different customers tell different versions, and team members hear different things.

Without a structure to organize what interviews reveal, discovery produces a pile of observations rather than a coherent picture. Teams argue about which stories to include. Friction points get noticed without being located within the larger flow of the job or without appreciating the downstream effects.

Job mapping is the discipline that imposes structure on this complexity. It is the act of documenting the customer's work, literally, step by step. It captures the full sequence from the moment the job begins to the moment it is complete. A job map does not describe a product. It describes a process. It shows what the customer is trying to accomplish at each stage of the work, independent of any tool or solution. *Not what they are doing, but what they are trying to achieve.*

What Job Mapping Is — and Is Not

A job map has three defining characteristics that distinguish it from other tools teams commonly use.

It avoids solutions*.* A job map describes what the customer is trying to accomplish at each step, not how they accomplish it with a specific product. This means avoiding tool-specific language: not "insert the pole into the sleeve" but "assemble the tent structure." Not "hammer stakes into the ground," but "secure the stakes." There is some grey area here. Specific technologies can appear in a job map, but each one narrows the map's applicability. The goal is to stay as solution-free as possible.

It uses the customer's perspective. The verbs and framing of a job map reflect what the customer is trying to do, not what the product does or what the company delivers. The customer is not "shipping a shelter," they are "receiving a shelter." This distinction keeps the map anchored in customer experience. While this sounds trivial, it's a common misunderstanding for practitioners as they begin to map their first jobs.

It is universal. A well-constructed job map applies across technologies, across product categories, and across time. The job of establishing shelter at camp was performed by backpackers decades ago with canvas and rope, and it will be performed decades from now with materials and systems not yet imagined. The map captures the job, not the current solution for it.

These characteristics are what make job maps strategically useful. A map that is solution-free and customer-centered reveals friction points that a product-focused analysis will miss, because it is looking at the customer's objectives rather than the product's performance.

Some practitioners resist the discipline of job mapping, finding its rules unnecessarily rigid. What they often miss is the strategic value of the artifact that results.

The Eight Universal Steps

Most jobs, when examined carefully, follow a recognizable structure. Regardless of industry, category, or customer, the work of accomplishing a goal tends to move through a consistent sequence of phases: from defining what needs to happen, through executing the core action, to concluding and resetting for the next cycle.

Lance Bettencourt and Tony Ulwick identified this structure through extensive research in customer-centered innovation, and it has proven durable across a remarkable range of contexts. Understanding it gives discovery teams a scaffold for constructing job maps that are comprehensive rather than partial.

Define: The customer clarifies what success looks like and establishes the parameters of the task. For the backpacker, this means choosing where to set up camp: evaluating the terrain, the wind direction, the proximity to water, and the flatness of the ground. Common verbs include plan, select and determine.

Locate: The customer gathers the inputs, tools, and resources needed to perform the job. For the backpacker, this means retrieving the tent from the pack: finding it among the other gear, extracting it without losing components, and laying out the pieces. Common verbs include gather, access, or retrieve.

Prepare: The customer organizes and stages everything needed before the core action begins. For the backpacker, this means clearing and preparing the ground: removing rocks and debris, smoothing the surface, and positioning the footprint. Common verbs include set-up, organize, or examine.

Confirm: The customer verifies that everything is in order before proceeding. For the backpacker, this means locating and separating the tent components: confirming that stakes, poles, the inner tent, and the rainfly are all present and accounted for. Common verbs include validate, prioritize, or decide.

Execute: The customer performs the core transformation: the central action the job exists to accomplish. For the backpacker, this is pitching and staking the tent: assembling the poles, attaching the tent body, and securing the structure to the ground. Common verbs include perform, transact, or administer. However, typically, the Execute step is a restatement of the job being mapped.

Monitor: The customer tracks progress and results, checking that things are going as they should. For the backpacker, this means assessing the shelter after setting up, checking tension, testing stability, and evaluating protection from wind and rain. Common verbs include verify, track, or check.

Modify: The customer adjusts when something is not right. For the backpacker, this means correcting problems: re-tensioning guy lines, repositioning stakes, and opening or closing ventilation as conditions change. Common verbs include update, adjust, or maintain.

Conclude: The customer wraps up, stores, and resets for the next cycle. For the backpacker, this means breaking down and packing the tent: dismantling the structure, folding or stuffing the components, and returning everything to the pack. Common verbs include store, finish, or close.

For more on this structure, read the landmark HBR article by Lance Bettencourt and Tony Ulwick, ***"The Customer-Centered Innovation Map."***

One observation deserves emphasis. Most product innovation focuses on the Execute step, which is the central action of the job. But the research behind this framework consistently finds that snags often live in the surrounding steps: Define, Prepare, Confirm, Monitor, Modify, and Conclude. These are the steps most likely to be underexplored in discovery and underserved by existing solutions. A job map that captures all eight steps ensures that those overlooked moments are visible and available for analysis.

Most product innovation focuses on the obvious step, but the best opportunities often live around it.

By the way, there can certainly be more than eight steps, or fewer than eight steps. Many misunderstand the purpose of the eight common job step templates, incorrectly interpreting this to mean that every job has eight steps. Instead, practitioners should think of these as triggers to ensure that they have covered the job completely.

The Big Sky Outdoors Job Map

Applying this structure to the Big Sky discovery effort produces a job map for the job of pitching a tent, the cluster of Product Jobs at the heart of the shelter experience for weekend backpackers.

Define: Select a tent site.

Locate: Retrieve the tent from the backpack

Prepare: Prepare the ground for the tent

Confirm: Locate tent components

Execute: Pitch the tent

Monitor: Monitor conditions (tension, stability, airflow, weather protection, etc.)

Modify: Adjust the tent (re-tension, open or close ventilation, service stakes, etc.)

Conclude: Pack up the tent.

Here we have a complete sequence from the moment the backpacker begins thinking about shelter to the moment the tent is returned to the pack the following morning.

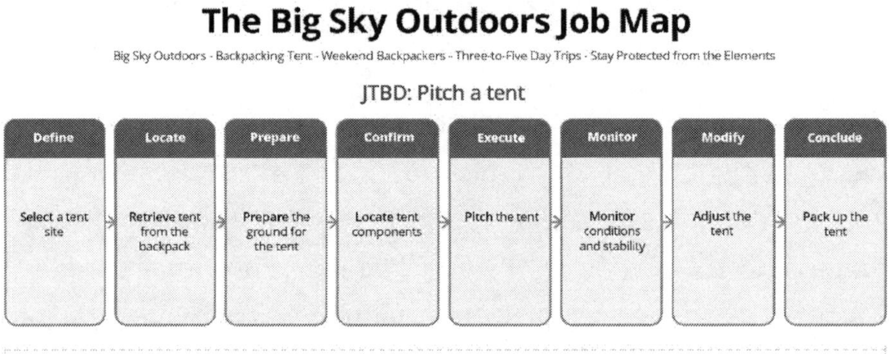

What this map makes visible immediately is the breadth of the job. Pitching a tent is not a single action. It is a process with distinct phases, each of which can go well or badly, each of which represents a potential challenge, and each of which may generate its own set of Job Success Criteria. The team that designs only for the Execute step, the physical act of assembly, has addressed merely a portion of the job.

The map also surfaces something that would be otherwise easy to miss: the Conclude step. Packing the tent the morning after is not glamorous, and customers rarely lead with it when asked about tent frustrations. A job map that captures Conclude ensures that issues remain visible through the discovery process. It also establishes where the job map ends.

Building a Job Map in Practice

Constructing a job map is iterative rather than definitive. Teams rarely produce a finished map in a single session. The process moves through multiple passes, each one adding clarity and correcting gaps.

The work begins by naming the job clearly, defining the state the customer starts with and the state they are trying to reach. For Big Sky, the job begins when the backpacker arrives at camp without shelter and ends when protective shelter is established. That boundary defines what belongs on the map and what falls outside it.

From there, the team sketches the core flow, the major steps of the job in rough sequence. This first pass is intentionally incomplete. The goal is to establish the backbone and the scope, not to capture every nuance. The eight universal steps serve as a useful scaffold here, prompting the team to look for definition, preparation, confirmation, and conclusion activities that might otherwise be overlooked.

The true job map is then actually built through early customer interviews, which are as much a calibration of the map as they are a source of success criteria. Customers will describe steps the team missed, collapse steps the team separated, or reveal that the boundaries of the job are different from where the team drew them. A backpacker who describes the job as beginning not at arrival but at the moment they start scouting the campsite while still hiking is telling the team something important about where Define actually starts.

The finished map, typically from eight to 16 steps for most jobs, becomes one of the most durable artifacts of the discovery effort. It gives the team a shared picture of the customer's work that transcends any individual interview or data point, and it provides the organizing structure for generating and later refining the Job Success Criteria that will drive prioritization.

Product Jobs and Core Jobs: Which to Map

One practical question that arises when constructing job maps is whether to map the Core Job, a specific Product Job, or something of a hybrid. The answer depends on the innovation question the team is trying to answer.

Mapping the Core Job — *staying protected from the elements*, produces a broad view of the customer's fundamental goal, largely independent of any specific product interaction. This level of analysis is most useful when the team is exploring where more ambitious innovation opportunities exist, potentially including solutions that look quite different from the current product.

Mapping a Product Job — *pitching a tent*, produces a more focused view of the customer's interaction with a specific product category. This level is most useful when the team is looking for opportunities to improve the experience of using and interacting with a product across its lifecycle.

For most discovery efforts, a hybrid approach serves best: Begin with a Product Job that sits close to the core action, then ensure the surrounding steps of the job map capture enough of the broader context to reveal friction that a narrowly product-focused map would miss. The Big Sky map does exactly this. It focuses on the pitching experience while capturing the full sequence from campsite selection through morning pack-out, preserving the context that makes the most consequential pitfalls visible.

What Comes Next

With the job map in hand, the Big Sky team had something they did not have before: a frame of the customer's work. The sequence of steps was visible. The full scope of the job, from campsite selection to morning pack-out, was on the board.

But a map of the job is not yet a map of customer needs.

That raises an important question: **What is a customer need, exactly?** Is it a requested feature? A product improvement? A complaint? A preference? Or is it something more precise?

What is a customer need, exactly?

In Prism, customer needs are expressed as the criteria customers use to judge success. They are the standards customers apply, often without consciously naming them, when deciding whether they can accomplish the job well and whether a product helps or gets in the way.

The next task in the Discovery Engine addresses exactly that. It's time to turn the structure of the job into an initial set of Job Success Criteria that can be tested, refined, and ultimately measured across the market.

Key Takeaways

- Without a structure to organize what customer interviews reveal, discovery produces a pile of observations rather than a coherent picture. A job map imposes that structure by documenting the customer's work step by step: what they are trying to accomplish at each stage, independent of any particular product.
- A strong job map has three defining characteristics: it is as solution-free as possible, written from the customer's perspective, and universal enough to remain valid regardless of which product the customer uses or what future technologies may replace it.
- Most jobs follow a recognizable eight-phase structure: Define, Locate, Prepare, Confirm, Execute, Monitor, Modify, Conclude. Most product innovation focuses on Execute, the central action, while significant friction often lives in the surrounding steps that teams rarely examine.
- The job map is built iteratively. The team's first version is a structured hypothesis. Early customer conversations will refine it, revealing steps that were missed, boundaries that were drawn in the wrong place, and sequences that unfold differently than the team assumed. It will never be complete until updated with actual customers.
- A completed job map becomes one of the most durable artifacts of the discovery effort. It is the organizing structure for generating success criteria, designing a discussion guide, and interpreting what customers reveal in conversations.

Where We Are in DISCOVER

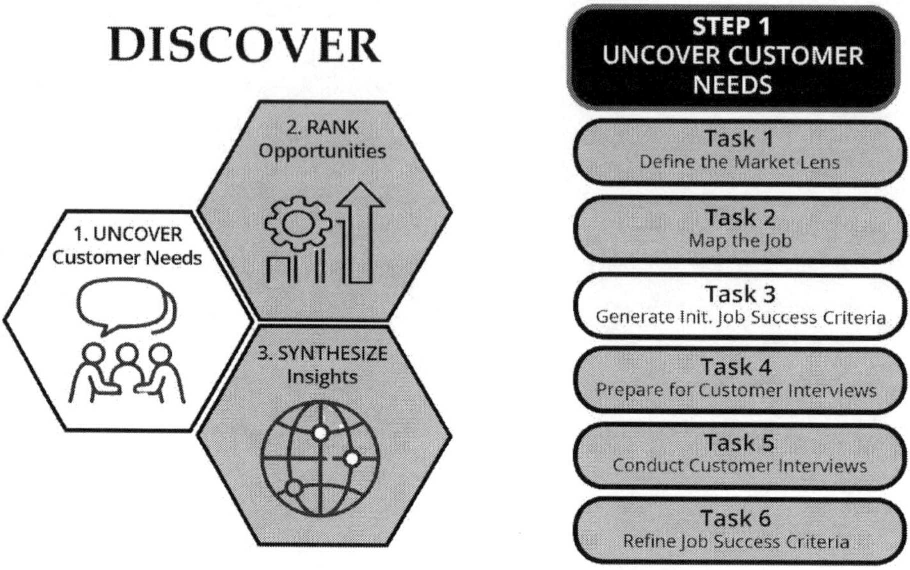

Step 1, Task 3: Generate Initial Job Success Criteria

What this chapter helps you do

Clarify what a customer need really is: not just a feature request, complaint, or preference, but the "Job Success Criteria" that customers use to judge how well they can accomplish their job-to-be-done.

What you will have by the end

A first draft of customer need statements, called "Job Success Criteria" that can be tested, challenged, and improved through customer interviews.

Coming next

Task 4: Prepare for Customer Interviews

Chapter 8: Task 3, Generate Initial Job Success Criteria

Visualizing Success

THE WHITEBOARD IN THE CONFERENCE ROOM was now divided into eight columns, one for each step of the job map the team had built the day before. Choose a campsite. Retrieve the tent. Prepare the ground. Separate components. Pitch and stake. Monitor conditions. Adjust. Pack out.

Shelton stood back and looked at the process. "Okay," he said. "We understand the steps. Now the real question. What does success look like for each one?"

Luis crossed his arms. "You mean performance targets?"

"Not... exactly. Not yet anyway," Shelton said.

Jenna looked down at her notes. "I thought the point of this step was to gather customer needs."

"It is," Shelton said.

"Then I guess I'm asking a basic question," Jenna replied. **"What is a customer need, exactly?** Is it a feature they ask for? A complaint? A preference? A benefit?"

Luis nodded. "Because if a customer says they need a more durable zipper, is that the need? Or is that their idea for fixing something?"

Shelton paused for a moment. "That's the question we have to answer before we go much further. If we define customer needs too loosely, we'll collect a pile of opinions. If we define them precisely, we'll have something we can test, compare, and eventually build a strategy around."

He turned back to the job map.

"First, we need to understand what backpackers are trying to accomplish at each moment. And what makes something go badly? What makes a step slow? Unpredictable? Inconsistent? A..."

Tom leaned forward. "A pain!"

Shelton laughed. "Yeah. A pain."

Tom continued, "That reminds me of something a guy told me last summer. Ryan Carter was an engineer from Fort Collins. He was describing a trip into the Indian Peaks."

Jenna looked up. "What happened?"

"Nothing super dramatic," Tom said. "But he did talk about rocks. Rocky ground. Couldn't get the stakes in. Storm clouds are building while he's trying to get the tent up." He paused. "But the way he described it stuck with me. He said the worst feeling wasn't when sleeping through the storm. It was before then, when the rain started while setting up the tent. His gear was getting wet, and the shelter wasn't ready. As the clouds gathered, he felt more and more rushed. The trip was getting off to a bad start. Wet gear. Wet head.

Wet clothes. And not even a dry tent to climb into. And it all began with the stakes."

Tom paused and continued, "He's actually on our recruiting list. I figured if we're doing this right, we should talk to him for real."

Shelton replied, "Let's get him into the sample. But also, for now, let's consider what you learned, even with that brief story."

He picked up a marker.

"Ryan might say he needs better stakes. Or a lighter tent. Or an easier setup. But underneath those statements are the criteria he's using to judge whether the tent is helping him accomplish the job."

Shelton wrote the first line on the board beneath the Pitch column.

Minimize the time to establish shelter when the weather deteriorates.

Then he added another beneath Execute.

Minimize the likelihood of rain exposure inside the tent during setup.

Luis stepped forward. "And something about pitching on rocky ground." Shelton nodded and wrote again.

Minimize the time to secure stakes in rocky terrain.

It was just a start. Three statements. But they were precise in a way that the earlier feedback lacked. Nothing unclear, such as better, easier, more sustainable, etc. They described specific moments of failure in the customer's job, framed as standards that the backpacker was applying.

Tom looked at the board. "That does look better. I know what each of those means. And if I read them a year from now, I'll know what they mean. And Ryan could read them, and we'd all have the same interpretation."

Jenna looked back at the board. "So a customer need isn't just what they ask for."

"Right," Shelton said. **"Customer needs are the criteria they use to judge whether they can accomplish the job successfully, and whether a product helps them do it well."**

Jenna nodded slowly. "That's much more useful."

Then she looked at the eight columns still waiting on the board. "But now what?"

Shelton capped the marker. "We're just starting. But... this, friends, is what we're looking for. This is progress."

"Customer needs are the criteria they use to judge whether they can accomplish the job successfully, and whether a product helps them do it well."

The Purpose of Generating Initial Success Criteria

At this point in the Discovery Engine, the team has defined the Market Lens and mapped the structure of the job. They know whose world they are studying and what the work looks like step by step. What they do not yet have is a clear picture of how customers judge success at each step. That is, the specific standards they apply when evaluating whether the job is going well.

Generating initial Job Success Criteria is the work of producing that picture. The word "initial" is deliberate. At this stage, the criteria are not validated. They have not been created through structured customer interviews. They are informed guesses, a starting set of the team's best current thinking. **Put simply, the team is drafting a first set of customer needs. These needs are written as the criteria customers use to judge two things: whether they can accomplish the job successfully, and whether a product helps them do it well.**

This task is possible, even this early, because starting from zero Job Success Criteria is inefficient and unnecessary. Before a team speaks with a single customer, relevant knowledge already exists. The team can infer many needs from competitive products, published reviews, and the team's own accumulated experience with the market. The right approach is to use it deliberately... as a starting point for divergence, not as a substitute for discovery.

The team is creating a first draft of what customers may need in order to accomplish the job successfully.

From Job-to-be-Done to Job Success Criteria

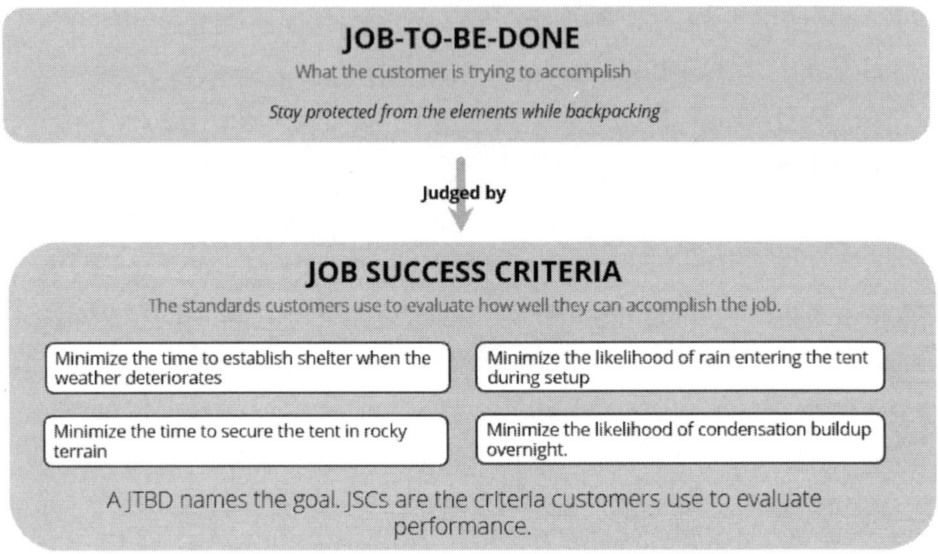

Three Essential Anchors

We can build initial criteria from three anchors. They do not guarantee that every criterion produced at this stage will prove valid; that is what customer interviews are for.

The first anchor is the Market Lens. Every candidate criterion must be evaluated against the specific customer, context, and goal that the lens defines. For Big Sky, that means the criterion must reflect the experience of a weekend backpacker on a three-to-five-day trip in variable weather, pursuing the goal of staying protected from the elements. The Market Lens is not just a scoping decision made at the beginning of the project. It is the scope, applied at every subsequent step, including this one. When an initial criterion is being considered, the test is simple: would this specific customer, in this specific context, pursuing this specific goal, care about this? Even if the answer is possibly yes, include it.

The second anchor is the Jobs-to-be-Done Pyramid. This reminds teams that customers both have tasks when interfacing with the product (acquisition, preparation, usage, maintenance, and disposal) in addition to the core job, the primary function the product serves. While it could also be a trigger for identity and emotional jobs that a customer has throughout the experience, we only capture Job Success Criteria for the jobs within the functional domain.

The third anchor is the job map. This provides the organizing structure for generating criteria. Each of the steps is a distinct zone of potential issues. Working through the map systematically ensures that criteria are generated for campsite selection, component retrieval, ground preparation, and pack-out, not just for the pitching moment that dominates product thinking.

It is worth noting that the job map, like the initial criteria themselves, has also not yet been validated with customers at this point. The team built it from internal knowledge and experience. It is a reasonable and structured hypothesis about how the job unfolds; however, customers may describe steps the team missed, collapse steps the team separated, or reveal that the boundaries of the job sit in different places than the team assumed. This does not undermine its value as a starting point. It simply means the map should be treated as a working structure that will be refined through interviews, not a confirmed account of the customer's experience.

How can we do this before interviewing customers?

The answer lies in remembering what divergence is for. Divergence is not about firm conclusions. The goal during divergence is completeness, through a comprehensive set of criteria. The cost of a false positive, an extra included criterion that turns out not to matter, is small compared to the cost of a false negative, a real criterion that was never surfaced. Generating candidates early protects against the second kind of error.

The cost of a few extra criteria is small compared to the cost of missing one that matters.

The job map helps. It is a knowledgeable guess about what customers are trying to accomplish, organized around the logical sequence of the job. That structure gives the team a principled basis for exploring: at this stage of the job, what would success look like? What could go wrong? What constraints might customers be navigating? Working through those questions systematically, before the first interview, produces a list that is grounded in the job itself.

This list becomes a starting point. No claims are being made yet about what matters most. Judgment is still suspended. The candidate criteria carry no weight until customers assess them in Step 2.

Writing Job Success Criteria

Before generating criteria, it is worth establishing the rules that govern what a strong criterion looks like, building on what was introduced in Chapter 3. These rules apply whether the criteria are being generated internally at this stage or refined from customer interviews later. A Job Success Criterion should follow a consistent grammatical structure: a direction of improvement, a performance metric, and, when helpful, a context.

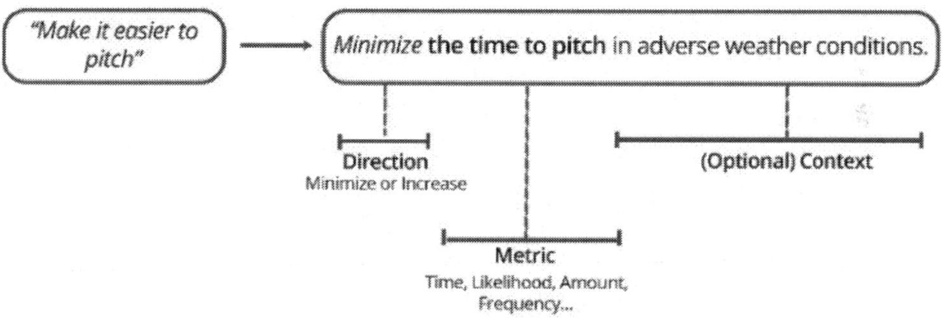

KEY PRINCIPLE
Frame criteria around what can go wrong
"Minimize the time...." is better than "Increase pitching speed" because it names the failure condition customers experience

Rule #1: Action-oriented, with a verb

A Job Success Criterion begins with a verb, most often "Minimize." Traditionally, Outcome-Driven Innovation allowed either "Minimize" or "Increase," but more recent practitioners have tightened this to "Minimize" nearly exclusively.

The recommendation for Prism is to use "Minimize" as often as possible. When strict adherence makes a statement significantly harder to read, due to "Minimize" producing a sentence with a double-negative, switching to "Increase" or "Maximize" is acceptable. Be aware, though, that varying the verb introduces the possibility of survey bias. The readability gain is real; so is the trade-off.

Key Principle: Minimize the Bad > Increase the Good

When Michelangelo revealed his statue of David to the world, the pope asked, "How did you create something so perfect?" His answer was, "I looked at the stone and removed everything that was *not David.*" And thus, we have a key principle that shapes how the strongest Job Success Criteria are written: Customers judge performance primarily by what goes wrong, not by what goes right. Innovation is not about adding good things; it is about removing bad things.

Customers judge performance primarily by what goes wrong, not by what goes right.

This may not seem intuitive, but it reflects something true about how experience works. When a job-to-be-done is going well, it tends to fade into the background. The tent goes up without incident, the stakes anchor cleanly, the shelter holds through the night, and the backpacker wants to think about dinner, not the tent. The memory fades.

It's when something fails, such as when the rain fly blows away in the wind, when the stakes are lost, or when the tent falls during the night, that performance becomes vivid and memorable. It becomes an experience locked with negative emotion.

Because of this, the most useful Job Success Criteria are framed around reducing failure rather than maximizing success. Consider the difference:

- Increase the number of trips that a tent can be used without leaking.
- Minimize the likelihood that the tent leaks.

Both point to the same underlying concern. But the second frames it as error reduction, which is how customers actually experience it. The first reaches toward an abstract measure of product life; the second captures the moment the customer dreads. This principle also provides a useful test when writing criteria: what could go wrong while performing this job, and what would it mean to minimize it? The answers tend to produce clear, grounded, actionable criteria.

Rule #2: Solution-independent, or as close to it as possible

A Job Success Criterion should describe what successful performance looks like, not how that performance is achieved. In its purest form, it does not refer to any product, technology, or design approach. A criterion written at that level of abstraction leaves the full solution space open and gives innovation the most room to work.

In practice, this is not always the best route. Product Jobs, in particular, involve direct interaction with the product itself, and the language of those interactions is sometimes unavoidably concrete. "Minimize the time to secure stakes in rocky terrain" names a stake. "Minimize the likelihood of poles bending under load" names a pole. These are solutions, not abstract performance standards. But they are also the honest language of the job as the customer experiences it, using technologies that, for the foreseeable future, are components of the world that the customer interfaces with.

The principle to apply is this: mention a specific solution only when the job genuinely cannot be described without it. But when you do, recognize that the scope of innovation has narrowed. A criterion that names a stake is still useful, but it is asking how to make staking better, not whether staking is the right approach at all, which is an inherent assumption.

When in doubt, try writing the criterion without the solution reference first. If the result is still specific enough to be meaningful and measurable, use that version. If it becomes too vague to be actionable, the solution reference is probably earning its place.

Rule #3: Measurable

A Job Success Criterion must be measurable, or at least as measurable as possible. It must be specific enough that different customers can interpret it consistently and respond to it meaningfully in a survey. "Improving the setup experience" is not measurable. "Minimize the time required to pitch the tent in adverse weather" is.

Summary: Job Success Criteria Guidelines

Job Success Criteria should follow these rules:

1. *Action-oriented, beginning with a verb*
2. *As solution-independent as possible*
3. *Measurable*

Plus: They should be worded to minimize bad things as opposed to maximize good things.

Job Success Criteria Examples

Weak: Make the setup faster.

Strong: Minimize the time required to pitch the tent when the weather is deteriorating.

Weak: Improve stake performance.

Strong: Minimize the likelihood of stakes failing to anchor in rocky terrain.

Weak: Strengthen rain protection.

Strong: Minimize the amount of rain that enters the tent interior during setup.

The strong versions are not just more precise. They are more useful at every subsequent stage of the Discovery Engine, from interview design through survey analysis.

Generating Criteria Across the Job Map

With the anchors in place and the rules clear, the team is ready to work through the job map systematically. For each step, they consider what could go wrong for this customer in this context.

There are many ways of asking "What goes wrong when trying to accomplish this job?", such as:

- What makes it slow?
- When is this inefficient?
- When does it go off-track?
- When does it have inconsistent results?
- When is it inaccurate?

Chapter 13 covers the 3D Probing Model, which thoroughly covers all the elements of probing questions, such as these. The product team can use the 3D Probing Model's questions to generate a healthy list of Job Success Criteria.

The following examples illustrate what this produces for the Big Sky job map. This is not a complete list. A thorough effort will generate far more, but it shows the range of criteria that emerges when the job map, the Market Lens, and the Jobs-to-be-Done Pyramid are applied together.

For the Define step — choosing a tent site:

- Minimize the time to identify a campsite suitable for tent setup
- Minimize the likelihood of choosing a site that proves unusable after unpacking
- Minimize the amount of exposure of the campsite to wind and weather

For the Locate step — retrieving the tent from the pack:

- Minimize the time to extract the tent from the backpack
- Minimize the likelihood of losing small components during retrieval
- Minimize the likelihood of misplacing other gear when extracting the tent

For the Prepare step — preparing the ground:

- Minimize the time to clear the ground of rocks and debris
- Minimize the likelihood of ground irregularities compromising tent stability

For the Confirm step — locating components:

- Minimize the time to separate all tent components
- Minimize the likelihood of losing components while unpacking

For the Execute step — pitching the tent:

- Minimize the time to erect the tent structure
- Minimize the likelihood of incorrect assembly in adverse conditions
- Minimize the time to stake the tent in rocky terrain
- Minimize the likelihood of the tent moving or collapsing during setup
- Minimize the amount of rain that enters the tent interior before the shelter is fully established

For the Monitor step — monitoring conditions and stability:

- Minimize the time to detect instability in the tent structure

- Minimize the time to determine whether the tent will hold overnight in the wind
- Minimize the likelihood of condensation buildup inside the tent overnight

For the Modify step — adjusting the tent:

- Minimize the time to correct instability
- Minimize the time to re-tension the corners
- Minimize the likelihood that adjustments need to be repeated

For the Conclude step — packing up the tent:

- Minimize the time required to break down the tent
- Minimize the likelihood of getting wet while folding and compressing a wet tent
- Minimize the likelihood of leaving components behind at the campsite

Notice that each of these criteria is framed around minimizing something that can go wrong. Notice also that they span the full experience of the job-to-be-done. Not just the pitching moment, but the moments before and after it that are equally real in the backpacker's experience.

Now consider the identity and emotional dimensions the Pyramid surfaces for the same job. Identity and emotional jobs surface alongside functional criteria, but they are captured differently. For example:

- Be someone who handles backcountry conditions competently
- Avoid appearing inexperienced or unprepared in front of hiking companions
- Avoid feeling anxious during setup
- Avoid uncertainty about whether the shelter will perform reliably overnight

- Feel proud when the tent is fully established

They are real motivations that influence how customers evaluate solutions, and they will likely not surface if the team only asks functional questions.

Sources Beyond the Team

Once the team has worked through the job map systematically, additional sources extend the list further.

AI analyses provide a highly complete list of job success criteria. With the Market Lens, the Job Map, and jobs-to-be-done framing, AI prompts, or interviews with synthetic customers can reveal a highly comprehensive list. Further, AI conversations can refine the writing for clarity, relevance, customer contexts and culture. This is often the best place to begin.

Competitive products and the customer language surrounding them are particularly rich. Every tent marketed in the category embodies a theory about what customers value. A tent advertised as pitching in sixty seconds implies a criterion: *minimize the time required to establish a protective shelter structure*, even if the advertisement does not phrase it that way. A tent that leads with storm-tested reliability implies a different one. Reading competitive claims and translating them from solution language into problem-space terminology surfaces needs that are already influencing market behavior.

Customer reviews, forum discussions, and community conversations extend this further. A backpacker who writes that a tent is nearly impossible to pitch alone in high wind is articulating a criterion. A forum thread about the anxiety of arriving at camp late with the weather coming in is surfacing an emotional job. A complaint about stakes that cannot be removed from rocky soil the following morning is pointing directly at the Conclude step of the job map. The team's job is to hear what's underneath the story and write it in measurable, solution-independent terms.

Prior research, support data, and institutional knowledge round out the picture. Organizations operating in a market for years have accumulated significant evidence about where customers struggle in many places, such as support tickets, warranty claims, and sales observations. Mining that knowledge systematically, filtered through the Market Lens, adds authentic depth to the working list.

A Working List is a Good Start

The output of this step is a working list. It's large, provisional, and imperfect. The criteria will be refined through customer interviews. Some will be reworded. Some will be split into more precise statements. Some will be found to reflect solution thinking and rewritten in problem-space terms. Many more will be added.

All of that is expected. The working list only needs to be complete enough to give the project momentum. To prepare the team for what they will hear later from real customers. For most jobs, a thorough effort at this stage could produce hundreds of criteria. That number may feel large, but that is not a problem to be managed *yet*. It is the natural output of studying a job-to-be-done with the seriousness it deserves. Proper convergence will eventually reduce the list and provide priorities. But that prioritization can only be as good as the list it is applied to.

For the Big Sky team, the wall is now covered. Criteria span every step of the job map, every level of the Jobs-to-be-Done Pyramid, and every source the team has been able to access. The hypotheses are in place. The next task is to test them against the lived experience of real backpackers.

What Comes Next

A working list of initial criteria and jobs is an initial draft of what matters to customers. The next step in the Discovery Engine is to add the experience of real backpackers, to find out what the list got right, what it missed, and what corrections to make.

That requires customer interviews. But interviews conducted without deliberate preparation produce scattered stories rather than structured insight. Before the Big Sky team schedules a single conversation, they need to think carefully about who to talk to, how to structure the discussion, and what they are specifically trying to learn.

Preparing for those interviews well is the subject of the next several chapters.

Key Takeaways

- Generating criteria and jobs before customer interviews is not a shortcut; it is a deliberate head start. The team already possesses knowledge from competitive products, published reviews, and domain experience. Using it systematically as a starting point makes the subsequent interviews more efficient and more directed.
- Three anchors keep initial criteria generation disciplined: the Market Lens (to filter for relevance), the Jobs-to-be-Done Pyramid, and the job map (to ensure criteria cover every step of the job, not just the obvious Execute step).
- A strong Job Success Criterion begins with "Minimize," names a specific metric, and optionally specifies the context in which performance matters most. They are framed around reducing failure rather than maximizing an abstract positive.

Where We Are in DISCOVER

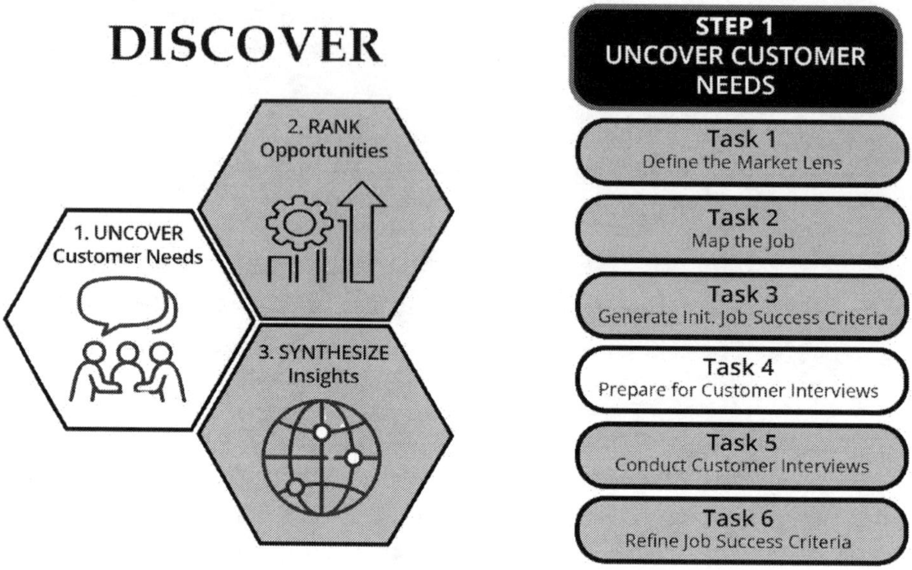

Step 1, Task 4: Prepare for Customer Interviews
Part 1: Getting Started

What this chapter helps you do

Plan the structure, logistics, and conditions needed for effective customer interviews.

What you will have by the end

A practical plan for organizing the team, context, documentation, and logistics needed to produce useful, trustworthy customer insight.

Coming next

Task 4 continues with the Moderator's Mindset.

Chapter 9: Task 4, Prepare for Customer Interviews — Getting Started

The Fastest Way Forward

SHELTON HAD BARELY SAT DOWN WHEN THE MESSAGE APPEARED on his phone. It was a text from Mark Reynolds, the CEO. Short and sweet.

> **How soon can we start talking to customers? Thx.**

Shelton read it twice. And a third time. The words glared back at him.

He knew exactly what was behind it. The company had spent weeks on innovation training. The kickoff meeting was weeks ago. Leadership was eager to see "progress." In most organizations, progress in discovery meant getting out of the building. Talking to customers as soon as possible, generating visible activity that proves a project is moving.

He typed a short reply but didn't yet send:

We're finalizing the prep now. We should be ready within a few weeks.

The team began to gather in the conference room. Luis noticed Shelton staring at his phone. Shelton exhaled a long breath and finally sent the text.

"Everything okay?" Luis asked.

"Mark wants us out there interviewing customers soon. Well, really soon," Shelton said.

Tom laughed. "That sounds about right."

Jenna leaned forward. "I'm not surprised. Can we start scheduling?"

Tom turned back to the group. "If we start interviewing tomorrow, we'll definitely move fast." He paused. "But we might not learn anything we can use."

Luis crossed his arms. "I know. We're not ready."

"Right," Shelton said. "Once we start, people will see that discovery is underway. If we rush, it will look good for a while. But eventually, we'll need to make sense of what we heard. We'll need data for a product strategy. A strategy to focus the engineers and developers."

Jenna looked up and said, "It's not just product. Marketing will use it for the website. The leaders will use it for strategic planning."

Luis added, "Did you know that John was promoted to CFO? He told me at lunch that he wanted our results when they're searching for M&A targets next fall. *Next fall.*"

The conference room felt expansive. Total silence. The little birds outside the window seemed suddenly quite loud.

Tom thought about the retailers and trail contacts he knew. "I could probably get a few backpackers on a call this week. But they'd all be people I already know, all local. Those guys use similar gear since they know what they're talking about. They've been around."

Jenna added quietly, "And what are we going to ask them? We haven't worked through that. We've been spending time focusing on what market to target."

Shelton nodded. "And that time was well spent. I'm taking a bit of a risk on this. But no one will remember an additional few weeks spent preparing. If we rush into interviews without being ready and our results aren't actionable, nobody will want to support this work ever again."

Jenna sighed, brushed loose strands of hair over her right ear, and added, "For sure."

Luis started to speak, then stopped.

Shelton capped the marker.

"It's alright. It's ok. It really is. I'll need to be tactful in communicating that we need time. More time. But we have to stay committed to the path. If we stray, we'll never be able to justify the poor results later. Mark has a lot of pressure on him, too, for speed. He's a good guy, actually. The good news is that with excellent insights, product development will go much faster than what we've seen before."

Shelton sat down and opened a blank page in his notebook.

He said, "But the fastest way forward is to slow down first."

Jenna raised her eyebrows.

Why Preparation Determines Quality

The quality of a discovery effort is not determined only by what happens during the interviews. The seeds of success are sown before then.

This sounds logical, but to an impatient organization, it feels off the mark. The interviews are what seem like real research. They are the visible, active part that generates results. Preparation weighs heavily like overhead. It seems like the planning and logistics are the procedural activities before the "real work" begins.

But this framing gets the causality backward. Interviews produce insight only when the conditions for insight have been established in advance. A poorly designed sample produces biased data regardless of how skillfully the interviews are conducted. A discussion guide that leads customers toward predetermined answers will confirm what the team already thinks, regardless of how open-minded the moderator tries to be. An interview team that has not agreed on roles will produce inconsistent data across sessions that resists synthesis.

Preparation is not merely overhead. It is the foundation that determines whether the interviews produce something of value.

The fastest way forward is to slow down first.

The following three chapters prescribe the preparation steps, beginning in this one, with assembling the team.

Assembling the Interview Team

A discovery interview works better as a team activity. Different roles contribute different cognitive functions during a session, and separating those functions across team members produces substantially better insight than asking a single person to do everything at once.

The Moderator

The moderator leads the conversation. They ask the primary questions, control the flow of the session, manage time, and maintain the neutrality that good discovery requires. The moderator's job is to be curious about the customer's experience, not to confirm hypotheses, not to advocate for the product, and not to fill silence with reassurance. The moderator needs to be comfortable with ambiguity, willing to follow unexpected threads, and disciplined enough to know when to stick to the plan and when to follow the customer.

Moderating well is a skill that develops with practice. For teams conducting their first qualitative discovery, it is worth investing time in a practice session, such as a mock interview with a colleague playing the role of customer, before the real sessions begin. The goal is not to script the conversation but to develop the muscle memory of asking short, neutral questions, listening without interjecting, and probing with curiosity.

The moderator is the only person who should direct new lines of questioning. Others should generally refrain from asking follow-up questions unless invited to do so. The recommended cadence is for the moderator to periodically pause and ask the team if anyone has questions to ask the customer. This gives the moderator a brief moment to review notes and determine where to go next, while allowing observers to raise anything that might otherwise be lost.

The Notetaker

The notetaker captures what the customer says, as close to verbatim as possible. The notetaker should, on the whole, avoid summarizing, because the specific words customers use often carry meaning that a paraphrase loses. When a backpacker says the tent *felt like it was fighting me*, that phrase is more analytically useful than a note that says the customer found the setup difficult. The notetaker treats the customer's words as raw material: language that eventually will be refined into criteria.

The notetaker also watches for emerging Job Success Criteria, marking moments where the customer's language suggests a measurable performance standard worth capturing. As a general rule, the notetaker's attention is better devoted to capturing notes than to asking questions. If clarification is needed to ensure accurate capture, a brief question is acceptable, but it should be consistent in tone and neutrality with the moderator's approach.

The Observer

The observer watches the session from a different cognitive position than the moderator. While the moderator is focused on the flow of the conversation, the observer is watching for dropped threads, moments where an interesting topic was raised and not pursued, where the customer's body language suggested something their words did not say, or where a connection to an earlier part of the conversation might be worth revisiting. After the session, the observer's notes often surface the insights most easily missed in the moment.

The Documentation Specialist

The documentation specialist manages recording, ensures audio quality, creates transcripts, and compiles session materials. In remote interviews, this means managing the recording platform and confirming that the audio is clean enough to transcribe reliably. In in-person interviews, it may mean operating a separate recording device. The documentation specialist reduces the cognitive load on the rest of the team by owning the technical and administrative dimensions of the session.

Staffing the Team

In practice, not every discovery effort will have the resources to staff all four roles. The minimum viable configuration is a moderator and a recording. Everything else represents an upgrade that improves insight quality. When resources allow only one additional person beyond the moderator, the notetaker role is the highest-value addition because preserved customer language is the raw material from which criteria are refined and synthesized.

On the upper end, be sensitive to how many people the customer is facing. There are no rigid rules, but a customer who feels like they are in a fishbowl will not give natural, revealing answers. An extra person or two beyond the core team generally causes no harm. More than five begins to create that risk.

Selecting the Interview Context

Where and how interviews are conducted shape what can be learned from them. There is no universally correct interview context. The right choice depends on research goals, the customer population, and available resources. But the trade-offs between contexts are worth understanding clearly before recruiting begins.

Remote interviews conducted via web conference are the most common format for qualitative discovery. They are fast to schedule, inexpensive to conduct, and allow teams to reach customers across geographies without travel. For most discovery work, remote interviews are a practical and effective choice. Their primary limitation is a lack of immersion. The moderator cannot observe the customer's environment, cannot see the artifacts and workarounds that often reveal things unspoken, and may find that the conversational dynamic is slightly more constrained than it would be in person.

In-person interviews at a neutral location, such as a coffee shop, a research facility, or a conference room, will offer richer conversational dynamics and stronger rapport. The moderator can read body language and physical cues more reliably than through a video screen, and there is often a natural warm-up period before the formal session begins that loosens the conversation. For customers who are less comfortable with technology or less accustomed to formal research settings, in-person interviews often produce more natural and revealing conversations. The trade-off is time and cost. Scheduling, travel, and logistics add friction that limits how many interviews can be conducted.

Contextual or field interviews, conducted in the environment where the job-to-be-done actually occurs, are the highest-value format when logistics allow. For Big Sky, this might mean observing backpackers at a trailhead, at a campsite, or even watching them pitch a tent in a park or backyard. The ideal would be to accompany a customer on an actual trip.

Field interviews reveal things better than mere conversational questioning can easily surface: the actual sequence of steps a customer follows, the workarounds they have developed without realizing it, the environmental conditions that shape their experience, and the physical and cognitive demands of the job as it is performed rather than as it is remembered. *The environment becomes the discussion guide.* Workarounds can be seen. Frustrations can be felt.

Every team conducting discovery about a physical product or an embodied experience should include at least a small number of field interviews alongside their remote or in-person sessions.

The practical recommendation for most discovery efforts is a blended approach: conduct most interviews remotely for efficiency, and invest in a smaller number of field or in-person sessions for depth and contextual richness. The field sessions will often produce insights that reframe what the remote sessions suggested, and they will almost certainly surface job steps, friction points, and criteria that were otherwise missed.

Documentation and Logistics

Before the first interview, the team needs to establish the documentation practices and logistical protocols that will allow insight to be captured consistently across all sessions and synthesized reliably afterward.

Recording is essential. Memory is not a reliable research instrument. Even skilled moderators with strong notes will miss things, misremember language, and gradually collapse the specificity of what customers said into summary and interpretation. Recordings allow the team to return to exact phrasing, verify their impressions, and surface details that were not noticed in the moment. Every interview should be recorded, with the customer's explicit consent obtained before the session begins.

Transcription converts recordings into searchable, annotatable text that the team can work with during synthesis. Automated transcription tools have become accurate enough for most discovery purposes. What matters is that transcripts exist and that the team knows how they will be used, which team members will review them, when they will be reviewed relative to the interview schedule, and how initial criteria identified in transcripts will be captured and organized.

The debrief is perhaps the most underappreciated practice in qualitative discovery. Immediately after each interview, before the team's memory of the session begins to fade, the team should spend time capturing their initial impressions and cleaning up their notes.

What surprised them? What Job Success Criteria emerged? What identity or emotional signals appeared? What follow-up questions should be added to the discussion guide for future sessions? The debrief is not an analysis. It is capture, preserving the freshness of immediate reaction before subsequent sessions, and the passage of time overwrites it.

But capture only works if there is time and mental space for it. Two interviews are the most a team should attempt in a day. More than that makes it difficult to debrief properly and nearly impossible to carry what was learned from one session into the next. The debrief is also the perfect time to make adjustments: modifications to the discussion guide, areas deserving more focus in subsequent sessions, or planned role rotations.

Common Preparation Mistakes

Even teams that understand the principles of interview preparation make missteps. The following are common and consequential.

Skipping the pilot interview. The first interview with a real participant should not also be the first time the moderator has run the discussion guide. A pilot interview, conducted with a colleague, a friend, or a participant whose data will be set aside, reveals problems with question phrasing, sequencing, and timing that are impossible to anticipate from the guide alone. It also gives the moderator practice with the format before the insights start to count.

Conflating roles during the session. When the notetaker begins directing questions or the observer interjects without invitation, the customer becomes confused, and the moderator loses control of the session. Roles can be rotated across sessions, just not within the same one, and not without intention.

Waiting too long to debrief. Teams that schedule back-to-back interviews without debriefing between them find that sessions blur together in memory. Takeaways and lessons from the third interview begin to contaminate recollections of the first. Debriefing immediately after each session should not be viewed as optional; it is what separates research that can be synthesized from research that has to be reconstructed from recordings after the fact.

Allowing stakeholder pressure to compress preparation. The most common reason teams rush preparation is external pressure from leadership, timelines, and the organizational belief that talking to customers is more valuable than preparing to talk to customers. This pressure is understandable and should be managed rather than simply resisted.

One effective approach is to make the preparation timeline visible to stakeholders early, explaining specifically what each step accomplishes and what risk is created by compressing it. Leaders who understand that a poorly designed sample will ultimately require more interviews to correct are usually willing to invest the time to design it well the first time. If leaders are kept informed, they will become advocates for executing the process well, not just fast.

What Comes Next

The practical foundations are now in place: a clear goal, a defined team, a chosen interview context, and the documentation protocols that will preserve what is learned. These are merely the initial checklist items to get ready. Chapters 11-12 continue with additional tasks in planning interviews and creating a discussion guide.

However, before moving forward, it's worth exploring *the moderator's mindset.* That topic is not another checklist item. It is something to reflect upon to be mentally prepared to begin research. It is the subject of the next chapter.

Key Takeaways

- The quality of a discovery effort is not determined only by what happens during interviews. It is also determined by what happens before them. Preparation is the foundation that determines whether the conversations that follow produce something usable.
- Discovery interviews work best with distinct roles: a moderator who leads and stays neutral, a notetaker who captures customer language as close to verbatim as possible, and an observer who watches for dropped threads and non-verbal cues. One person cannot do all three easily.
- Interview context shapes what can be learned. Remote interviews offer speed and reach. In-person interviews offer richer conversational dynamics. Field interviews, conducted in the environment where the job occurs, reveal things no amount of conversational questioning can surface. Most discovery efforts benefit from a blended approach.
- A common preparation failure is allowing stakeholder pressure to compress the timeline. Make the preparation work visible to stakeholders early, explaining specifically what each step accomplishes and what risk is created by skipping it.

Where We Are in DISCOVER

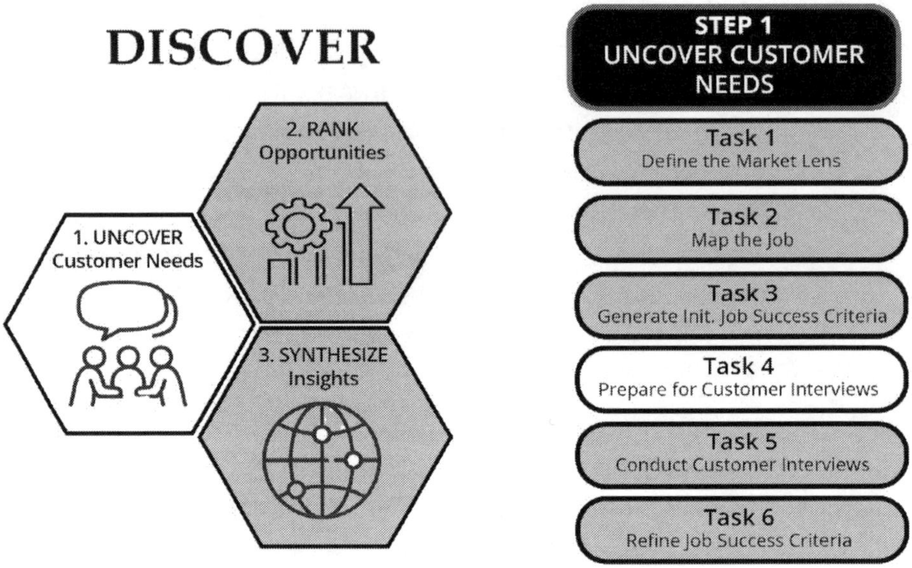

Step 1, Task 4: Prepare for Customer Interviews
Part 2: The Moderator's Mindset

What this chapter helps you to do

Recognize confirmation bias and adopt the mental frame needed to listen and learn without steering the customer.

What you will have by the end

A practical mindset for conducting interviews with curiosity, discipline, and restraint.

Coming next

Task 4 continues with deciding which customers to interview and how many interviews are enough.

Chapter 10: Task 4, Prepare for Customer Interviews — The Moderator's Mindset

A Head Start

TOM WAS ALREADY AT THE TABLE WHEN THE OTHERS ARRIVED, his notebook open in front of him.

"I have a confession," he said.

Shelton set down his coffee. "Go on."

"I ran into my buddy, Derek, this weekend. He does a lot of backcountry camping. We were at his place Saturday night, and I thought, *he's exactly the kind of person we're trying to talk to*. So I wanted to try some things out. I started asking him questions, you know, for this project."

Jenna looked up. "You interviewed him?"

"Yes. Well, I tried to." Tom turned his notebook toward them. The page was covered in notes, but several lines had been crossed out, and there were question marks scattered through the margins. "Honestly, it was kind of frustrating. Derek wasn't very helpful."

Shelton glanced at the notebook. "What do you mean, not helpful?"

"He just kept pushing back on everything. I asked him about the new DCF tents. You know, Dyneema Composite Fabric, the ultralight stuff. He basically dismissed it even though he had actually read about it. Said it was too expensive." Tom shook his head. "I tried to explain that the weight savings more than justify the cost on longer trips, but he didn't want to hear it. Just kept saying it wasn't for him. And then I asked him about carbon fiber poles and..."

Luis frowned slightly and jumped in, "Wait, you tried to *explain it to him*?"

"It would be better to say that I was trying to help him. These fabrics are a genuine breakthrough. I've been following the space for months." Tom leaned back. "But he just shut down after that. One-word answers. I had to drag everything out of him. We'll need to find better customers than him to interview."

The room was quiet for a moment.

Jenna spoke carefully. "Tom, what were you hoping to learn from Derek?"

"Stuff for our project, of course. What backpackers want in a tent. What frustrates them. You know, like we've been saying."

"And did you ask him that?"

Tom opened his mouth, then closed it. He looked down at his notebook. Two pages of notes, most of them about fabric weight and cost comparisons. He flipped forward. Then back.

"I think so. I mean, I thought I did," he said, more slowly.

"What did you find out frustrates him?" Shelton asked.

Tom stared at the page for a moment. "I have something here somewhere. I can't remember offhand."

Shelton nodded, not unkindly. "Derek wasn't giving you wrong answers," he said. "He was giving you answers you weren't expecting. Answers that didn't seem right to you. And when that happened, you did less interviewing and more advising."

Tom set the notebook down.

Shelton laughed before continuing, "Tom, you didn't do anything wrong by getting started or by having some ideas. I mean, but no, that wasn't a great interview performance. But still, I'm glad you had that experience."

Tom explained, "I see what you mean by advising. I think you're right. But why are you glad it happened?"

Shelton replied, "Because it's time for a talk about our mental frame. And how to not accidentally sabotage these sessions."

Shelton stood and turned to the whiteboard.

"What happened in that room has a name. And we all have to learn to manage it. All of us," he said, and wrote two words.

Confirmation Bias.

The Mental Posture

Discovery interviews require a different orientation than most business conversations. In most professional contexts, the goal is to demonstrate knowledge, advance an argument, or persuade someone toward a conclusion. Discovery interviews invert this dynamic. The moderator's job is to demonstrate curiosity, not expertise. The team's job is to be attentive, not judgmental. The entire purpose of the session is to learn something the team did not already know.

This is harder than it sounds. Teams entering interviews with a pre-developed Job Success Criteria list and a job map already in hand have formed ideas about what they expect to hear. The pull toward confirmation, toward noticing what fits the existing framework and discounting what does not, is a cognitive tendency that operates below the level of conscious intention.

A moderator who believes setup speed is the most important issue in the backpacking tent market will, without intending to, ask more follow-up questions about setup speed than about other topics, spend more time on answers that confirm that belief, and remember those answers more vividly during synthesis.

The corrective is not to pretend that preconceived ideas don't exist. They do exist, and they are useful. The corrective is to treat them explicitly as possibilities rather than conclusions. The discussion guide, the subject of a future chapter, is a structural tool for doing this. But the disposition must come first. A team that approaches interviews with genuine openness to being wrong will produce better discovery than a team that approaches them looking for confirmation, regardless of how well the guide is written.

The Moderator's Orientation

Conducting a discovery interview well begins not with technique but with orientation, with how the moderator understands their role and what they are trying to accomplish.

The moderator's role in discovery is the inverse of the expert role. The moderator is not the authority in the room; the customer is. The moderator's job is not to demonstrate what they know but to uncover the customer's experience. The questions should be simple, almost naive, because naive questions invite expansive answers. Silences should be tolerated, because silence gives the customer space to keep talking. The moderator's reactions should be neutral, because neutral reactions do not indicate which answers are more welcome than others.

One nuance deserves attention here. Neutrality does not mean coldness. Many customers arrive at a discovery interview with quiet uncertainty: they are not sure whether their experience is relevant, whether they are speaking at the right level of detail, or whether what they have to say is useful at all. A moderator who responds to everything with silence or a blank expression can inadvertently suppress the very openness they are trying to create.

Small, carefully chosen encouragements, such as "that's helpful" or "interesting," serve a different purpose than substantive reactions. They are not a commentary on the content of what was said. They are signals that the customer is doing the right thing by talking, that the conversation is going well, and that they should keep going. Used sparingly and applied broadly rather than in response to specific answers, they help maintain the customer's confidence and keep them in a talkative, exploratory state.

The risk is real, however. The same phrase that reassures a hesitant customer can also, if timed carelessly, signal that one answer was more welcome than another. The discipline is to offer encouragement in response to the act of sharing, not the substance of what was shared.

This orientation, curiosity combined with humility about what the team does not yet know, is the foundation on which every other moderating skill is built. Technique without this orientation produces technically competent conversations that nonetheless miss the most important things. Orientation without technique produces open conversations that fail to cover the right territory. Both are necessary. But orientation comes first.

Understanding Confirmation Bias

Confirmation bias is the tendency to notice, remember, and interpret information in ways that confirm what we already believe. It is not a character flaw or a sign of intellectual dishonesty; it is a fundamental feature of human cognition that affects everyone, including experienced researchers who are actively trying to avoid it.

Tom's conversation with Derek is a clean illustration of how it operates. He entered the conversation with a strong view that ultralight fabrics represent a genuine breakthrough, and that view shaped everything that followed. He steered the conversation toward it, pushed back when Derek didn't agree, and came away with two pages of notes that reflected his own beliefs more than Derek's experience. Derek's actual issues never surfaced. The conversation became frustrating for both.

The answers we did not expect are often the ones that teach us the most.

In discovery, confirmation bias operates through several distinct mechanisms that practitioners should be able to recognize and counter.

The first is selective questioning. Moderators who have strong notions tend to ask more follow-up questions in areas that confirm those hypotheses and fewer in areas that do not. A moderator convinced that fabric weight is the primary purchase driver will probe weight-related comments extensively and move quickly past comments about setup difficulty or overnight stability. The transcript will appear to confirm the hypothesis, not because the data supports it, but because the moderator created more data about weight than about anything else.

The second is selective noticing. Even when customers raise topics that contradict the team's expectations, those topics register less vividly than topics that confirm them. A customer who mentions in passing that they have never once thought about tent weight because they care far more about how quickly it goes up will register less strongly in the moderator's memory than a customer who confirms that weight matters. Confirming data feels significant. Disconfirming data feels like an outlier.

The third is selective interpretation. Ambiguous customer statements, which are most of them, tend to be interpreted in ways that fit preexisting ideas. When a customer says, "I want a tent that performs," a moderator focused on weather protection will hear that as being about weather protection. A moderator focused on setup speed will hear it as being about setup speed. The statement supports whatever the moderator already believes.

The fourth is selective recall. When the team debriefs after a session, the comments that get remembered and repeated tend to be the ones that fit the prevailing ideas. The surprising or contradictory remarks, which are often the most analytically valuable, fade more quickly from memory and receive less airtime in the debrief.

Understanding these mechanisms is the first step toward countering them. Awareness alone does not eliminate confirmation bias, but it does create a productive skepticism: a habit of reflecting, when a pattern begins to emerge, on whether that pattern exists in the data or in the questions that produced it.

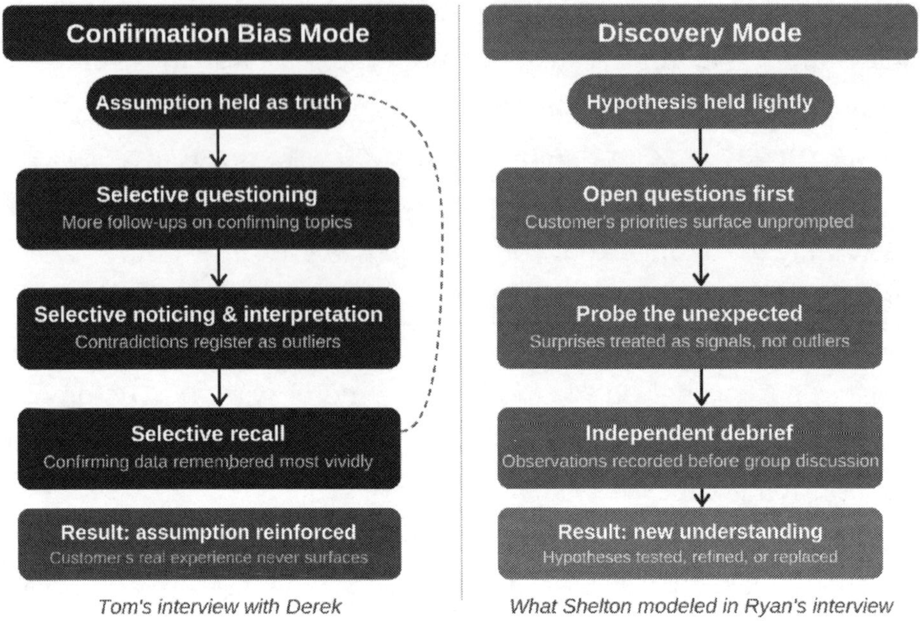

Practical Strategies

Because confirmation bias cannot be eliminated through good intentions alone, practitioners need a plan to counteract it during conversations and during synthesis.

The most powerful in-conversation strategy is to treat unexpected or contradictory responses as clues to something significant rather than anomalies. When a customer says something that does not fit the team's hypotheses, the instinct is to move on, to note it briefly and return to more familiar territory.

The disciplined response is the opposite: pause, probe, and seek to understand. What exactly did the customer mean? In what context does this arise? How important is it relative to other things they have described? The unexpected response may be an outlier. It may also be the most important thing said in the session. The moderator cannot know which until it has been explored.

A second strategy is to structure the discussion guide so that the customer's unprompted commentary is captured before the moderator's hypotheses can shape the conversation. Chapter 12 addresses this in detail, but the principle is simple: ask open, broad questions first and let the customer determine what is worth discussing before introducing any specific topics.

A third strategy is to rotate moderators across sessions when the team has more than one person capable of leading interviews. Different moderators have different assumptions and different attentional biases. A pattern that appears consistently across sessions led by different moderators is more likely to reflect something real in the data than a pattern that appears only in sessions led by the same person.

A fourth strategy is to compare independent observations during the debrief before group discussion begins. The debrief, covered as a logistics practice in Chapter 9, is also one of the most effective defenses against selective recall.

Body Language and Non-Verbal Signals

Confirmation bias does not operate only through questions and verbal responses. It also works through body language. And customers are highly attuned to non-verbal signals about *which answers are welcome.*

A moderator who leans forward slightly when a customer mentions a particular topic, raises their eyebrows when a specific concern comes up, or nods more enthusiastically in response to certain answers is signaling interest, which encourages the customer to provide more of what triggered the signal. The reverse is equally true: a moderator who glances at their notes, shifts in their seat, or responds with shorter follow-ups when a topic does not align with their expectations signals disinterest, which discourages the customer from pursuing that direction.

These signals are largely unconscious on both sides. The moderator is not deliberately communicating preference, and the customer is not consciously adjusting their responses. But the dynamic is real, and its effects on the data are meaningful.

The practical discipline is to maintain consistent body language across all responses, the same level of attentiveness, the same quality of eye contact, the same pace of follow-up, regardless of whether the customer is saying something expected or unexpected, confirming or contradicting.

This is not about being expressionless or clinical. Warmth and genuine interest are entirely compatible with consistency. The goal is to be equally interested in everything the customer says, which is the appropriate orientation for discovery. Every response is valuable, and the ones that feel least relevant in the moment could ultimately be the most important.

In remote (web conference) interviews, the same principle applies. Camera presence, facial expressions, and response timing are all visible to the customer and carry the same signaling risk as in-person body language.

What Comes Next

The practical foundation is now in place, and so is the mental frame that makes it useful. Two things are both true: the team has done real preparation, and that work has inevitably produced assumptions. The work from here is to hold those theories lightly, using them as a starting point for curiosity rather than a destination to confirm.

The next task is to return to the Market Lens and refine who to talk to. A sample plan that is thoughtfully built, one that reflects the range of customers whose experiences define the market, is what ensures that the mental frame developed here gets applied to the right conversations. That is the subject of the next chapter.

Key Takeaways

- Confirmation bias is not a character flaw. It is a feature of human cognition that affects everyone. Confirmation bias operates through selective questioning, selective noticing, selective interpretation, and selective recall. Understanding the mechanisms is the first step toward countering them.
- The moderator's role is the opposite of the expert role. The goal is not to demonstrate knowledge, advance an argument, or steer toward a conclusion. The goal is to be curious about the customer's experience.
- Unexpected or contradictory customer responses are evidence, not anomalies. When a customer says something that does not fit the team's presumptions, the disciplined response is to pause, probe, and understand, not to move on.
- Hypotheses formed during preparation are useful starting points, not destinations to confirm. The team should enter every conversation aware of its presuppositions and deliberately hold them loosely, using them to know what to listen for rather than what to find.
- Structural defenses against confirmation bias, such as open-ended questions before specific ones, independent debrief notes before group discussion, and rotated moderators across sessions, are more reliable than good intentions alone. The guide and the debrief process are tools for keeping bias from corrupting the research.

Where We Are in DISCOVER

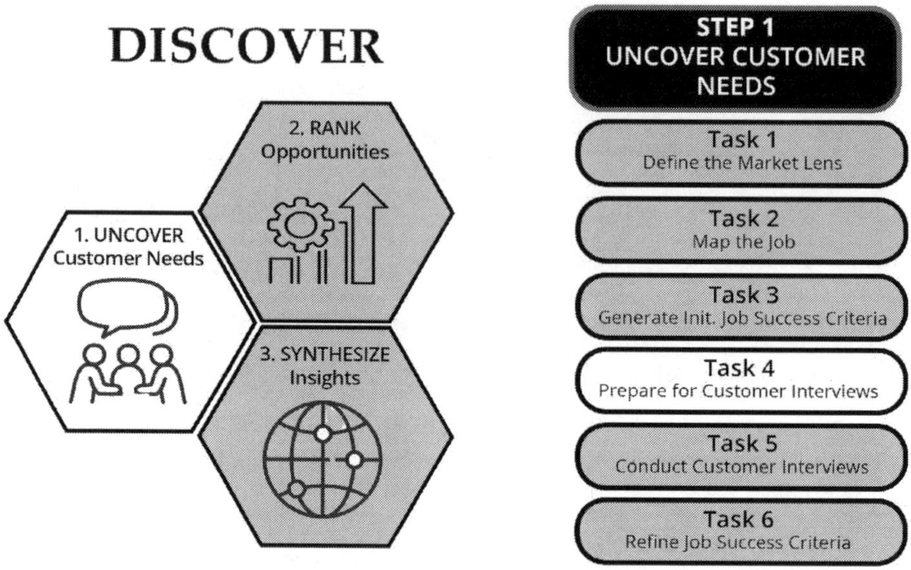

Step 1, Task 4: Prepare for Customer Interviews
Part 3: Sampling

What this chapter helps you to do

Decide which customers to interview, how many interviews are enough, and how to recruit a useful mix of participants.

What you will have by the end

A practical sampling plan for finding customers who can help you test, challenge, and improve the Job Success Criteria.

Coming next

Task 4 continues with building the discussion guide.

Chapter 11: Task 4, Prepare for Customer Interviews — Sampling

Who Should We Talk To?

THE WALL WAS COVERED WITH JOB SUCCESS CRITERIA.

Shelton stepped back and counted the statements clustered under each column of the job map. Eighty-three so far, and the team had not yet exhausted the Modify and Conclude steps. By the time they finished, the list would reach well over 100.

"Okay," Jenna said, studying the wall. "This is a start. But we need to find out which are real."

Tom said, "I can line up backpackers this week for our interviews. I know people through the retailers I work with, regulars who come in every spring before the season starts."

Shelton nodded slowly. "How many could you get?"

Tom thought about it. "Eight, maybe ten. Good people. They know their gear."

Luis looked up from his notebook. "So, we start with them?"

Shelton picked up a marker and wrote on the board.

DIVERSE VS REPRESENTATIVE

"Those are two different things," he said, turning back to the group. "And right now, we need the first more than the second."

Tom frowned. "What do you mean?"

"The people you know," Shelton said, "are they all weekend backpackers? Same region, same experience level, same kind of trips?"

Tom paused. "Pretty much, yeah. Pretty similar, now that you mention it. Colorado Front Range crowd mostly. But they could tell us a lot because they're all more experienced than average."

"That's exactly the problem," Shelton said. "Not with the people themselves, they'd be great interviews. But if we talk to ten very similar people, with the same background, even the same typical trips, we'll hear the same things. We won't know if what we're hearing is universal or specific to one kind of backpacker in one kind of context."

Jenna leaned forward. "But I thought we were supposed to find the most typical backpacker to target with this new tent. You know, weekend warriors and all that."

"Yeah, but there's more to it than that. I'm glad you said that, though, because it's my point exactly," Shelton said. "Right now, we're trying to find out everything that could matter to a backpacker in our Market Lens. *But within that, we need variety.* We need different customer types within the frame of the Market Lens."

Tom asked, "Different?"

Shelton confirmed, "Different."

Tom continued, "To get different answers? For what reason?"

Shelton replied, "Differences in customers, *because we are searching for full range of answers.* Here's the thing: with more variation, we can cover our Market Lens with fewer people. And I'll bet you know how we can get that done."

Jenna sat up tall. She nodded, "I believe I do. We're going to build a screener and work with that recruiter from the last VoC project, right?"

Shelton replied, "That's the fastest route. Yes, I'd say so."

Tom looked at the wall of criteria. "And we're designing the mix that we need before anyone starts lining up customers."

Jenna cut in, "Mix, yes, but the word the recruiter used was '*sample*.'"

"You got it. You've all got it. And Jenna, you're right, the recruiter can help us," Shelton confirmed.

Sampling Decisions

Among the decisions that determine the quality of a discovery effort, few have more impact than who gets interviewed. Yet sampling is often treated as an afterthought, a matter of contacting whoever is available, willing, and accessible. Teams recruit from their existing customer lists, rely on colleagues to suggest names, or accept whoever responds to a general call for participants.

The result is convenience sampling. It's fast and easy, and it produces real information about real customers. The problem is not that those customers are wrong to talk to. The problem is incompleteness. A sample built from convenience rather than design will systematically cluster around customers who are most accessible, most engaged, most vocal, or most similar to the team's existing relationships. Those customers tend to share characteristics, experiences, and priorities. Their feedback echoes.

In qualitative discovery, persistent echoes indicate that completion is near. When interviews start to sound alike, it can feel like saturation, like the team has heard enough. But if the sample lacks diversity across the Market Lens, what the team is actually hearing is a narrow slice of the market speaking in unison. Discovery that stops there will miss the segments, contexts, and use cases that would have complicated, enriched, and ultimately strengthened the findings.

Deliberate sample design, deciding in advance who to talk to and why, is the structural defense against this. It requires more planning than convenience sampling. It also produces better discovery.

Best Practice: Use a Recruiter

The best practice is to use a market research recruiter. They will be skilled in building screeners and, therefore, will help walk the team through the process of ensuring that they have a well-crafted sample.

If the team has been working through the Discovery Engine, they will be a dream client for a recruiter. With the Market Lens in hand and a solid understanding of jobs-to-be-done, the team may very well even teach the recruiter a thing or two.

But in practice, product managers and other practitioners have a day job. Recruiting customers for interviews takes time, and they are rarely the fastest or most effective at it. Yet the insights are valuable, expectations are high, and timelines are tight. In that context, relying solely on internal recruitment is usually a poor economic choice.

However, in some cases, such as industrial B2B or when there's a highly concentrated market, even recruiters may not have good access to customers. In those cases, teams may be working with business development or sales to line up interviews. A team in those situations should invest substantial time with BD/sales leadership to ensure that adequate time and priority are devoted to scheduling sessions.

Qualitative Sampling Is Different from Quantitative Sampling

Before designing a qualitative discovery sample, it helps to understand how it differs from the quantitative sampling most practitioners are used to in surveys.

Later, in Step 2, the Discovery Engine will turn to quantitative research. In quantitative research, often informally shortened to "quant," practitioners use surveys, usage data, market measurements, etc., to produce results that can be generalized to a broader population. **For that generalization to be valid in a quantitative phase, the sample must be representative**: its composition must mirror the composition of the population being studied. A survey of backpackers should include roughly the same proportion of experienced and novice hikers, weekend warriors and thru-hikers that exist in the market of interest. Statistical confidence depends on this representativeness.

Qualitative discovery operates on a different logic. Its goal is not to measure how widely needs are distributed across a population. That is the survey's job, which comes later. The goal of qualitative discovery is to uncover the full range of needs that exist, ensuring that every important customer need, friction point, and Job Success Criterion is captured before measurement begins.

To do that efficiently, diversity is essential. A sample that stretches the boundary of the Market Lens, reaching somewhat beyond a representative mix, will surface new needs faster than one that simply mirrors the target population.

Here's why. A purely representative sample of weekend backpackers will skew toward the most common type: moderately experienced, fair-weather hikers taking occasional trips in accessible terrain. Interviewing ten people in that profile will produce strong coverage of their needs. But across those interviews, the same needs will appear again and again. The list deepens, but it does not expand. The result is repetition, which slows discovery and increases cost without expanding what is learned.

Contrast that with a more intentionally diverse sample. Backpackers who camp in extreme weather. Those with physical limitations that affect setup. First-time hikers who struggle with what more experienced hikers take for granted. More advanced users pushing into technical terrain. Each group brings a different set of constraints, tradeoffs, and workarounds, along with different needs.

Skill level is one of the most important dimensions of this diversity. In many cases, *a person's skill and knowledge are effectively part of the product*. An experienced user may not mention common issues because their expertise has allowed them to work around or eliminate those frustrations. A less experienced user, facing the same situation, will surface those needs immediately. Including both perspectives ensures those needs are not missed.

This is why diversity accelerates discovery. New needs emerge more quickly, and the path to a complete list becomes shorter. In practice, this approach surfaces the full range of Job Success Criteria far faster than a purely representative sample could.

Qualitative discovery values diversity over pure representativeness. The sample should be designed to maximize the range of customer experiences, contexts, and perspectives that are heard, not to mirror their distribution in the market.

A diverse sample helps the team learn more from fewer conversations.

The practical implication is significant: qualitative and quantitative sampling require different instincts. Practitioners who are accustomed to thinking about sample representativeness alone need to balance that during the qualitative phase with a different question: who would bring a perspective to this job that we have not yet heard?

A diverse sample helps the team learn more from fewer conversations.

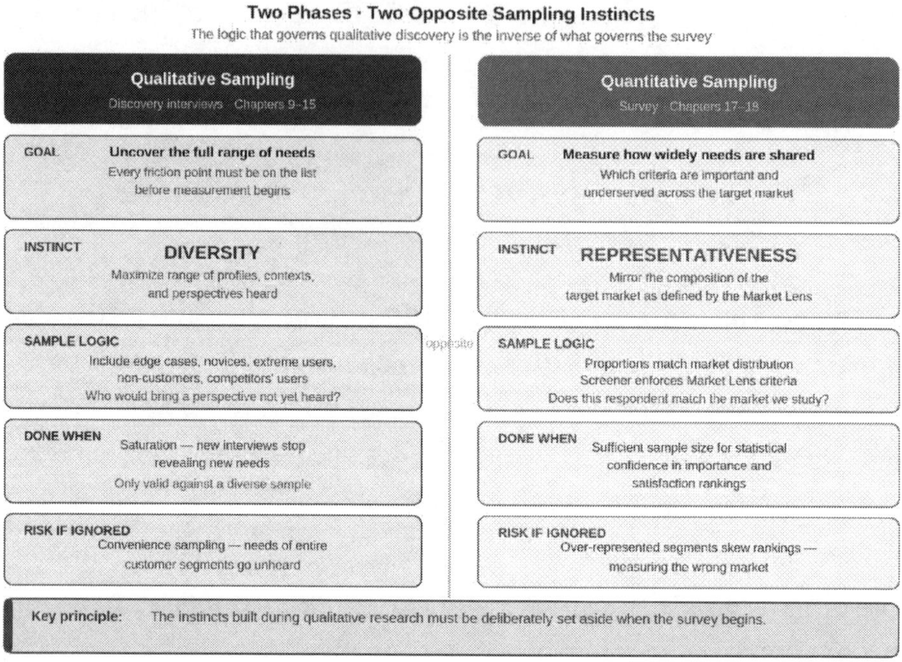

When are we finished? (The Concept of Saturation)

The question teams most commonly ask about qualitative sampling is: *how many interviews are enough?*

The honest answer is that the right number depends on both the diversity of the sample and the number of interviews conducted. These are two codependent variables. But there is a concept that helps teams know when they are approaching completion: saturation.

Saturation occurs when new interviews stop revealing new needs. When the team conducts an interview and finds that everything the customer describes: every challenge, every success criterion, every identity and emotional job, is already somewhere on the working list, the sample is approaching saturation for that market. Additional interviews begin only confirming what is already known, rather than expanding the possibilities.

Saturation sounds straightforward, but it carries an important caveat: it only works if the sample was designed well, with sufficient diversity in the first place. A team that interviews ten people with nearly identical profiles will reach apparent saturation quickly, because the same needs keep appearing, and new ones do not. But that saturation is an artifact of the sample's homogeneity, not evidence that the full landscape of needs has been covered. True saturation, the point at which additional interviews are genuinely unlikely to surface new needs, can only be assessed against a well-designed, diverse sample.

For most qualitative discovery efforts in a reasonably well-defined market, a sample of eight to 30 interviews, designed with intentional diversity, is sufficient to approach genuine saturation. Fewer interviews may be adequate when the job is narrowly defined and the customer population is relatively homogeneous. More may be needed when the job occurs across significantly different contexts or when the customer population is broad and varied.

These are guidelines, not rules. Assuming good sample design, a team that reaches interview number 15 and is still regularly hearing new needs should keep going. Meanwhile, a team that reaches interview number 12 and finds that the last three interviews have added nothing new has probably covered the territory.

Designing the Sample: A Practical Framework

Designing a qualitative sample requires identifying the dimensions along which the customer's experience of the job meaningfully varies and then ensuring the sample includes representation across those dimensions. The process moves through five steps.

The first step is to return to the Market Lens and confirm the boundaries. Who's in? Who's out? The sample should center on customers who match the defined job executor, use context, and core job. A few spots can be held for participants just outside those boundaries, but choose the edges deliberately: the most useful outliers are those whose situations create more friction, not less. For Big Sky, the core should be weekend backpackers taking multi-day trips in variable conditions, with a handful of spaces reserved for participants who stress-test the product's assumptions in concrete ways, such as ultralighters pushing for minimal weight, inexperienced backpackers still building their systems, or older hikers who may struggle with vision or manual dexterity.

The second step is to identify the diversity dimensions, the variables along which the customer's experience of the job is likely to vary in ways that matter for discovery. Different diversity dimensions will surface different needs, different friction points, and different success criteria. For the Big Sky study, relevant diversity dimensions might include:

- **Experience level:** novice backpackers encountering setup challenges for the first time versus experienced backpackers with established routines and higher performance expectations
- **Trip context:** solo backpackers versus groups, since social dynamics, including identity and emotional motivations

around competence and image, differ significantly between the two

- **Terrain and weather exposure:** backpackers who primarily camp in mild conditions versus those who regularly encounter high wind, rain, snow, or alpine terrain
- **Physical profile:** backpackers who are in excellent physical condition at camp versus those who arrive fatigued, older, or dealing with physical limitations that affect their setup experience
- **Geographic region:** different terrain types, rocky alpine, forested, desert, create different staking, site-selection, and weather challenges
- **Equipment familiarity:** backpackers who have used the same tent for years versus those who recently changed equipment and are still learning

Not every diversity dimension will prove equally important. The team's judgment about which dimensions are most likely to surface meaningfully different needs should guide which ones are prioritized.

The third step is to construct a sample matrix, a simple grid that maps the diversity dimensions against the number of interviews planned. It ensures the sample is distributed across the dimensions rather than clustered within them. A sample matrix does not need to achieve perfect balance across all dimensions. Its purpose is to make the diversity of the sample visible and intentional, so that gaps are identified before recruiting begins rather than after the interviews are complete.

The fourth step is to determine the total sample size. Working from the sample matrix, the team estimates the minimum number of interviews needed to cover the meaningful intersections of the priority diversity dimensions. Generally, no single diversity dimension should be represented by only one participant. A single voice is too thin to distinguish personal idiosyncrasy from genuine pattern. At least two or three participants per meaningful dimension provides a more reliable representation. Most projects fall between eight and 30 interviews, with 10 to 15 being typical.

The fifth step is to design the screening criteria, driving the questions used during recruitment to verify that a candidate matches the Market Lens and contributes to the diversity the sample is designed to achieve. Screening criteria should be tight enough to exclude participants who fall outside the study scope, and specific enough to guide recruiters toward the right diversity dimensions. For the Big Sky study, screening questions might include:

- How many multi-day backpacking trips do you take per year, and what is a typical trip length?
- Do you typically backpack solo or with a group?
- Describe the terrain and weather conditions you most commonly camp in.
- How long have you been using your current tent, and how comfortable are you with your setup process?
- Have you camped in significant wind, rain, or snow in the past year?

Participants who answer these questions in ways that confirm they match the Market Lens and contribute to the sample's diversity are the right candidates. Participants who are enthusiastic and available but do not match the lens should be thanked and politely denied.

Big Sky Sample Matrix

Qualitative discovery · target 20 participants · planned distribution across 6 dimensions

Diversity Dimension	Values within Dimension (planned participant count)			Total planned
Experience Level	Novice 6	Intermediate 8	Experienced 6	20
Trip Context	Solo 10	Group 10		20
Terrain & Weather	Mild conditions 8	Adverse conditions 12		20
Physical Profile	Fit at camp 14	Fatigued / Limited 6		20
Geographic Region	Rocky Alpine 9	Forested 7	Desert 4	20
Equipment Familiarity	Long-term user 12	Recently changed 8		20

Cell shade = relative weight within dimension:

Primary emphasis (50%+ of sample) · Secondary emphasis (30-49%) · Minority representation (under 30%) — still required

Design rule: No value should have fewer than 2-3 participants. A single voice cannot distinguish personal idiosyncrasy from genuine pattern. The matrix makes gaps visible before recruiting begins — not after interviews are complete.

Common Sampling Mistakes

Even teams that understand the principles of qualitative sampling make predictable errors. The following mistakes are easy to make and have compound effects across the entire discovery effort.

Relying on existing customers exclusively. Current customers are accessible and motivated to participate. They have already been filtered by the decision to purchase, which means their needs may differ systematically from the needs of customers the company has not yet won. A qualitative sample should include non-customers and users of competitive products alongside existing customers.

Recruiting from a single channel. Teams that recruit entirely from one source, such as a customer email list, a retailer's database, or a single online community, tend to get participants who share characteristics associated with that channel. Recruiting from multiple channels reduces this concentration effect.

Overweighting vocal customers. The customers most willing to participate in research are often the most engaged, the most opinionated, or the most dissatisfied. Each of these groups has something valuable to contribute, but none of them alone represents the full market. A deliberate sampling design helps counteract the self-selection bias that comes from relying on volunteers.

Ignoring edge cases. Customers who use the product in unusual ways, extreme conditions, or non-standard contexts are often dismissed as outliers not worth studying. In discovery, edge cases frequently reveal needs that are present but less visible in the mainstream population. The backpacker who regularly camps in conditions that most weekend hikers would avoid may surface friction points that affect less extreme backpackers more quietly and less obviously.

Treating the sample plan as fixed. The sample plan is a starting point, not a commitment. Early interviews may reveal that a diversity dimension the team anticipated is less relevant than expected, or that a dimension they did not anticipate is surfacing meaningfully different needs. The plan should be updated as the interviews progress.

Applying This to Big Sky

A trusted recruiting firm guided Shelton's team. When they finished designing the sample, the recruiting list looked quite different from Tom's initial suggestion of eight familiar faces from the Front Range retail circuit.

The final sample plan called for 18 to 22 participants distributed across the following dimensions: a mix of solo and group backpackers; novice, intermediate, and experienced hikers; participants from different geographic regions with different terrain profiles; backpackers who regularly camp in adverse weather and those who primarily camp in mild conditions; participants in strong physical condition and those who arrive at camp fatigued or physically limited; and users of several different tent brands, including Big Sky's own products and those of key competitors.

Tom looked at the recruiting criteria. "I'm glad the recruiter is in the lead here to set up these appointments. This would take us an eternity."

"Yep. Give them a couple of weeks. They'll all be lined up," Shelton said. "In the end, we'll know we've heard from the full range of people who live in this market, not just the ones we happened to know."

Jenna was looking over the screening questions. "And when the survey comes," she said, "we'll know our criteria actually came from the whole market, not just one corner of it."

That was the point. The sample was not just a logistical decision. It was a research design decision that would determine the completeness of everything the Discovery Engine produces from this point forward.

What Comes Next

With a sample plan complete and a recruiter in place, it's time to wrap up preparation and think about structuring the discovery conversations.

The team begins to imagine themselves talking to customers when, naturally, questions arise, such as:

- What will we talk with them about?
- What questions will we ask?
- Do we keep it open-ended, or should we script it tightly?

These are all natural questions. In the next chapter, we pick up with the team as they wrestle with this, as they learn how to design a Discussion Guide.

Key Takeaways

- Qualitative sampling and quantitative sampling require opposite instincts. Quantitative research requires a representative sample that mirrors the population. Qualitative discovery needs a diverse sample that maximizes the range of customer experiences heard.
- Convenience sampling, recruiting whoever is available, known, and willing, can produce biased insight. It clusters around the most accessible, most vocal, and most similar customers, producing echoes rather than the diversity that qualitative discovery requires.
- Saturation, the point at which new conversations stop revealing new needs, is the best indicator for completion. But saturation can only be assessed honestly against a well-designed, diverse sample. A homogeneous sample reaches apparent saturation quickly, but that convergence reflects the sample's limits, not the market's.
- A recruiter with a well-constructed screener will produce a better sample faster than internal sourcing in almost every case.
- The sample plan is a research design decision, not a logistics decision. Who gets interviewed determines the completeness of everything the Discovery Engine produces. This includes the criteria set, the survey population, and ultimately the opportunity rankings that will guide strategic decisions.

Where We Are in DISCOVER

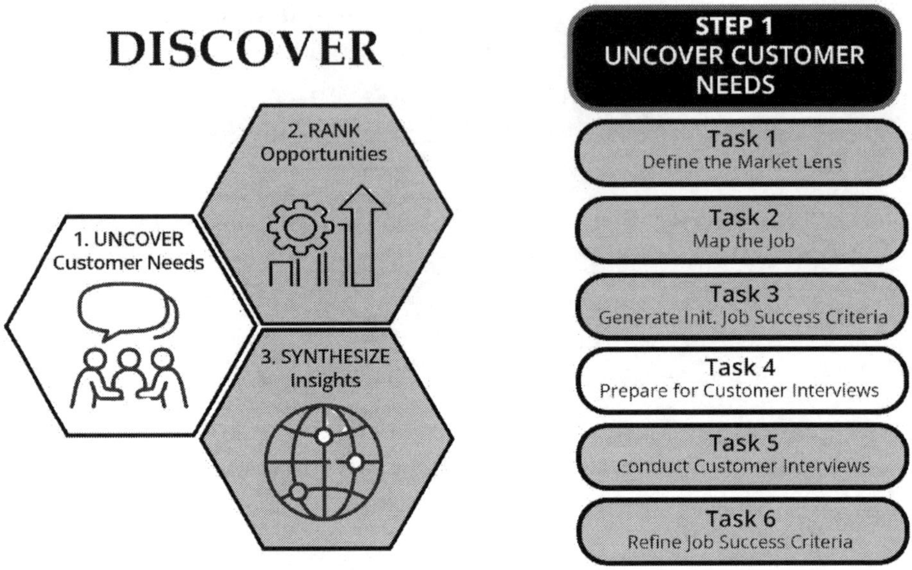

Step 1, Task 4: Prepare for Customer Interviews

Part 4: Build the Discussion Guide

What this chapter helps you do

Build a discussion guide that turns the Market Lens, Job Map, and initial Job Success Criteria into a structured conversation.

What you will have by the end

A practical interview guide that helps you explore the customer's job, probe for deeper insight, and test your early understanding without over-scripting the conversation.

Coming next

Task 5: Conduct Customer Interviews.

Chapter 12: Task 4, Prepare for Customer Interviews — Discussion Guides

Do we need a script?

NOTEBOOKS OPEN, THE TEAM ASSEMBLED.

Shelton began writing on the whiteboard.

Luis glanced at his laptop, noted the agenda item, *Build the Discussion Guide*, and leaned back in his chair.

"Do we really need that?" Luis asked. "Wouldn't it be better to keep things open-ended? Just talk to people and see what comes up. Is that what we were taught in that Design Thinking training course?"

Tom nodded. "I agree. Backpackers tell great stories when you let them talk. I've had some really revealing talks just by asking how their last trip went."

Across the table, Jenna shook her head. "Sorry, guys, I have to disagree. If every conversation goes in a different direction, we'll end up with twelve different exchanges about twelve different things. We won't be able to compare them or do anything with them. It will be a mess."

She pulled out a notebook. "I think we should write down every question we want to ask. That way, nothing gets skipped. Look, I've already got a start on it from my flight yesterday."

She flipped through page after page. Jenna had a lot of questions written down.

Luis grimaced and said, "Well, I don't know. That sounds like a survey, not the open sessions we've been told these are supposed to be."

The room went quiet.

Shelton turned toward the group. "You're both right, sort of. But you're both describing the same mistake from opposite directions."

Luis and Jenna looked at him.

"If we only ask for stories without a plan," Shelton said, "the conversations drift. We'll learn plenty of things, but remember our goal: *a complete list of Job Success Criteria.* Pure storytelling won't get us there. On the other extreme, if we script every question, the conversation feels mechanical. Customers give short answers instead of telling us what actually happened. And we won't leave room to explore the challenges they bring up on their own. We will limit what we could have learned."

He drew a small box on the whiteboard.

"The Discussion Guide is not a script. It's a structure. It organizes the conversation so we cover the right territory, but the customer still leads within that structure. We're not throwing purposeless questions at them. But we do need something to keep us on track, to guide us across the breadth of the job. And with the customer, we will explore additional depth based on what they share."

Tom leaned forward. "So the discussion guide keeps us on track. It shows where we're drifting, and what we still haven't covered."

"That's part of it," Shelton said. "Without it, we'll spend too much time on the topics we find interesting and miss the ones we didn't think to ask about. But it does more than that. It gives shape to how the session unfolds. If you'll forgive the term, it 'scripts' the flow."

Tom frowned slightly. "Scripts it? I'm not sure about that. Is this supposed to be an interview or a conversation?"

Shelton smiled. "It's a bit of both. But the best way to think about it is a *guided conversation*."

Interviews are Guided Conversations

Before examining how a discussion guide works, it is worth examining what kind of interaction it is designed to support because the word "interview" carries connotations that can subtly undermine discovery.

An interview might imply a formal, structured exchange in which an interviewer asks questions and a subject provides answers. The power dynamic is clear, the format is predictable, and the subject's role is to respond rather than to lead. This dynamic is useful for many purposes. But it is not ideal for discovery.

What discovery requires is something closer to a *guided conversation*, an interaction in which the moderator has a clear agenda and a plan. This is a session in which the customer feels comfortable enough to speak freely, follow their own associations, and share experiences they were not specifically asked about. The best discovery conversations feel, from the customer's perspective, more like talking with a genuinely curious friend than being formally questioned. The moderator is guiding the conversation with intention and discipline that the customer may not fully perceive. The customer is simply telling their story.

This distinction has practical implications for how the discussion guide is written, how the moderator introduces the session, and how the interview is conducted. The goal is to understand the customer's experience as fully as possible, which requires the customer to feel relaxed, engaged, and willing to say things that were not asked for.

What a Discussion Guide Does

A discussion guide is the backbone of a qualitative discovery interview. As opposed to a script, it is a methodical framework that ensures the moderator covers the research objectives across sessions while preserving the flexibility to follow unexpected and revealing threads when they emerge.

The distinction matters because these interviews are not data collection exercises where consistent stimuli produce comparable responses. They are structured interactions where the moderator's job is to understand the customer's experience within the time available.

A script prevents the moderator from pursuing the most revealing moments: the unexpected admission, the casual detail, the emotional signal that surfaces briefly and disappears.

A rigid question-and-answer format never allows customers to develop their thinking, tell the story behind a response, or connect one experience to another in ways the moderator did not plan for.

What the guide does is organize the conversation into a logical sequence of topics, provide the moderator with starting questions for each topic, and prompt where follow-up probing is likely to be valuable. Within that structure, the moderator exercises judgment. They will move faster through areas where the customer has little to say, slowing down and probing deeply when a rich vein of insight appears.

Inputs Required Before Writing the Guide

A discussion guide is an artifact of the preparation work that, to this point in the process, has already been completed.

The Market Lens defines the scope of the conversation. The guide should be anchored in the specific customer, context, and job-to-be-done as defined by the lens. Questions that fall outside the lens, that would be relevant for a different customer profile or a different use context, should not be in the guide.

The job map provides the backbone of the conversation. Each step in the map represents a distinct zone of the customer's experience, and the guide should ensure that the full sequence is ultimately covered. Without the job map as an organizing reference, discussion guides tend to cluster around the most visible moments of the job, the Execute step in the backpacking tent example, and neglect the steps before and after it, where equally important issues live.

The initial Job Success Criteria list prepares the moderator for what they may hear. Having thought through the criteria in advance, the moderator will recognize when a customer's language points toward one of them and will be better equipped to probe naturally in that moment.

The Jobs-to-be-Done Pyramid™ provides a full range of signals the team should be alert to. A well-designed guide creates space not just for functional friction but for the identity and emotional jobs that live higher in the Pyramid. Customers rarely volunteer these spontaneously. The guide's job is to create the conversational conditions in which they can emerge naturally.

The IROW Structure

Every discovery discussion guide follows a four-part structure. **The memory aid is IROW: Introduction, Rapport, Objectives, Wrap-up.** Each section serves a distinct purpose, and understanding those purposes helps moderators execute each one effectively.

Introduction

The Introduction establishes the ground rules for the conversation. It covers who is conducting the research and why, what the session will cover and how long it will take, confidentiality, the assurance that there are no right or wrong answers, and permission to record the session. If an incentive is being paid, this is the moment to confirm that arrangement as well.

The Introduction should be brief, just a few minutes, and it is acceptable to read this section from the prepared Discussion Guide. It functions as the official agreement for the session, and consistency matters. Its primary purpose is to reduce the customer's uncertainty about what they are being asked to do and why. Customers who understand the context and feel comfortable with the format give richer, more candid responses than customers who are uncertain about how their words will be used.

Big Sky Example — Introduction

"Thank you for making time today. My name is Shelton, and I'm here with my colleague, Tom, who will be taking notes. We're doing research to better understand the experiences of backpackers, specifically around camp setup and shelter. We're not testing a product or trying out our theories. We just want to understand your experience as well as possible.

There are no right or wrong answers. Everything you share will be kept confidential, and we won't attribute anything to you by name. The session will take 60 minutes, and with your permission, we'd like to record the conversation so we can review it later. Is that okay?

Before we begin, do you have any questions for me?"

Rapport

The Rapport section's purpose is to warm up the conversation, establish the customer as the expert on their own experience, and create the relaxed, open dynamic that the Objectives section depends on. Without it, customers often remain slightly guarded, giving technically accurate but emotionally thin responses that lack the depth and specificity discovery needs.

Rapport questions should be easy to answer and relevant to the project without venturing into the territory that belongs in the Objectives section. A natural approach is to invite the customer to talk about themselves, their background, and their relationship to the activity, establishing early that this is a session in which the customer's perspective is valued, and the moderator is listening with interest.

Importantly, planned Rapport questions should avoid problems, frustrations, pain points, or any topic that belongs in the Objectives section.

They must be broad, open and general. Rapport is for context and connection, not for early data collection.

Big Sky Example — Rapport

- Tell me a bit about your backpacking experience. How long have you been doing it, and what kinds of trips do you typically take?
- What draws you to backpacking? What do you like about it?
- Tell me about your kit. What are some of your favorite pieces of gear?

These questions work well for several reasons. They are easy to answer. Any backpacker can describe their experience and their gear without effort or anxiety. They are open-ended, inviting narrative rather than yes/no responses. They establish the customer as an experienced person whose perspective is worth hearing. And they reveal useful context: how experienced the customer is, what kind of trips they take, what they value about the activity, and the products they rely on. That context will help the team interpret everything the customer says in the Objectives section later. Notice, too, that none of these questions ask about problems, frustrations, or things that could be improved.

Adapting Rapport to the Customer

Rapport should generally run no more than 5 to 10 minutes, but the exact right length depends on both the customer and the clock.

When a customer is reserved or slow to warm up, the moderator can invest more time in Rapport, staying with easy, open questions until the customer is visibly relaxed and speaking freely. A customer who gives short, careful answers during Rapport will give short, careful answers during the Objectives section too. The time spent warming up the conversation is the investment that makes the rest of the session productive.

On the other hand, when a customer is naturally talkative, engaged, and comfortable, Rapport can move faster. The moderator can follow the energy, acknowledge what the customer has shared, and transition to the Objectives section once the conversational dynamic is established. Forcing a lengthy Rapport section on an already-engaged customer wastes time and can feel patronizing.

Even better, when the moderator already knows the customer (a colleague, a regular retail contact, a previous research participant), Rapport can be minimal. A brief acknowledgment of the relationship and a statement of what the session will cover is usually sufficient. The familiarity that Rapport would normally establish already exists.

When the Customer Wanders into Objectives Territory

Sometimes during Rapport, a customer will spontaneously begin describing a problem or a frustration without being asked. This is not necessarily a disruption.

When this happens, the moderator can choose to follow the customer into the topic rather than redirecting them back to Rapport. A natural transition, *"That's really interesting. Tell me more about what happened"*, allows the moderator to begin the Objectives exploration early and organically, led by the customer's initiative. The moderator can note where in the Objectives section this topic falls and adjust the remaining time accordingly.

This flexibility is one of the advantages of treating the discussion guide as a navigational tool rather than a fixed sequence. The guide defines the territory to be covered. The order in which that territory is explored can follow the customer's natural lead when the customer offers it.

Objectives

The Objectives section is the core of the discussion guide. This is where substantive discovery happens, where the moderator explores the job, surfaces friction and Job Success Criteria, and listens for the identity and emotional jobs.

This section is organized by themes. A theme might correspond to a step in the job map, a dimension of the customer's experience, or a specific area the team has flagged as likely important. Within each theme, the guide provides a starting question and a set of follow-up probes. The moderator opens the theme with the starting question, then follows the customer's lead by probing for depth.

Themes are sequenced so that the discussion flows naturally, with broad experiential themes first, followed by more specific themes later. Each theme connects logically to the next while following the least-aided to most-aided principle described below.

The job map often shapes this sequence, since it provides a natural organizing logic for interviews about how a job unfolds step by step. But the job map is just one template, not a mandate. In some cases, organizing by context, by phase of the customer's relationship with the product, or by type of experience will produce a more coherent conversation. The goal is that moving from one theme to the next feels like a logical progression, not an abrupt topic change.

What Gets Covered with Each Customer in Objectives?

Here is one of the most important things to understand about the Objectives section: The Discussion Guide typically covers more territory than can be addressed with any single customer.

The team's goal is not to cover every topic with every customer. It is to cover all the topics across all interviews. Trying to force complete coverage in a single session comes at the expense of depth and exploration. A team that rushes through themes to hit every point will come away with shallow data from many topics rather than rich data from the ones that mattered most to that particular customer.

Changes in What's Covered During the Objectives Section Across the Series of Interviews

In practice, the team's focus shifts across the arc of the full series of interviews. Early sessions, typically the first several, are focused on refining the job map and capturing the highest-level friction points. The team is orienting itself to the customer's world and calibrating the guide.

Within a typical guide organization, the team methodically explores each step of the job map in greater depth, probing for Job Success Criteria within each. By the time the team reaches the second half of its sessions, the criteria list should be nearly complete. The remaining interviews focus on filling the last gaps, ensuring that the criteria are balanced across the job steps, and confirming that each step of the job map has been explored.

In the final portion of the sessions, roughly the last 15%-20%, the focus shifts to language. Are the criteria clear? Unambiguous? Written in the customer's terminology? These final sessions are where the team refines the Job Success Criteria into something precise enough to survive the scrutiny of a survey instrument.

A Governing Principle: Least to Most Aided

Questions must be sequenced from least to most aided. Everything else in the Objectives section flows from this principle, and violating it disrupts the learning process.

To understand why, consider what happens when the sequence is reversed. Suppose a moderator opens a discovery interview by asking: "We've heard from some backpackers that setup speed in bad weather is a major frustration. Can you tell us about your issues there?" The customer now thinks the team is especially interested in that topic. From that moment forward, every subsequent response is shaped by that belief. The customer emphasizes weather-related setup experiences, connects other frustrations back to weather, and unconsciously de-emphasizes topics the question did not frame as important. As a result, the moderator has not learned what the customer cares about.

Ask broad questions first, before your hints teach the customer what answer you are hoping to hear.

At the least-aided end of the spectrum, questions are maximally open. They invite the customer to describe their experience in their own terms, bring up whatever is most salient to them, and lead the conversation wherever their experience naturally takes them. What surfaces in response to these questions is the most honest result the interview can produce: the customer's unprompted concerns, the experiences that are most vivid and consequential, the language they naturally use to describe the job.

As the interview progresses, questions become progressively more specific. The moderator moves from broad experience questions to questions about steps of the job, from general frustrations to specific moments of difficulty, from the customer's own priorities to depth within already established Job Success Criteria. By this point, the customer has already described their experience in their own terms. The more specific questions are filling gaps rather than shaping the overall picture.

This sequencing principle applies not just to the overall structure of the Objectives section but within each theme. When opening a new theme, the moderator should begin with the broadest possible question and narrow from there. Not "what makes setup difficult in bad weather?" but "walk me through your setup process." Let the customer describe what happens. Then probe the specific dimensions that did not arise spontaneously.

The most important insights in a discovery interview often emerge from the first half of the Objectives section, before the moderator has asked anything specific. When teams lead with their most important questions, eager to validate the theories they care about, they tend to steer the conversation too early, limiting what could have been learned and reducing the breadth of insight the interview might have revealed.

Writing Questions That Work: The SQLA Principle

Within each theme, the quality of the starting question and the follow-up probes determines what the interview will produce. **A governing discipline for an excellent question is SQLA: Short Question, Long Answer.**

The moderator's questions should be brief and open, ideally no more than one sentence, and designed to produce extended responses from the customer. Long questions signal the interviewer's assumptions, constrain the customer's response, reveal too much about the moderator's biases, and reduce the chance of hearing something unexpected. Compare these two versions:

Long version: "When you're setting up your tent and the weather is starting to change, and you're feeling pressure to get shelter established quickly, what specifically makes that process difficult, especially with the stakes and poles? For example, the openings of the pole sleeves, muddy sites, or the type of bad weather coming in?"

Short version: "What can make setup difficult?"

The short version invites the customer to tell a story. The long version tells the customer what story to tell and presumes the answer. Short questions preserve the discovery space. Long questions close it. When a long question forms in the moderator's mind, the discipline is to find the core of it and ask only that, stripping away the context, the qualifications, and the implicit framing that the customer never gave.

The Discussion Guide: IROW Structure

Not a script · Not a questionnaire · A structured framework for a guided conversation

SECTION	PURPOSE	KEY PRINCIPLE
I Intro	**Establish ground rules** Confidentiality · recording consent No right or wrong answers Not testing a product or concept	Brief — 3 to 5 minutes · reading from notes is acceptable Removing the expectation of product evaluation is one of the highest-leverage acts a moderator can perform
R Rapport	**Warm up the conversation** Easy, open questions about background Establish customer as the expert Build the candid dynamic Objectives needs	5 to 10 minutes · Do NOT touch problems or frustrations Any topic that belongs in Objectives stays there If customer wanders into Objectives territory, follow them — don't redirect
O Objectives	**Core discovery work · 40 to 45 minutes** Explore the job step by step Surface friction and success criteria Listen for functional, identity, and emotional signals **Least aided to most aided** Broad open questions first Hypothesis testing last **SQLA: Short Question, Long Answer** One sentence · strip every question to its core	Guide covers more than any one session can reach Cover all topics across all conversations — not all topics with every customer Question families: Tell me a time · Extremes A vs B · Process · Magic Pill · Workaround JTBD: What makes [job step] difficult / time-consuming / unpredictable? After every response: "What else?" before probing deeper
W Wrap-up	**Close and safety net** Signal session is ending Final open door for anything not covered Request permission to re-contact	5 to 7 minutes · "Is there anything we haven't talked about that would be useful to understand?" "What should we have asked you that we didn't?" Honor the time commitment

Total session: 60–90 minutes · First 1–2 sessions treated as pilots — update the guide before the main series begins

Question Templates That Work

Discovery practitioners can draw on two distinct families of questions in the Objectives section: voice-of-customer questions from traditional market research, and jobs-to-be-done-specific questions developed as part of Tony Ulwick's Outcome-Driven Innovation methodology. They can be used in combination or independently.

Traditional Voice-of-Customer Questions

These question types have been proven across decades of qualitative research. They work because they invite narrative, surface authentic experience, and create the conditions for customers to reveal what matters most in their own words.

Tell me about a time when...

Tell me about a time when... invites the customer into a specific story. Rather than asking for opinions or preferences, this question asks for an experience, which is where the most useful data lives. "Tell me about your most recent backpacking trip."

Extremes

Extreme experience questions ask about the best or worst the customer has encountered. "Tell me about the worst time you've had with your tent." "Tell me about a trip when everything just worked." Extreme experiences reveal the edges of performance, the conditions under which the job is most difficult and those where it feels effortless.

Both are analytically valuable, and the contrast between them often brings information to light that neither alone would reveal.

A vs. B

A vs. B questions ask the customer to compare two options. "Why would you choose Product A over Product B?" And after fully exploring that response, continuing with, "And why might you choose B over A?" The answers to comparative questions are always Job Success Criteria. Customers explain how a product performs better against their criteria, thus revealing those criteria. Asking for the comparison in both directions unearths more.

Process

Process questions ask the customer to walk through a sequence of steps. "Walk me through the process of packing your tent up in the morning." Process questions are powerful for revealing job map steps, some of which customers rarely volunteer because they have accepted those steps as routine. Walking through the process step by step exposes friction that conversational questions miss.

Magic Pill

Magic Pill questions ask the customer to describe their ideal solution. "Tell me about the attributes of your perfect tent." These questions need to be handled carefully as the customer's answer will almost certainly be in solution space, naming features or designs rather than needs. The value of the Magic Pill question is not the feature that the customer names so much as the follow-up that comes after: *"And how would that help you?"* That follow-up reliably converts solution language back into problem language, surfacing the underlying Job Success Criteria the customer was reaching for. This type of probe, "And how would that help you?", is but one of the many probing responses revealed in the next chapter.

Purchase Experience

Purchase experience questions explore the journey of a recent buying decision. "Walk me through how you chose your current tent." Probing the purchase experience reveals the criteria the customer applied when evaluating alternatives, which are often the same ones they use to judge performance in the field.

Workarounds

Workaround questions are among the most powerful in a discovery conversation. "Have you made any modifications to your gear or your process?" A customer who has developed a workaround has identified an unmet need and solved it imperfectly using what was available.

Every workaround is evidence of a gap between what the job-to-be-done requires and what current solutions provide. When the interview is happening in the environment where the customer performs the job, the team should ask to see the workaround, if possible. Observing it directly is more revealing than any description. The team should document those workarounds with pictures or videos if possible.

Learning

Learning questions explore the customer's earliest experience with a product or a job-to-be-done. "Tell me about your first time setting up this tent. What did you learn that you've applied ever since?" New users encounter friction that experienced users have learned to work around and no longer consciously notice.

Learning questions recover that friction and often reveal the steepest parts of the learning curve that the current product has failed to flatten. Another version of this is, "If you could go back in time and advise your inexperienced self, what would you say?"

Jobs-to-be-Done and ODI Questions

Outcome-Driven Innovation (ODI) questions, developed by Tony Ulwick, are structured to keep discovery grounded in the customer's job-to-be-done and to surface what makes it difficult in specific, measurable terms.

When customers struggle with a job, breakdowns fall into five categories:

- **Execution** — What makes this job hard to do?
- **Reliability** — What makes this job inconsistent?
- **Output** — What makes the results fall short?
- **Control** — What makes this job difficult to manage?
- **Risk** — What could go wrong?

Question Structure

Most questions follow a single template, pairing the job or job step with an adjective drawn from the appropriate category:

What makes [job or job step] [adjective]?

For example: "What makes pitching the tent time-consuming?"

Two categories require a slight variation in phrasing to stay natural and precise. Output questions focus on the result rather than the process: *"When pitching the tent, what errors do you find with the result?"* Control and risk questions often work better as event-based probes: *"When there's an error pitching the tent, what makes it hard to detect?"*

Adjectives by Category

1. Execution — hard to do

- Slow/time-consuming
- Difficult
- Inefficient
- Costly
- Physically demanding

"What makes pitching the tent physically demanding?"

2. Reliability — doesn't work consistently

- Unpredictable
- Inconsistent
- Error-prone
- Unreliable

"What makes pitching the tent error-prone?"

3. Output — result falls short

- Incomplete
- Low-quality
- Limited
- Delayed

"When pitching the tent, what errors do you find with the result?"

4. Control — hard to see or manage

- Unclear
- Unobservable
- Hard to fix
- Hard to adjust

"When there's an error pitching the tent, what makes it hard to detect?"

5. Risk — something could go wrong

- Unsafe
- Risky
- Stressful

"What makes pitching the tent unsafe?"

Applying the ODI Template Across the Job Structure

Following the least-aided to most-aided principle, a moderator begins broadly with the job-to-be-done and works progressively toward more specific job steps. They can also use the Jobs-to-be-Done Pyramid, starting broad with a Core Job, and from there, continuing either to Product Jobs or to individual job map steps.

Starting with the Core Job Anchor, **Stay protected from the elements while backpacking:**

- What makes staying protected from the elements while backpacking challenging?

- What makes staying protected from the elements while backpacking time-consuming?
- What makes staying protected from the elements while backpacking go off-track?
- What makes staying protected from the elements while backpacking require a lot of physical effort?

From there, the same template applies to each Product Job in the lifecycle:

- What makes purchasing a tent challenging?
- What makes purchasing a tent time-consuming?
- What makes purchasing a tent problematic?

This last one could also be rephrased as "What problems do you have when purchasing a tent?"

And then to each step of the job map:

- What makes choosing a campsite area challenging?
- What makes pitching the tent slow?
- What makes adjusting the tent go off-track?
- What makes packing the tent difficult?

The template is simple and repeatable. Its power comes from applying it systematically across the full structure of a job-to-be-done, not just the obvious central steps, but the surrounding steps where friction would otherwise be left unexamined.

Wrap-up

The Wrap-up closes the conversation and ensures nothing important has been missed. It should also indicate that the session is nearing its end. Customers are aware of the time just as the team is, and honoring the requested commitment matters for the relationship and for future research access.

Beyond managing the close, Wrap-up questions also serve as a safety net, a final opportunity for the customer to raise topics the guide did not cover, to name things they have been thinking about throughout the conversation but were not asked, or to speak directly to whatever matters most to them. In a sense, Wrap-up questions are mirror images of Rapport questions: easy to answer, low pressure, but with the additional quality of offering the customer an open door if there is something they want to add.

Further, the Wrap-up should close with a sincere expression of gratitude. It can optionally also include a request for permission to re-contact if follow-up conversations or survey participation may be needed later.

Big Sky Example Questions — Wrap-up

- Is there anything about your experience with backpacking that we haven't talked about that you think would be useful for us to understand?
- What should we have asked you that we didn't?
- If the president of a major tent manufacturer were sitting here with us, what would you want to tell them?

"Thank you so much for your time. This has been helpful. Would it be okay if we reached out again if we have follow-up questions, or if we conduct a survey later in our research?"

Timing and Pacing

A complete discovery interview typically runs 60 to 90 minutes. As an example, here's a rough allocation for a 60-minute session:

- Introduction: 3 to 5 minutes

- Rapport: 5 to 10 minutes, adjusted to the customer
- Objectives: 40 to 45 minutes across themes
- Wrap-up: 5 to 7 minutes

For a session over 60 minutes, the additional time should mostly be allocated to Objectives.

When writing the guide, the team should reference the expected time for each theme and consider those estimates before the conversations begin.

What about Internal Hypotheses?

Discovery teams sometimes need to ensure that particular topics get covered. A senior stakeholder wants to know whether customers experience a specific problem. A product leader has a hypothesis they feel strongly about. A business question has been sitting unanswered long enough that someone insists it gets addressed directly.

The recommendation is to handle these sparingly and carefully. A discussion guide built around specific questions to confirm will produce confirmation, not discovery. The better home for hypothesis testing is outside of the qualitative discovery phase, such as concept testing or surveys, where specific criteria can be measured across a large population with statistical rigor. Qualitative discovery is better suited to uncovering what the team does not yet know than to verifying what it suspects.

When specific questions cannot be avoided, the rule is simple: place them at the very end of the Objectives section.

After the customer has described their experience in full and unprompted, a specific question can probe territory that did not surface naturally. The absence of spontaneous mention is itself meaningful data, and it is only meaningful if the question was not asked earlier. A customer who never raises setup difficulty in adverse weather, then confirms it matters when asked directly, has told the team something different than a customer who volunteers it within the first five minutes.

The number of such questions should be small. A long list of specific questions is a signal that the guide has drifted from discovery toward validation.

When these questions are asked, the moderator should do their best to frame them neutrally. Not "we've found that setup in bad weather is a major problem, has that been your experience?" but "how does weather factor into your setup experience?" The moderator should reveal as little as possible about the underlying assumption.

Refining the Guide

No discussion guide survives first contact with a real interview unchanged. Questions that seemed clear in writing prove ambiguous in practice. Themes that seemed important prove unproductive. The pacing that seemed right in the planning room takes twice as long in the field.

The team should expect to refine the guide as the study progresses. Early conversations may reveal that certain questions need tightening, that a theme deserves more time, or that a topic the guide didn't anticipate keeps surfacing. Those are signals worth acting on.

More significantly, later interviews should reflect what earlier ones established. As Job Success Criteria take shape and certain themes become well-understood, the guide can go deeper on those areas and wider across job steps and themes that haven't yet been fully explored. The guide is a living document, precise enough to produce consistent, comparable data, but flexible enough to sharpen as the team's understanding grows.

A Note on Flexibility

A discussion guide is a tool. The moderator and team are still in charge. The moderator's highest obligation in a discovery conversation is to understand the customer's experiences and issues, not to complete the guide. When a customer raises something unexpected and genuinely revealing, the moderator can follow it as long as it's still within the project's scope.

The guide exists to ensure coverage of the research objectives when the conversation does not spontaneously go there. The discipline is to follow interesting threads while tracking where in the guide the conversation currently sits, and returning to uncovered territory when the thread has been fully explored.

What Comes Next

With the discussion guide written, another task from the preparation phase is complete. The team has defined the Market Lens, mapped the job, generated Job Success Criteria, designed the sample, and built the tool that will structure every conversation.

The guide tells the moderator what territory to cover and in what sequence. What it cannot fully prepare for is the moment when a customer describes a problem, and the moderator must decide, in real time, where to go next. Should they probe why the problem matters? What causes it? When is it worse? What would success look like?

Those decisions require a navigational framework of their own. That framework is the subject of the next chapter.

Key Takeaways

- A discussion guide is neither a script nor a questionnaire. It is a structured framework that ensures the moderator covers the research objectives in every session while preserving the flexibility to follow unexpected and revealing threads when they emerge. The guide keeps the conversation honest. It tells the moderator when certain topics have not been covered yet.
- The interaction the guide is designed to support is a guided conversation, not an interview. The customer should feel relaxed, engaged, and free to share experiences they were not specifically asked about. The moderator's structure should be largely invisible to the customer.
- The Objectives section of every guide must be sequenced from least aided to most aided. Broad, open questions come first. Specific hypothesis-testing questions come last. Violating this sequence poisons the most valuable data the conversation can produce: the customer's unprompted priorities.
- SQLA — Short Question, Long Answer — is the governing discipline for every question in the Objectives section. Long questions signal the moderator's assumptions, constrain the customer's response, and reduce the chance of hearing something unexpected. Strip every question to its core before asking it.
- No guide survives first contact with a real conversation unchanged. The team should expect to refine it as the study progresses: tightening questions, adjusting pacing, and expanding into themes that earlier interviews didn't fully reach. The guide is a living document, and improving it is not a sign of inadequate preparation. It is the expected output of a good process.

Where We Are in DISCOVER

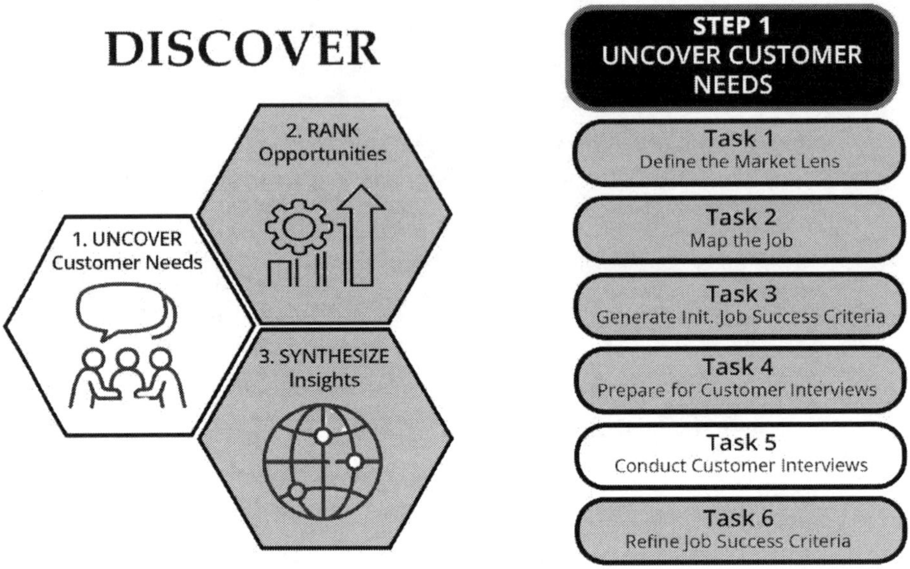

Step 1, Task 5: Conduct Customer Interviews
Part 1: The 3D Probing Model

What this chapter helps you do

Respond to customers in real time, ask better follow-up questions, and probe across the customer's job.

What you will have by the end

A practical way to move beyond surface answers by exploring what customers do, why it matters, what gets in the way, and how they define success.

Coming next

Task 5 continues with probing beyond functional needs.

Chapter 13: Task 5, Conduct Customer Interviews — The 3D Probing Model

A Backpacker's Tale

RYAN CARTER WAS THE BACKPACKER Tom had mentioned back in an earlier team meeting. Ryan was the engineer from Fort Collins who'd described getting caught on rocky ground in a building storm. Tom had made sure he was on the recruiting list.

Now, two weeks later, Ryan stirred his coffee while the team settled into their seats by a table in the small café near the trailhead parking lot.

Shelton opened his notebook and proceeded through the Introduction and Rapport sections of the guide. The awkwardness faded away, and except for the notes being taken, it appeared just like a group of friends grabbing coffee.

Entering the Objectives section, Shelton said, "Tell us about your last trip."

Ryan shrugged. "Nothing unusual. A couple of friends and I went up into the Indian Peaks for a long weekend."

"How far in?" Shelton asked.

"About nine miles the first day," Ryan said. "We got to camp late afternoon."

Shelton looked back up. "What happened when you got there?"

Ryan thought for a moment. "Well, the first problem was the ground. Rocky. Every place that looked flat had stones under the soil."

"Walk me through what happened," Shelton said.

"The tent stakes for a start," Ryan said. "I had to move them around a few times and put rocks on top of a couple. I could hammer them in with a rock, but I didn't want to risk bending them."

"What part of the setup did that affect most?" Shelton asked.

"Everything downstream," Ryan said. "Once you can't get the stakes in, you can't tension the tent properly. And I was running out of time."

"What was driving the time pressure?"

Ryan pointed toward the window. "A little rumble of thunder, a long way off. You could see the clouds building over the ridge, the temp was starting to drop, and the wind was picking up."

Jenna glanced at Shelton, noticing the pattern. Shelton was not just asking about tents. He was asking what happened, and following each answer into the next layer of the problem.

"Why was that such a problem for you?" Shelton asked.

Ryan's expression changed slightly. "Because if the shelter isn't up before the rain starts, your gear gets wet. And once that happens, the whole evening goes sideways. You're cold, your sleeping bag is damp. It compounds."

"When is that worse?" Shelton asked. "What conditions make it more stressful?"

"When it's late in the day, and you're already tired," Ryan said. "With the rocky ground, then you're fighting two problems at once. The terrain and the clock."

"And then it got worse," Ryan added. "A few raindrops on my unpitched tent. It's such a bad feeling. Your gear starts getting wet before the tent is even up."

Shelton leaned forward slightly. "How quickly does setup need to happen for it to feel manageable in those conditions?"

"Under 20 minutes," Ryan said. "Much past that and in the rain, you've got a problem."

"What time would be ideal?"

Ryan didn't hesitate. "If I could get the tent up fast enough that nothing inside gets wet, I'd consider that a win. That's the bar. But you said, ideal? Probably 7-10 minutes."

Tom was writing quickly. Two criteria had emerged:

Minimize the time required to establish shelter when conditions are deteriorating.

Minimize the likelihood of gear exposure to rain during setup.

"Is there anything else you'd like to let us know about that challenge?" asked Shelton.

Ryan replied, "Did I mention that I put rocks on top of the stakes? I worry about those stakes coming up in the night."

Shelton continued, "Tell me more about that."

Throughout the rest of the morning, Ryan did most of the talking while the team listened, pages of notes accumulating as the coffee cups were emptied and refilled.

Why Most Probing Falls Short

The most common failure in discovery conversations is not asking the wrong questions. It's stopping too soon after asking the right ones.

A customer says, "Setting up my tent in bad weather is a nightmare." The moderator notes this as a problem and moves to the next question. The interview has only captured a complaint. It has not captured any criteria. It has not revealed why the difficulty matters, what produces it, when it is worse, or what success would look like. The data is real but shallow, too thin to survive synthesis and too vague to generate a measurable Job Success Criterion.

The problem is not a lack of questions. Most moderators have plenty of questions. The problem is not knowing where to go next once a customer says something important. Without a way to navigate, the conversation either drifts into territory that does not matter or stays on the surface of territory that does.

Moderators don't need scripted probing questions. *They need direction.*

Where to go next?

Most teams approach discovery interviews with one of two extremes. They follow a rigid discussion guide, asking questions in a fixed order. Or they keep things loose, hoping good follow-up questions will come to mind. Neither works particularly well. Scripted probing questions produce shallow answers because they prevent the moderator from following what matters. Unstructured interviews miss the dimensions that matter most because there is no framework to notice what has not yet been explored.

What a moderator needs is something in between: a way to work with a customer's initial problem statement and help them to explore it together.

At its core, the 3D Probing Model is built on a simple idea. When a customer shares an experience, there are a handful of meaningful directions the conversation can go. The moderator can clarify what is failing, understand why it matters, uncover what is getting in the way, identify when it becomes most difficult, or define what success would look like. These five directions form the foundation of the model.

The Five Core Probing Questions

The 3D Probing Model is built around five questions. They are the navigational options available to a moderator at any moment, each one opening a different window into the customer's experience.

What is failing? This question grounds the conversation in a specific, located breakdown. Before the moderator can explore anything meaningfully, the problem itself must be precise. Vague problems produce vague criteria.

Why does it matter? This question reveals consequences and importance. It moves the conversation from the problem toward the larger goal the customer is trying to accomplish. It can also begin to surface the identity and emotional dimensions of the experience.

What is preventing resolution? This question surfaces root causes and constraints. It asks what is blocking the customer from resolving the problem themselves, whether through the nature of the problem itself or through the limits of available solutions.

When is it worse? This question uncovers context and variability. Problems are rarely uniform. The conditions that make a problem severe or irrelevant are often the key to writing a criterion that is precise enough to be actionable.

What does success look like? This question defines the desired state. It converts everything the conversation has revealed into a measurable performance standard, the metric the customer applies and the range they consider acceptable.

These five questions are the practical, in-the-room version of the 3D Probing Model. Everything else in this chapter is a fuller expression of them.

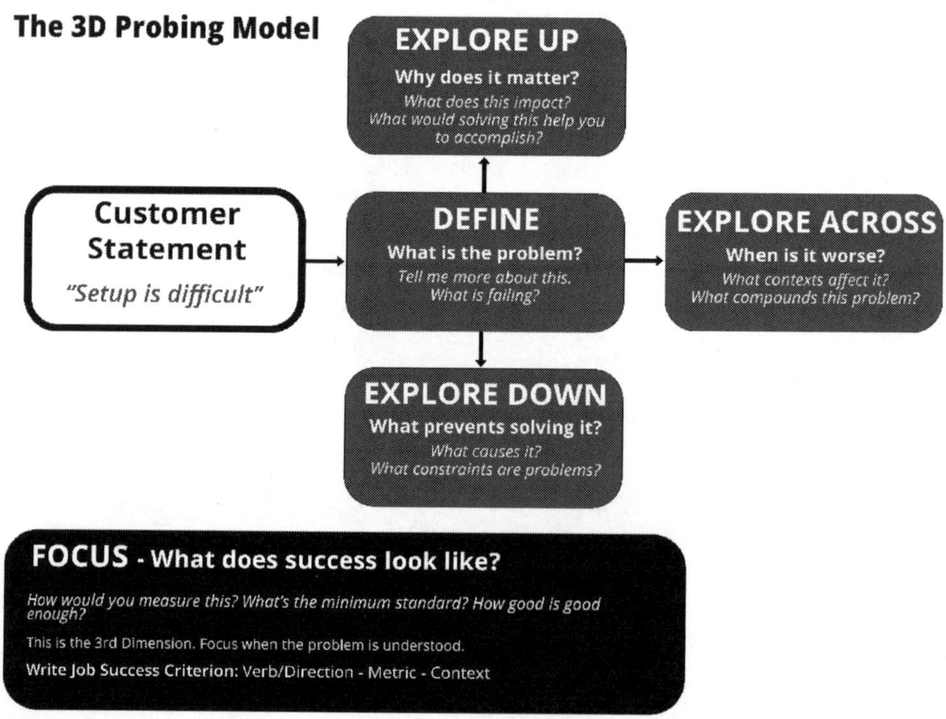

Why It's Called The 3D Probing Model

The model is called 3D because a moderator is exploring a problem across multiple dimensions, not just one. A helpful way to think about those dimensions is through the lens of photography.

First, the moderator frames the subject: *What exactly are we looking at?* That is Define. Then the moderator moves around it, viewing the problem from different angles and in different conditions. That is Explore. Finally, the moderator brings it into focus and captures it, making the problem clear enough to act on. That is Focus.

The moderator is not merely observing the problem. They are capturing it in a form that can be acted on, and that captured form is the raw material of Job Success Criteria.

Follow the Cues

The five questions are not a hard-coded sequence. They are options. In practice, once a customer has offered a problem, a good moderator does not mechanically move to the next. They listen, notice what is still missing from the picture, and choose the direction that best serves the conversation at that moment.

- If something sounds important but the reason is unclear, why does it matter?
- If something sounds blocked, what is preventing resolution?
- If the problem seems situational, when is it worse?
- If the description is still vague, what is failing?
- If the problem is well understood, what does success look like?

The model expands the moderator's choices by providing options for where to go next. And for moments when the right direction still isn't clear, four universal rescue probes covered later in this chapter will ensure a moderator is never without good options.

This is what makes the model useful under pressure. It ensures that critical dimensions such as why the problem matters, what is constraining its resolution, and when it is most severe are not accidentally skipped. Plus, it gives the moderator something to reach for in the moment, when a customer's answer is unexpected, and there is no prepared question that fits. Structure with flexibility.

The best probes follow the customer's cues and are inspired by genuine curiosity.

Three Anchors: Define, Explore, Focus

To make the five questions easier to navigate in real conversations, the model organizes them into three anchors.

DEFINE corresponds to the first question: what is failing? It is where the moderator locates the problem precisely before delving into anything else.

EXPLORE corresponds to the middle three questions: why does it matter, what is preventing resolution, and when is it worse? It is where the moderator moves outward in multiple directions to understand the full landscape of the problem.

FOCUS corresponds to the final question: what does success look like? It is where the moderator moves inward to the measurable core, establishing the performance standard the customer actually applies.

In practice, most conversations begin with *Define* because a moderator needs to know what the problem actually is before going deeper. Most time is spent in *Explore* because understanding a problem from multiple angles takes more effort than locating it or measuring it. *Focus* comes when the problem is well enough understood that it is time to establish what better would look like.

But the moderator is always free to move between anchors as the conversation requires. New information may call for a return to Define. A customer's answer may skip past Explore and arrive at Focus unprompted. The model is a navigational aid. The anchors tell the moderator where they can go next, not where they must go next.

Summary of Define-Explore-Focus with the Five Questions

- Define
- What is failing?
- Explore
- Why does it matter?
- What is preventing resolution?
- When is it worse?
- Focus
- What does success look like?

Where Probing Begins

Before the 3D Probing Model can be applied, a customer needs to have said something worth probing. That happens through the opening phase of the interview, where the moderator asks a set of Objectives questions drawn from an initial, open-ended set of questions, often from either general VoC Questions or Tony Ulwick's

Outcome-Driven Innovation process, as covered in the previous chapter on developing the discussion guide.

Those are not probing questions. They are invitations. Their purpose is simply to give the customer an opening to provide a problem.

As a reminder from the previous chapter, some general VoC questions include:

- **Tell me about a time:** Tell me about a time when you...
- **Extremes:** Tell me about your worst/best experience with...
- **A vs. B:** Why would a person select Product A over B?
- **Process:** Walk me through the process of...
- **Magic Pill:** If I could give you a magic product to help, what would that be?
- **Purchase Experience:** Tell me about how you chose your recent purchase of Product A.
- **Learning:** What advice would you give to a person with less experience who's performing this task for the first time?

Additionally, the ODI questions cover:

- **Execution:** What makes this job hard to do?
- **Reliability:** What makes this job inconsistent?
- **Output:** What makes the result fall short?
- **Control:** What makes this job difficult to manage?
- **Risk:** What could go wrong?

Once the customer responds, the moderator has something to work with. **This is where 3D Probing begins.**

DEFINE — What Is Actually Breaking Down?

Define is the natural starting point for most probing sequences. Before exploring why a problem matters or what is stopping the customer from solving it, the moderator needs to know precisely what the problem is and where in the job it occurs.

Customer descriptions of difficulty are often vague. When a customer says “setup is difficult,” the moderator does not yet know whether the difficulty is physical effort, sequencing, time, likelihood of error, or something else entirely. Each is a different problem with different implications for the criteria list.

Define converts vague descriptions into specific, located performance gaps. The questions clarify the nature and location of the breakdown, not its cause, not its consequences, and not the customer’s preferred solution.

General Define Questions:

- Tell me what you mean by that.
- Walk me through what happens when it goes wrong.
- What part of the process breaks down?
- Where specifically does it get complicated?
- What does that look like in practice?
- What is it that actually fails?

These questions do not ask why the problem happens, what the consequences are, or what the customer wishes were different. They locate the breakdown.

Customers often offer vague terms, for which specific “Define” probes work well. These can be categorized as vague negatives or vague positives.

“Define” Probing for Vague Negatives

Vague negative examples include words like difficult, troublesome, and failure-prone. These don’t sound vague to the customer because in their minds, they knew exactly what they meant. The probe is simply to ask for clarification, such as:

- Can you tell me what you mean by difficult?
- In what way is it troublesome?
- Failure-prone? What do those failures look like?

"Define" Probing for Vague Positives

Vague positive examples are when a customer says they want something to be good in unclear terms, such as easier-to-use, more comfortable, or more stylish. Moderators should be prepared for vague positives because these are perhaps the most common phrases that customers say. And it can seem intimidating, because the probing question may not appear as obvious as when hearing a vague negative. However, the technique in these cases is quite simple:

- You'd like it to be easier to use? Tell me, what makes it difficult to use?
- You'd like it to be more comfortable? Tell me, what makes it uncomfortable?
- You'd like it to be more stylish? What makes it unstylish?

Once the moderator recognizes this pattern, they can easily navigate through any vague terms that the customer presents.

Define, the common first anchor

In the Big Sky conversation, Ryan's initial description, difficulty with stakes on rocky ground, is a starting point, not a finished definition. Shelton's probe, "walk me through what happened," begins the Define work. Ryan's response, repositioning stakes, improvising with rocks, and risking bent equipment, gives the team a picture of what failing looks like at that step of the job.

Define is the most common first anchor. However, if a customer opens a conversation with a detailed, specific, already-located problem, the moderator may begin exploring immediately.

EXPLORE — Three Directions

Explore is where much of the work happens. Once the problem is located, the moderator has three directions available.

Explore Up: Why Does It Matter?

Exploring upward means moving from the problem toward its consequences, understanding what the difficulty threatens and why it matters enough to be worth discussing. This is not about the mechanism of the problem but about its meaning, what larger goal it interferes with, and what happens downstream when it occurs.

This is also where the higher levels of the Jobs-to-be-Done Pyramid™ can surface. A staking problem on rocky ground is a Product Job issue. But upward probing often moves the conversation toward the Core Job, and eventually toward the Identity and Emotional Jobs that give the Product Job its power to improve the entire experience.

Explore Up questions:

- Why is that a problem for you?
- What does that affect?
- What becomes harder when this happens?
- What does that slow down?
- What does it make harder to accomplish?
- What happens as a result?
- How does that affect the rest of what you're trying to do?
- If this got worse, what would that mean for you?
- What are you trying to accomplish when this is going wrong?

- Who else does it impact?

In Ryan's case, exploring upward from the staking problem reveals the Core Job urgency, shelter must be established before the weather turns, and the downstream cascade: wet gear, a cold sleeping bag, and an evening that gets worse. Further upward probing surfaces the identity domain, the discomfort of being the last person still struggling while the group watches.

Explore Down: What Is Preventing Resolution?

Exploring downward means moving from the problem toward what is blocking its resolution. The governing question is: what is stopping the customer from solving this problem?

That question has two kinds of answers.

The first is the root cause, which produced the problem in the first place. Moving down through the problem hierarchy reveals progressively narrower issues. The tent's ceiling is leaking. Move down: there is a hole in the tightened seam. Move down again: it's old and has been in an attic for years. The vertical axis is relative. The moderator can enter the hierarchy at any level and move in either direction, since a problem at any level always has causes beneath it and consequences above it.

The second is constraints, the point at which the customer hits a floor. They know the problem exists, may even know its cause, but something prevents them from fixing it. If they've developed a workaround, it is likely that they have only partially addressed the problem. The constraint is the boundary of what the customer can solve with what currently exists, and it can be where significant unmet needs live.

Both root cause and constraints answer the same governing question. Root cause reveals the nature of the barrier. Constraints reveal the limit of what is currently available to overcome them.

Root cause questions:

- Why does that happen?
- What produces that difficulty?
- What is it about the situation that makes this hard?
- When you think about why this is difficult, what comes to mind?
- What would need to be different for this not to happen?

Constraint questions:

- What prevents you from doing this as well as you'd like?
- What do you wish you could change about how this works?
- When does the situation not fit well with your environment or setup?
- What stops you from fixing it?
- Why hasn't this been solved already?

One practical note: new moderators like to ask the question, "What do you do about that now?" This is not a disaster, but it's also not a great question. It invites the customer to describe a workaround, which is a solution, not a constraint. It's "ok" because it keeps the customer talking about the issue, but it's not great because it will not be as revealing as a better question would be. And with the clock ticking, it's significant to lose precious minutes learning about the construction of the customer's DIY backpack, with custom tent attachment points.

However, when a customer spontaneously brings up a workaround, this is completely different and productive. The follow-up is to *Explore up*, such as "Why that approach?" "What are you trying to accomplish when you do that?", or "How does that help?" This surfaces the underlying problem rather than cataloging the improvised solution.

Solvable Constraints vs. Environmental Constraints

Not all constraints are the same kind of barrier, and recognizing the difference is important.

Some constraints are solvable. The stake design could be improved, the setup sequence could be redesigned, and the pole connection mechanism could be simplified.

Other constraints are permanent fixtures of the environment. Rain is unpredictable. Rocky terrain exists. Fatigue after a long hike is inevitable. These are immutable. Treating them as solvable elements rather than part of the environment leads innovation teams astray.

When an environmental constraint surfaces, the moderator should resist probing what would fix it and instead probe what the customer needs in order to succeed despite it. For Big Sky, the innovation question is not how to eliminate fatigue but what a backpacker needs to establish shelter when the ground, the weather, and their low energy level are all working against them.

Questions that shift the frame productively: "What would make this manageable even when conditions are bad?" or "What would give you confidence that you could handle this regardless of the terrain?" Alternatively, *Exploring up* from the environmental constraint can be productive: "In what ways does this cause a problem?"

A constraint's value as a potential criterion increases when it appears repeatedly across a diverse sample. One that surfaces consistently and unprompted across many different customers in many different contexts is a market-level indicator, indicating that existing solutions have failed to address a widely shared need.

Explore Across: When is it Worse?

Exploring across means moving from the problem toward the conditions that shape it, understanding when the difficulty is most severe and what factors drive the variation. Teams often treat a problem as uniform when it is actually highly condition-dependent, generating criteria that are too broad to be actionable.

Explore Across questions:

- What circumstances make this more difficult?
- When or where is this hardest?
- With whom, or in what situations, does this become a bigger problem?
- Are there times when you avoid doing this, or put it off?
- Is there a situation where this isn't a problem at all?
- What's different when it works well versus when it doesn't?
- What conditions have to be present for this to become unacceptable?

In Ryan's case, *Exploring across* reveals that the staking problem is specifically acute when the soil is rocky, and the weather is deteriorating simultaneously. On flat, soft ground in good weather, staking is easy. This contextual specificity transforms "Minimize the likelihood of staking difficulty" into the more precise and actionable "Minimize the time to secure the tent on rocky terrain."

When to Move Between Directions

The three Explore directions are options for an in-charge moderator. After each customer response, the moderator considers: What is still missing from the picture?

- If the reason the problem matters is unclear, Explore up.
- If what is producing it remains unclear, Explore down.
- If the problem varies across situations, Explore across.

The model expands the moderator's choices. At any moment in the conversation, there is always another direction available. The goal is a complete picture: what the problem is, why it matters, what is stopping the customer from solving it, and when it is most consequential.

Focus works differently. Where Explore moves up, down, and across within a topic, Focus moves inward, pressing toward precision. It is not a stage that necessarily has to wait until the end. A moderator may feel the pull toward a Focus question at any point in the conversation, and following that instinct can be the right move. The practical guidance is simply this: a problem that has not been explored is not ready to be focused on. But once a moderator senses that the shape of a problem is clear enough, the door to Focus, the third dimension of the 3D model, is open.

FOCUS — What is the Job Success Criterion?

This anchor sharpens the boundary of the fuzzy problem. Focus has three moves. The first establishes what the customer is measuring when they evaluate performance. The second drafts a Job Success Criterion and checks it with the customer in real time. The third establishes the range, where acceptable performance begins and where it ends.

Move 1: The Metric Question — What Are You Actually Measuring?

The metric question asks the customer to name the dimension they use to evaluate performance. Customers often know intuitively how they judge a job's performance without having made that standard explicit.

The best approach is often to just be direct and ask, "If you were going to measure this, what would you measure?"

Or, if the customers are technical in nature, "What metric do you use?"

However, here are some more subtle Metric questions:

- When you think about whether this went well or badly, what are you actually paying attention to?
- How do you know when this has gone wrong?
- What is the first sign that something is off?
- What does the difference between a good experience and a bad one come down to?

In Ryan's case, the metric question surfaces *time*. He knows almost immediately whether the setup is going well based on how quickly the shelter is taking shape relative to the deteriorating conditions. Once the metric is established, the moderator can move to another probe.

Move 2: The Criterion — Drafting Job Success Criteria with the Customer

Once the metric is identified, the moderator can attempt to draft a Job Success Criterion in real time and test it with the customer.

This is not note-taking; it's still an interviewing technique. The moderator proposes a criterion and checks it directly.

In Ryan's case, Shelton had established that Ryan was tracking two things: time and whether anything got wet. Rather than writing that down and moving on, he first checked it.

"So, if I were to say the goal is to minimize the time required to establish shelter before gear gets wet — does that capture what you're describing?"

Ryan didn't hesitate. "Yeah. That's exactly it. Fast enough that nothing inside gets wet before the fly is on."

The customer's response is data. Ryan confirmed the criterion and sharpened the language in the same breath, "before the fly is on" adds a precision Shelton hadn't included. That refinement would not have surfaced without the check.

For moderators early in their practice, a simple heuristic helps with the initial draft. Ask internally: Is this primarily about time and efficiency, or about avoiding a problem?

If it's about time or efficiency: *"Minimize the time to..."* is usually the right opening.

If it's about avoiding something going wrong: *"Minimize the likelihood of/that..."* is usually the right opening.

As the team gains experience, a wider range of verbs and metrics will come naturally. The full framework for constructing Job Success Criteria, including the complete verb set and criterion structure, is covered in Chapter 8.

Move 3: The Range Question — What Does the Acceptable Range Look Like?

The range question establishes the performance envelope: the lower bound below which the experience becomes genuinely unacceptable, and the upper bound at which the customer would consider the problem fully resolved.

Barely acceptable threshold questions:

- At what point does this go from frustrating to genuinely unacceptable?
- When does this cross the line from an annoyance to a real problem?
- What is the worst you can tolerate?

Fully satisfied threshold questions:

- What would fully satisfied look like to you?
- At what point would this stop being a concern for you at all?
- What would make this feel completely resolved?

In Ryan's case, the barely acceptable threshold is low: worse than 20 minutes of rain exposure before shelter is established crosses into genuinely problematic territory. The fully satisfactory threshold is equally clear: shelter up before any gear gets wet, something that can be accomplished with a tent that can be pitched in 10 minutes. A product that performs worse than the barely acceptable threshold fails the customer. One that performs at the fully satisfactory threshold, or better, has solved the problem. Everything in between is where the market rewards each marginal unit of improvement.

To an engineer that will later be tasked with addressing this problem, the value of this ten-to-twenty-minute range is massive.

Keeping "Focus" Conversational

The range question carries a specific risk: it can start to feel like a survey. If a moderator were to ask, "On a scale of one to ten, how important is setup speed?", the customer moves from storyteller to respondent, and the richness of the exchange collapses.

The purpose of the range question in an interview is not to collect precise measurements. It is to understand the shape of the customer's performance standard. A survey could collect precise numbers later. The interview is collecting the lived sense of what the range feels like from inside the customer's experience.

Keep range questions grounded in the customer's story. "At what point does it go from frustrating to genuinely unacceptable?" is a story question. "What number on a scale of one to ten represents unacceptable?" is a survey question. When a customer offers a specific number spontaneously, capture it. Do not engineer that response by asking for it directly.

This is why *Focus* is more than a closing move. It is where the language of the customer's experience begins to translate into Job Success Criteria. Everything the conversation has produced, such as the located breakdown, the consequences, the constraints and the conditions, converges here into a performance standard that can be measured, ranked, and acted on. Capture it with the same precision the customer used to describe it.

Keep Going with "What Else?"

Within any anchor, one of the most productive moves a moderator can make *is simply to remain there*. Before shifting direction, before moving to a new problem, before advancing the discussion guide, the moderator should consider whether the current line has been exhausted.

The question is always some version of: what else?
When Exploring down, that sounds like: *"What else makes this difficult?"*
When Exploring up: *"What other problems does this create for you?"*
When Exploring across: *"In what other situations does this become worse?"*

Even within Define, once a customer has described one aspect of the breakdown, the moderator can ask: "What else falls apart when that happens?"

The same logic applies inside Focus. Once a customer has described one performance standard, they may hold another. A moderator who moves on after the first criterion surfaces may leave the second one on the table.

This is cognitively easy for the customer because they are already inside the problem. With one question type on the table, a second response comes more readily than it would cold. In Big Sky terms, once Ryan has described the staking difficulty, he is primed. "What else makes shelter setup harder under those conditions?" feels like building on the current conversation, rather than processing a new question.

The pattern holds across anchors, job steps, and the full arc of the interview. The moderator's instinct to move on is often premature. Exhausting a direction before changing it is almost always the better discipline.

The 3D Probing Model

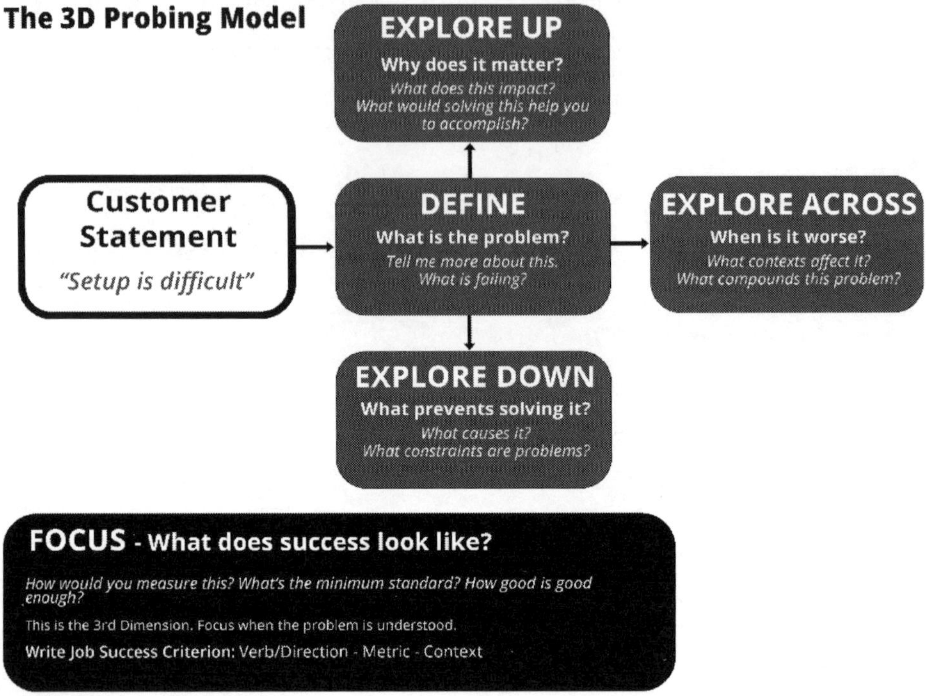

Putting the Model Together: A Walkthrough

Ryan's interview illustrated the model in motion, but it entered mid-stream. To see the full sequence from a customer's opening statement through to a complete set of criteria, consider the exchange below.

Watch for the five questions at work throughout: what is failing, why does it matter, what is preventing resolution, when is it worse, and what does success look like. The moderator begins with Explore Down, not because Down always comes first, but because the customer's opening statement most immediately raised a question about the mechanism. The first direction chosen should be the one that addresses what seems to be missing most at that moment.

Customer: "Setting up my tent in the wind is miserable."

Define: "What part of the setup does the wind affect most?"

Customer: "The tent fabric flaps everywhere. I'm trying to get the poles in while the whole thing is billowing around. Getting the poles seated is nearly impossible when the tent is moving."

Explore Down — Root Cause:

Moderator: "Why does the fabric move so much during setup?"

Customer: "It's so light. It catches all the air. But it's a problem because I have to pitch the inner tent first. The insides are completely exposed before the fly goes on."

Explore Down — Constraint:

Moderator: "What prevents you from setting it up differently?"

Customer: "There's no other way to do it. That's just how the design works."

Moderator: "Tell me more about that."

Customer: "If I could get the fly on first somehow, or if the whole thing went up as one unit."

Note that the customer has offered a feature request, a fly-first design. Rather than accepting this as a criterion, the moderator moves up.

Explore Up:

Moderator: "How would that help you?"

Customer: "The inner would stay dry. And the whole structure would be more stable during setup. Quick setups are usually sloppy, and without proper tension, then the thing can come down later, in the night."

The moderator has now converted the feature request back into two underlying criteria: "Minimize the likelihood of the tent interior getting wet during setup," and "Minimize the likelihood of tent instability due to setup errors."

Explore Across:

Moderator: "When is this problem worse?"

Customer: "When I arrive late and have to pitch in the dark while it's windy. The wind can blow the tent fly around, and it can be hard to see with my headlamp."

Moderator: "Are there times when wind during setup isn't really a problem?"

Customer: "If I can find a sheltered spot, sure. But in alpine terrain, that's not always possible."

Explore Up:

Moderator: "Why is the wet inner such a problem for you?"

Customer: "Because if the inner gets wet, the inside of the tent is damp all night. That's the biggest thing, but it's not the only thing."

Moderator: "It's not? What else?"

Customer, "No. If I'm fumbling with setup in the dark, my friends are already in their tents, comfortable and snug. I feel a bit out of sorts when I'm the only one still messing around with the tent. I feel like a rookie."

Focus — Metric Question:

Moderator: "How do you judge how well the setup went?"

Customer: "How long it takes, mostly. And, in those conditions, whether anything got wet."

Focus — Criterion:

Moderator: "Would it be fair to say the goal is to *Minimize the time to set up the shelter*?"

Customer: "Yeah, exactly. Faster is always better. It's just more important, a lot more important, when the weather is turning."

The customer has done two things at once: confirmed the criterion and sharpened it. The conditional context, specifically when the weather is turning, was not in Shelton's draft. It surfaced only because the criterion was checked out loud. That refinement makes it more precise and more actionable than anything the moderator wrote down privately.

Focus — Range Question:

Moderator: "For the setup, at what point does the time it takes go from annoying to unacceptable?"

Customer: "Honestly, anything past 20 minutes can put you at risk. I'd say 20 minutes is unacceptable."

Moderator: "Let's think about it the other way. What's your ideal setup time?"

Customer: "Getting the shelter up and everything inside dry before the rain really comes in. That's the bar. If you're better than 10 minutes, that probably gets you there."

From this single exchange, the 3D Probing Model has produced at least three distinct Job Success Criteria candidates:

- Minimize the time required to establish a fully protected shelter structure in wind and rain
- Minimize the likelihood of the tent interior becoming wet during setup in adverse weather
- Minimize the likelihood of instability in the tent structure during pole assembly in the wind

Each criterion is specific, measurable, solution-independent, and grounded in the customer's experience. None of them would have been accessible from the customer's opening statement alone. Additionally, Shelton uncovered the range of performance for setup, from ten to twenty minutes. This will be vital later in concept ideation, development, testing, and benchmarking.

3D Probing, Simplified

The 3D Probing Model is detailed by design. Real discovery conversations are complex, and a moderator who understands the model fully will be equipped to handle whatever a customer brings into the room. But complexity on the page should not produce hesitation in the conversation. The model is meant to be internalized, not feel oppressive.

Here is what to carry into the room: Five questions. Three anchors. One principle.

The five questions:

- **What is failing?** Ground the conversation in a specific, location-based breakdown before going anywhere else.
- **Why does it matter?** Move toward consequences, importance, and the larger goal the customer is trying to accomplish.

- **What is preventing resolution?** Surface root causes and constraints, both what produced the problem and what prevents the customer from resolving it.
- **When is it worse?** Identify the conditions that make the problem severe, situational, or irrelevant.
- **What does success look like?** Establish the metric and the range that define what better actually means to this customer.

The three anchors: *Define* corresponds to the first question. *Explore* corresponds to the middle three. *Focus* corresponds to the last.

The one principle: follow the clues, not the script. When a customer says something, ask yourself where the conversation needs to go next. The five questions tell you what your options are. Just follow the customer's cues and energy from there.

If the moderator embraces a genuine curiosity, the next direction to go will appear.

Patterns Worth Watching

A few recurring patterns can be disruptive to the interview. None are fatal. Most self-correct with a properly curious moderator. Still, they are worth knowing as patterns to watch for and generally avoid.

Generally avoid these:

Treating environmental constraints as solvable ones. When a customer describes a condition that cannot be changed, such as rain, rocky terrain or fatigue at the end of a long day, the productive question shifts from what would fix it to what the customer needs in order to succeed despite it. That reframe often leads directly to actionable criteria.

Letting Focus become a survey. Scaled responses and numerical ratings pull customers out of their stories. Range questions work best when they stay grounded in the customer's experience. Specific numbers that emerge naturally are worth capturing. Numbers that are engineered by asking for them directly are not.

Staying in one Explore direction longer than the conversation warrants. When a customer begins repeating territory, that is usually a signal to move. Every direction has a point of diminishing returns.

Overuse of "For example." This feels helpful in the moment. It is not. A moderator facing silence is tempted to fill it with examples, believing they are making the question easier to answer. What they are actually doing is answering it themselves.

It sounds like this: "What makes it difficult to pitch the tent in the dark? For example, is it hard to find the stakes, find acceptable ground, or is it because your flashlight is buried in your backpack?"

The customer now has three options to choose from, *all of which were provided by the moderator*. Whatever they say next is shaped by that list. The moderator has traded an open question for a multiple-choice prompt and will never know what the customer would have said unprompted.

"For example" can be used sparingly, particularly late in a session when a customer needs a nudge to continue. But as a default response to silence or hesitation, it is one of the most reliable ways to contaminate a response. When the urge arises, the better move is the Universal Probe: "Can you tell me more about that?" Or simply silence.

Handling Feature Requests

Feature requests can surface at any time. Whenever they appear, the probe is the same: *Explore up*.

For example, a customer says one of the following:

- I wish the stakes were longer.
- It would be great if the tent could be pitched with fewer poles.
- They should make it so the fly goes on first.

These statements point toward real needs but describe the customer's proposed solution rather than the underlying problem.

The correct response is to Explore up:

- How would that help you?
- What problem would that solve?

The customer who says "I wish the stakes were longer" will, when asked how that would help, typically describe a performance problem: the stakes do not anchor reliably in rocky soil, or they pull out overnight in the wind. That performance problem is the criterion. The longer stakes are one possible response to it, and not necessarily the best one.

Whenever a customer volunteers a feature, treat it as a clue that, when prompted correctly, can reveal the real need beneath it, and *"Explore up"* to surface what that need is.

Four Special Probes for Anytime

A moderator should never be concerned about not knowing what to say back. Here are four probes that can be used most anytime: The Universal Probe, Silence, Repeat as a Question, and Paraphrase Back.

The Universal Probe

Skilled moderators always have the universal probe in their back pockets. It can work for most any part of the interview, but is especially useful during Define.

It's this: *Can you tell me more about that?*

Despite the apparent simplicity, the Universal Probe doesn't sound repetitive, even if used frequently. With that phrase, a moderator should never be lost for words. It is always revealing and exposes nothing about the moderator's thoughts or opinions.

Silence

One of the best probes is just to be silent. This takes a bit of restraint by the entire interviewing team, as it only takes one person to break the silence. But if the team refrains from speaking, let the customer's words hang out there; more often than not, the customer will continue to elaborate.

Repeat as a Question

This can be used almost anytime. The customer says, "It's difficult." The moderator replies, *"It's difficult?"* The moderator merely repeats the words back to the customer, adding inflection to make it sound like a question. This technique comes not from innovation research but from FBI hostage negotiator Chris Voss, in his book *Never Split the Difference*.

It works because moderators and hostage negotiators both seek to learn as much as they can while revealing as little as possible.

Paraphrase Back

This is similar to Repeat as a Question. But in this case, the moderator is paraphrasing the customer's words to check understanding. By changing the customer's actual words slightly, the customer can accept or correct the reframing.

For example:

Customer: I can never get the tent back in the stuff sack. It's always sticking out the top.

Moderator: I see. So, it's too long after you've rolled it up, *is that correct?*

Customer: Not exactly. It could be too long, or it could also be too fat. Both create problems.

It's the *"is that correct"* phrase that makes this powerful. The moderator keeps the customer in charge and ensures they have full permission to accept or modify the new framing.

What Comes Next

The 3D Probing Model provides the navigational framework for exploring functional problems, what is failing, why it matters, what is stopping the customer from solving it, when it is worse, and what success would look like in measurable terms. Used with discipline, it converts vague complaints into precise Job Success Criteria.

But functional problems are not the only thing worth probing in an interview. As the Big Sky team's conversation with Ryan demonstrated, the most revealing moments sometimes come when the conversation moves above the functional level, when a customer reveals not just what went wrong, but what it said about them, and how it made them feel.

Probing for identity and emotional signals requires a different kind of listening. That is the subject of the next chapter.

Key Takeaways

- The most common failure in customer interviews is not asking the wrong question. It is stopping too soon after asking the right one. A customer complaint captured at the surface is not a Job Success Criterion. It is a starting point. The 3D Probing Model is the navigational framework for moving from complaint to criterion.
- The model is built around five questions a moderator can ask at any moment: What is failing? Why does it matter? What is preventing resolution? When is it worse? What does success look like? These questions are not in sequence. They are options. The right one to ask next depends on what is still missing from the picture.
- The three anchors, Define, Explore, and Focus, organize the five key questions into a practical framework. Define locates the breakdown precisely before anything else. Explore moves outward in up to three directions: upward toward consequences and meaning, downward toward root causes and constraints, and across toward the conditions that make the problem worse. Focus establishes the metric and the range that define what better actually means.
- When the problem is well understood, draft the Job Success Criterion out loud and check it with the customer directly. The customer's response is data. They will confirm, correct, or sharpen the language in ways that private note-taking never produces. That refinement is not a courtesy check. It is part of the discovery.
- Environmental constraints cannot be removed. Rain, rocky terrain, and fatigue after a long hike are inevitable. When a customer describes an environmental constraint, the productive question is not what would fix it but what the customer needs in order to succeed despite it. That reframe typically leads directly to the most actionable criteria.

- Feature requests are starting points, not findings. When a customer names a preferred solution, the correct response is to Explore up: "How would that help you?" This converts solution language back into problem language and surfaces the underlying criterion the customer was reaching for.
- Four probes work in almost any moment: the Universal Probe ("Can you tell me more about that?"), Silence, Repeat as a Question (echoing the customer's words with upward inflection), and Paraphrase Back (restating and inviting correction). A moderator who has internalized these four will never be lost for where to go next.

Where We Are in DISCOVER

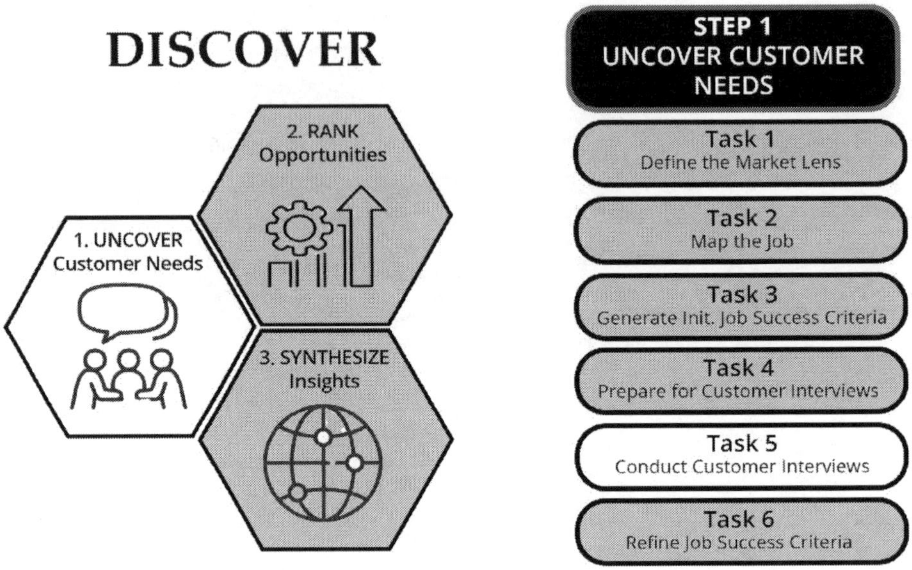

Step 1, Task 5: Conduct Customer Interviews
Part 2: Probe Beyond Function

What this chapter helps you do

Explore the identity and emotional motivations that sit beneath functional customer needs.

What you will have by the end

A practical way to see beyond functional performance, including how customers want to act, be seen, and feel.

Coming next

Task 5 continues with bringing the full interview approach together.

Chapter 14: Task 5, Conduct Customer Interviews — Probing Identity and Emotion

Something Deeper

RYAN TOOK ANOTHER SIP OF COFFEE.

"After the rain started," Shelton began, "what happened next?"

Ryan shrugged. "I got the fly clipped on and dove inside. Everything stayed mostly dry. I just sat there and caught my breath."

"You caught your breath?" Shelton asked.

"Yeah," Ryan said. "I was sweating. It's tiring. But I was also stressed thinking about how tightly I'd hammered those stakes in."

Shelton tilted his head slightly. "You were stressed about the stakes?"

"Yeah."

Shelton leaned forward. "Why?"

Ryan hesitated. "Well… the weather, partly."

Shelton noticed the pause. "What else was going on?"

Ryan smiled faintly. "Actually, the worst part would be the next morning. And I knew it."

"What were you expecting to be a problem?" Shelton asked.

Ryan sighed. "It played out exactly like I thought. Everyone's packed up and ready to hike. Coffee's done, packs are on... and I'm still messing with my tent."

"What was the issue?"

"If the ground's rocky and you've hammered the stakes in hard, they don't come out easily," Ryan said. "Sometimes they're wedged in or bent a bit from hammering."

Shelton nodded, letting him continue.

"You might not think about it," Ryan said, "but if they're stuck, it can take a while to get them out without breaking them or hurting yourself. I usually end up looking for a stick to pry them loose."

"What makes that a problem?" Shelton asked.

"Time."

"And what problem does that extra time create?"

Ryan shrugged. "Mornings are already a bit rushed. The part I hate is when everyone else is ready to go, and they're waiting. *On me.* The stakes are just part of it, but it doesn't take much to fall behind."

"Behind?" Shelton asked.

Ryan shrugged again. "Yeah. The other guys say it's fine," he said. *"But I hate being the one who slows everyone down."*

The table went quiet.

Shelton nodded slowly. "And that's why you feel rushed?"

Ryan nodded. "That's right. I feel rushed because everyone's waiting on me. You want to look like you know what you're doing out there."

The conversation had just moved beyond a product problem. It revealed how the moment shaped how Ryan saw himself in the group, and how he wanted to be seen by others.

Beyond the Functional Domain

The previous chapter introduced the navigational framework for probing customer problems. The 3D Probing Model showed how to move from a surface complaint to a performance standard through Define, Explore, and Focus, generating Job Success Criteria grounded in the customer's experience.

But Ryan's comment about *not wanting to be the guy who slows everyone down* did not emerge from a functional probe. It emerged from a pause, a follow-up question, and a willingness to listen and hear what the experience meant to Ryan rather than simply what it cost him in time and effort.

That distinction, between what an experience costs and what it means, is the territory this chapter covers.

As the Jobs-to-be-Done Pyramid establishes, customers pursue more than functional success when they perform a job. They are also trying to become a certain kind of person, manage how they are perceived by others, and feel a certain way. These motivations, organized within The Jobs-to-be-Done Pyramid across the Identity and Emotional domains, are real, consequential, and often more durable than functional preferences. They are also largely invisible to discovery teams that have not learned how to listen for them.

This chapter explains how to recognize identity and emotional jobs when they surface in a discovery interview, and how to uncover them productively when they do.

Why These Cues Rarely Appear Directly

Customers talk naturally about what they do and what goes wrong. They describe tasks, sequences, friction points, and frustrations. The language of functional experience, what happened, what was difficult, what took too long, is comfortable and familiar. It's the language of problem-reporting, and most people are fluent in it.

The language of identity and emotion is less comfortable in a professional or semi-formal research context. Customers will rarely say, "I was trying to reinforce my identity as a competent outdoorsman" or "I wanted to feel calm and in control in front of my friends." These are real motivations, but they are not the kind of thing most people say directly, especially to a researcher they've just met.

The true motivations are often hidden inside the practical complaint.

Instead, identity and emotional jobs appear embedded in functional language. They surface as asides, qualifications, and emotional coloring around descriptions of tasks and results. The moderator, who is listening only for performance language, times, frequencies, and likelihoods, will hear Ryan say "I hate being the last guy with his tent up" and register it as a setup-speed complaint. The moderator who understands the Jobs-to-be-Done Pyramid will also hear it as an identity cue worth probing.

This means that surfacing identity and emotional needs is less about asking the right questions and more about hearing the cues when they appear and knowing how to follow them.

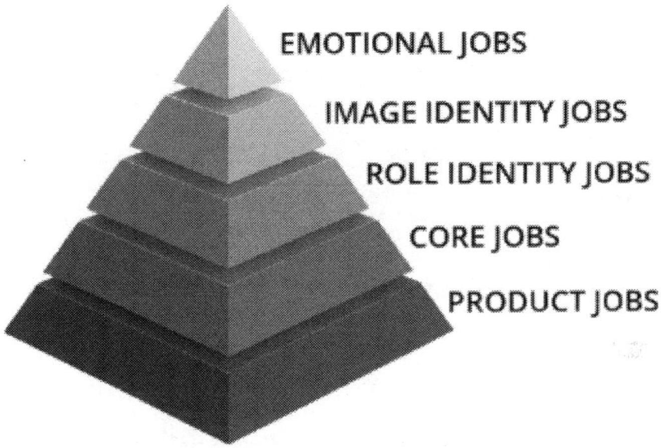

Exploring Up with the Jobs-to-be-Done Pyramid™

In the 3D Probing Model, **identity and emotional jobs can surface when the moderator Explores Up**, asking why a problem matters, what it affects, and what it prevents the customer from accomplishing.

When a moderator asks, "How does this impact you?" in response to a functional complaint, the customer's answer reveals what the complaint means at a higher level of motivation. It invites the customer, if so inclined, to connect the functional experience to something larger, a role they are trying to perform, an image they are trying to maintain, or a feeling they are trying to preserve or avoid.

Understanding this connection gives the moderator a tool: when a conversation has thoroughly explored a functional problem and produced solid criteria, a final upward probe, "Why does that matter to you, beyond the practical inconvenience?" can open something new.

The Identity Domain: Two Distinct Levels

The Jobs-to-be-Done Pyramid separates identity motivation into two levels, and the distinction matters for how jobs are recognized and how they're used.

Level 3 captures Role Identity Jobs, the roles customers are trying to live through their actions. A Role Identity Job is about becoming someone: being the kind of person who handles backcountry conditions competently, being a reliable member of the group, being someone who knows their gear and uses it well. Role Identity is persistent and internal; it's an internal standard the customer holds to, independent of whether anyone else is watching.

Level 4 captures Image Identity Jobs, how customers want to be perceived by themselves or others. Image Identity splits into two subcategories: Self-Image, which concerns how the customer wants to see themselves in the moment, and Reputation, which concerns how they want to be seen by others. These are related but distinct. A backpacker who feels privately embarrassed by a fumbled setup, even when no one is watching, is experiencing a failed attempt at a Self-Image Job. A backpacker who is acutely aware of their friends watching and does not want to appear inexperienced is likewise experiencing a failed attempt at a Reputation Job.

In practice, both levels can operate simultaneously. Ryan's comment, *"You want to look like you know what you're doing out there,"* contains elements of both. The desire to look competent in front of the group is a Reputation concern. The underlying standard, being someone who handles these situations well, is a Role Identity concern. Both are real, both are worth noting, and distinguishing between them matters when the team later considers how the insights apply to product design versus positioning and messaging.

Cues That Reveal Identity Jobs

Role Identity jobs, revealing who the customer is trying to become, typically appear as self-descriptions and internal standards:

- "I'm the kind of person who..."
- "I've always tried to be someone who..."
- "That's just how I operate."
- "I take pride in doing this right."
- "I want to make sure I'm doing this properly."
- "I feel like I should be able to handle this."

Image Identity jobs, revealing how the customer wants to be perceived, often appear as statements about social visibility, comparison with others, and awareness of the audience:

- "I want to look like I know what I'm doing."
- "People expect me to have this handled."
- "I hate being the one who can't figure it out."
- "My friends know gear — I don't want to look like a beginner."
- "I want to seem like I belong out there."
- "It's embarrassing when it takes me that long."

Role Identity language tends to be inward-facing: "I take pride in," "I want to be someone who." Image Identity language tends to be outward-facing: "I don't want to look," "people expect," "it's embarrassing."

Cues That Reveal Emotional Jobs

Cues appear when customers describe how they felt during an experience, not just what happened. They reflect the moment-to-moment felt quality of the job, the internal states that accompany the functional events.

The most common emotional markers in discovery conversations appear as:

Anxiety and tension: "I was stressed," "I was worried that," "I kept thinking about what would happen if," "That makes me nervous."

Relief and release: "Once it was up, I finally relaxed," "That moment when it all clicks into place," "I could breathe again after that."

Frustration and helplessness: "I hate when," "It drives me crazy that," "I just feel stuck," "There's nothing I can do about it."

Confidence and competence: "When it works right, I feel like I know what I'm doing," "That gives me confidence," "I feel prepared when I have that sorted."

Embarrassment and inadequacy: "It's embarrassing," "I feel like I should know better," "I look like I don't know what I'm doing."

Pride and satisfaction: "I take real satisfaction in," "It feels good when," "I'm proud of how I handled that."

These cues are data about a distinct layer of customer motivation that product design, messaging, and brand positioning can all address. A tent that allows Ryan to pitch quickly and competently in front of his friends does not just solve a functional challenge; it supports the emotional experience he is trying to have and the identity he is trying to maintain.

Probing Identity Cues

When an identity cue surfaces in the conversation, the moderator can follow it, but gently, and without introducing psychological language that the customer has not used themselves.

The goal of identity probing is to understand the role or image motivation well enough to capture it, not to conduct a deep analysis of the customer's self-concept. The questions should feel like a natural extension of the conversation, curious follow-ups that invite the customer to say more about something they have already raised.

Useful identity probing questions:

- "Why is that important to you?"
- "What does doing that well say about you?"
- "What does it mean to you when that goes right?"
- "What does it feel like when that goes wrong, beyond the practical inconvenience?"
- "How does that reflect on you, in your own eyes?"
- "What does that say about the kind of backpacker you are?"
- "Is that important to you personally, or more in terms of how others see you?"

When probing identity cues, the moderator should stay close to the customer's own language rather than introducing abstract terms. If a customer says, "I hate looking unprepared," the probe should follow that specific language: "What does looking unprepared mean to you in that moment?" rather than reframing it in terms the customer has not used.

Probing Emotional Cues

Where identity probing asks what the experience means to the customer, emotional probing asks what the experience feels like and what conditions produce or relieve those feelings.

The goal is to understand the emotional job well enough to write it: *Avoid feeling anxious overnight when the weather is deteriorating.* That requires understanding both the emotional state the customer is seeking or avoiding and the conditions that trigger it.

Useful emotional probing questions:

- What does that feel like in the moment?
- What's going through your mind when that happens?
- What makes that anxious feeling worse?
- When does that feeling go away?
- What would need to be true for you to feel confident about this?
- Is that a fleeting feeling, or does it stay with you?
- What's the opposite of that experience?
- When do you feel the way you want to feel?

When exploring emotional veins, the moderator should match the emotional register of the customer's language rather than escalating it. If a customer describes mild frustration, the probe should be mild and curious, not "that sounds really distressing," but "what does that feel like?" Matching the register keeps the conversation feeling natural and prevents the moderator from inadvertently amplifying an emotional response beyond what the customer described.

Capturing Identity and Emotional Jobs

After each conversation, identity and emotional jobs should be clarified in the debrief alongside functional criteria. Put them in a separate category, organized by the level of the Jobs-to-be-Done

Pyramid they reflect. The goal is to preserve the customer's exact language before it fades, because that specificity is what makes the patterns analytically useful later.

For identity cues, note what the customer said, which level of the Jobs-to-be-Done Pyramid it appears to reflect, and a draft job statement in the appropriate form. Role Identity statements follow the pattern "be someone who..." or "I am a person who..." Image Identity statements follow the pattern "be seen as..." or "see myself as..."

For emotional jobs, note what the customer said, the emotional state it describes, such as anxiety, relief, confidence, embarrassment, pride, etc., the conditions that trigger it, and a draft job statement following the form "feel..." or "avoid feeling..."

Why Identity and Emotional Jobs Matter Beyond Product Design

Identity and emotional insights can be the foundation of differentiation that is difficult to replicate. A competitor can match a functional specification, such as a tent that pitches in under five minutes or stakes that anchor reliably in rocky terrain. They cannot as easily match a product experience that is designed from the ground up to support a specific identity and emotional reality. A tent that makes a weekend backpacker feel capable and prepared in the moments when conditions are most demanding.

Identity jobs also directly inform messaging and positioning strategy. A product positioned around functional specifications speaks to one layer of customer motivation. A product positioned around the identity and emotional experience it enables speaks to a deeper and more durable layer. The most effective product positioning connects all three domains: here is what it does, here is who it is for, here is how it makes you feel. That connection is only possible if the discovery that precedes positioning has surfaced all three.

What Comes Next

The chapters covering probing have equipped the team with a complete toolkit for exploring what customers experience and why it matters. The 3D Probing Model provides the navigational framework for functional problems. The techniques in this chapter extend that framework for *Exploring Upward* into the identity and emotional territory where the deepest motivations live.

How all that technique comes together in an actual conversation, and what separates a great interview from a compromised one, is the subject of the next chapter.

In recent chapters, we followed the Big Sky Outdoors team as they conducted their first interview with Ryan and they tried out their interview methods. Going into the next chapter, we go back in time a few weeks as the team settles in for that first interview.

After all, once the session begins, it's showtime. I*t's time to listen*, and there are a handful of final elements to keep in mind.

Key Takeaways

- Identity and emotional jobs rarely appear as direct statements. The Jobs-to-be-Done Pyramid is a listening framework. The job is there, embedded in functional language. The moderator must know what to listen for.
- Identity jobs surface most reliably through Explore Up, asking why a problem matters, what it affects, and what it prevents the customer from accomplishing. When upward probing moves past consequences into meaning, the conversation has reached the identity or emotional layer of the Pyramid.
- The Jobs-to-be-Done Pyramid separates identity motivation into two distinct levels: Role Identity Jobs, about who the customer is trying to become, and Image Identity Jobs, about how they want to be perceived by others. These are related but distinct.
- Emotional jobs describe how a customer wants to feel in a specific moment, confident, capable, calm, or what they are trying to avoid feeling: anxious, embarrassed, inadequate.
- Identity and emotional insights are the foundation of differentiation that is genuinely difficult for competitors to replicate
- When an identity or emotional job surfaces, follow it gently and stay close to the customer's own language. For identity jobs, ask what the experience means: "What does that say about the kind of person you are?" or "Is that important to you personally, or more about how others see you?"
- For emotional jobs, ask what the experience feels like and what produces or relieves it: "What does that feel like in the moment?" or "What would need to be true for you to feel confident about this?" The goal is a job statement precise enough to act on.

Where We Are in DISCOVER

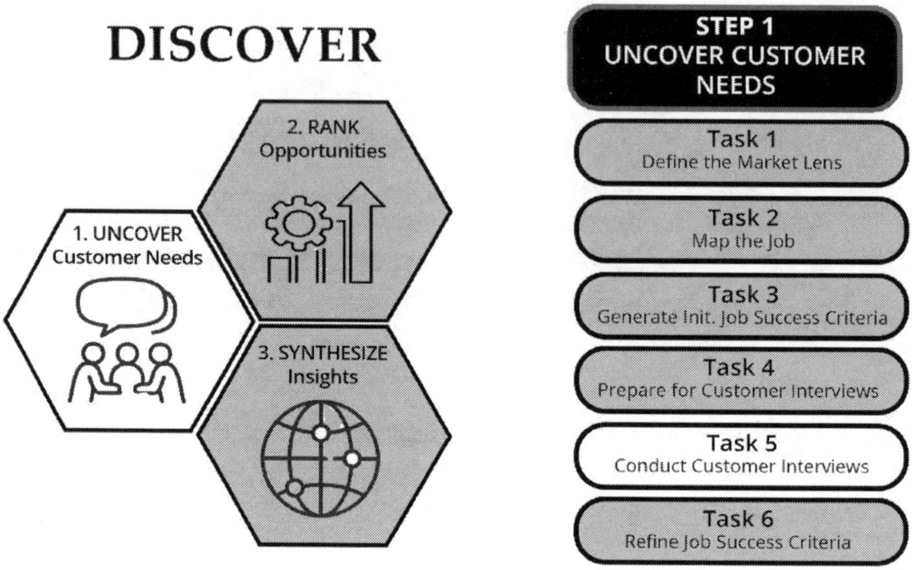

Step 1, Task 5 Conduct Customer Interviews
Part 3: Bringing It All Together

What this chapter helps you do

Put the full interview approach into practice, from preparation to probing, listening, adapting, and closing the conversation.

What you will have by the end

A practical model for conducting customer interviews with enough structure to stay focused and enough flexibility to follow what customers reveal.

Coming next

Task 6: Refine Job Success Criteria

Chapter 15: Task 5, Conduct Customer Interviews — Bringing It All Together

Today, We Listen

Three Weeks Earlier

THE PARKING LOT WAS MOSTLY EMPTY. A dust-covered black Ford F150, a green Subaru with bicycle racks holding expensive-looking bikes, and an open, rusty red Jeep rested in the few spots. A torn trail map was mounted on a post near the entrance, along with the smell of pine and cold air. The café sign was lit. Through the window, they could see a server wiping her hands on an apron as she moved behind the counter.

Nobody got out of the car right away.

Tom flipped through the pages of the discussion guide, making a few notes. Jenna looked out the window. Luis had his notebook on his knee, pen uncapped, but wasn't writing anything.

Shelton sat with his hands in his lap.

"You all ready?" Tom asked.

Nobody answered immediately.

"Do you have the opening questions handy?" Jenna asked.

"I do. And the rest of the discussion guide, too," Shelton said. He smiled.

"I know." She paused. "I was also reviewing the 3D Probing Model. But what if you turn to me for a follow-up question and I can't think of anything? What will you ask if you can't think of anything?"

Shelton smiled. "I'll ask, 'Can you tell me more about that?' The Universal Probes are always there. And they work. Simple questions will take you further than you might think. Remember, we don't have to be the experts. In fact, we shouldn't be the experts. Not today."

Luis capped his pen. "Yeah, but even with that, what if he doesn't say much?"

"Then we ask, and we wait. Silence is part of it." Shelton glanced over. "And if he says a great deal about something we didn't plan for, as long as it's about backpacking with a tent, we follow it. That's not losing control of the session. That's the session working."

Jenna asked, "But what if he starts talking about unrelated things?"

Shelton smiled. "If he tells us about his new puppy, we'll redirect him back to the scope, nicely, of course. As long as it's within the Market Lens we established, backpacking with a tent on short trips, we'll go with it."

Jenna said, "Yes, that's right. Sorry, I remember now. I'm just a bit nervous. We'll let him continue as long as it's not something we've already captured in detail from an earlier interview."

Shelton said, "True. But since this is our first interview, that's unlikely to be the case."

Jenna laughed. "Of course. I told you I was nervous!"

Tom was quiet for a moment. "I'm a little worried about looking like I don't know what I'm doing."

"In front of a backpacker at a trailhead café? Besides, today we're not the experts. If we come in here trying to show everything we know, our customer will talk less." Luis smiled slightly.

Tom said, "I know. I know."

Shelton turned to face them. "Here's what I want you to hold onto. This is not a performance. Ryan isn't grading us. We're not trying to conduct a perfect interview today, because there's no such thing." He paused. "We're here to learn. That's it."

Jenna looked up. "And if we miss something?"

"We'll have another session. And we'll be better in that one than we are in this one. That's how it works."

Shelton looked at each of them. "Think about where we started. Nothing but our own assumptions. We're about to change that. Whatever Ryan gives us today, we'll leave this café with Job Success Criteria we didn't have when we walked in. That's guaranteed."

Tom nodded.

"No pressure here. We're not getting everything from one customer anyway," Shelton continued. "He might be an expert or a casual weekend hiker. Ryan might be talkative, or he might be quiet. We can't control that. What we can control is whether we actually listen to what he tells us. Whether we follow his cues or our own expectations. Whether we go deeper when something matters."

He opened his door. "We're ready. Let's trust our preparation."

He stood, and the others followed.

"Notebooks ready," he said. "Our own ideas set aside. For now."

The team entered and settled at a corner table. The server picked up a pad and started to approach. Ryan looked toward the door, where a figure had just walked in and was scanning the room.

"Today, we listen."

The Market Lens, the discussion guide, the job map, and everything else covered in previous chapters are part of excellent preparation. This chapter is about what happens when that prep meets a real customer in a real conversation. The tools work. But they work best when the moderator has also made the shift Shelton named in that parking lot: from expert to listener, from hypothesis-holder to curious investigator. That shift was the subject of Chapter 10. What follows here is the conduct that expresses it, as there are a few things to keep in mind.

Hold the Discussion Guide Lightly

The moderator must balance two competing demands throughout the session: following the guide and following the customer. A moderator who follows only the guide will miss the most revealing moments. A moderator who follows only the customer will produce uneven coverage.

The practical discipline is to hold the guide lightly, to know its structure well enough to navigate it without consulting it constantly, and to track mentally where in the guide the interview currently sits. When the customer leads somewhere unexpected, as long as it's within the Market Lens, the moderator follows. When that thread has been explored, the moderator returns to the guide and picks up where the conversation left off.

Specific situations will require judgment in the moment.

When a customer gives a very short answer to an open question, the moderator should not move immediately to the next question. Short answers usually mean the question did not land, the customer is not yet comfortable enough to elaborate, or the topic is simply less relevant to this particular customer. The right response is a gentle probe, "Can you tell me more about that?", or simply silence, holding the space long enough for the customer to continue. Silence is one of the moderator's most powerful tools and one of the least used.

When a customer gives a long, free-ranging answer that moves across several topics, the moderator should resist the impulse to interrupt. Let the customer finish. Then note which themes from the guide were covered, which were not, and which new topics appeared that the guide did not anticipate. The long, free-ranging answer can be where the important cues live. The notetaker should attempt to flag distinct Job Success Criteria from that monologue within their notes. The moderator then has many options, amongst the stated problems, to dive into.

When a customer says something that directly contradicts an internal assumption, the moderator should make a point to go deeper, navigating with the 3D Probing Model. Understanding why this customer's experience differs from the team's expectation is as analytically valuable as understanding why another customer confirms it. Contradictions are not problems. They are data.

Be Wary of the Selling and Solving Instincts

Discovery teams are often composed of people whose professional identities are defined by doing: selling, engineering, designing and supporting. Those instincts do not disappear when the role shifts to researcher, and in a discovery interview, they can be actively harmful.

The selling instinct shows up when a team member with a sales background begins, consciously or not, to present the company favorably, to position the product as a solution to the frustrations the customer is describing, or to respond to complaints with reassurance that the company is working on the problem. All of these behaviors feel natural to someone whose professional habit is to build customer relationships and advance toward a close. In a discovery conversation, they are research-contaminating. The moment a customer understands that the team is developing a product that addresses their frustration, every subsequent response is shaped by that knowledge.

The solving instinct shows up when a team member with an engineering, design, or support background responds to a customer's description of a problem by engaging with the problem intellectually. They might give advice, suggest solutions or workarounds. This feels natural, normal and helpful. It is not. The goal of the discovery interview is to learn, and advising undermines learning.

The moment you start solving problems, the learning stops.

In business-to-business situations where the customer is an important account, the solving instinct can create an additional complication: the team member may feel a genuine obligation to help. The appropriate response in these cases is to acknowledge the customer's problem, note that it deserves proper attention, and commit to a follow-up outside the research context. Something like: "That's really important, and I want to make sure we address it properly. Can we set up some time after this to dig into it later?" This honors the relationship without allowing the research conversation to become a support call. And it has the added benefit of being entirely true: understanding the problem fully, which is what the discovery conversation is doing, is actually the prerequisite for addressing it well.

Both instincts, selling and solving, should be named and discussed with the team before the first session begins. Practitioners who know to watch for these impulses in themselves are better at managing them than practitioners who have not considered it in advance.

Receiving What the Conversation Offers

Some customers are natural storytellers. They provide rich, detailed, unprompted accounts of their experiences, make connections between topics, and volunteer context that the moderator did not ask for. These sessions are enjoyable and can produce dense, high-quality data.

Other customers are not. Some are reserved by temperament, cautious about sharing unsolicited opinions, or simply having a quiet day. These sessions require more patient silence, more gentle probing, and more careful cultivation of comfort. They may produce less insight as a result. The moderator should not take this personally or interpret it as a failure. Some reserved, perhaps more introverted customers also gather momentum as the interview progresses, as they become more comfortable with the process.

The same principle applies to evaluating the session while it is happening. Real-time judgment is counterproductive for two reasons. It consumes cognitive resources that should be devoted to listening, and it is made on incomplete data. A session that seems thin at the midpoint may ultimately reveal the most important insight of the study. One that feels rich and confirming may, on reflection, have produced mostly repeats of what had been stated by other customers.

The discipline is to stay fully present and reserve all evaluation for later. The moderator's job in every session is to receive what this customer offers, not to judge it against expectations or wish the customer were more forthcoming. Extract what is available and trust that the sample was designed to provide a range of voices.

When Executives or Leaders Are in the Room

Discovery conversations occasionally include senior leaders or executives who want to observe, or sometimes participate in, the research. Their presence is not inherently a problem. Leaders who observe discovery interviews often develop a more direct and durable understanding of customer needs than those who receive findings secondhand. When a leader hears a customer describe a frustration in their own words, it tends to land differently than reading about it in a report.

The challenge is that leaders and executives, by disposition and professional habit, are often exactly the wrong people to have speaking in a discovery interview. They are accustomed to asking direct, specific questions. They are comfortable expressing opinions. They are used to moving conversations efficiently toward conclusions. In a discovery context, all of these instincts work against the research.

An executive who interjects with a question about a specific feature mid-conversation has likely provided a current initiative. An executive who expresses enthusiasm when a particular frustration surfaces has just told the customer which frustrations matter most. An executive who asks why the customer hasn't considered a particular product has just introduced the solution space into a conversation that should be grounded in the problem space. These are extremely difficult, at best, to navigate during an interview, and essentially impossible to recover from.

The principle for managing executive presence is simple and should be communicated clearly before the session begins: observers speak last and least, if at all, and only when invited by the moderator. If an executive has a question they want asked, they should write it down and pass it to the moderator, who will decide whether and when to raise it. But by agreement, they need to be fine with their question not being asked. But if given, any direct executive questions should come only in the final minutes, after the moderator has completed the guide, and should follow the same neutrality principles that govern all discovery questions.

This is not a slight to the executive. It is an acknowledgment that the value of their presence is in what they observe, not in what they contribute.

The Moment After the Conversation

Imagine the Big Sky team immediately after finishing an interview with Ryan, the weekend backpacker introduced earlier. Ryan described several situations from a recent trip: pitching a tent on rocky ground, rushing to set up before a rainstorm, worrying about wind during the night, struggling to repack a wet tent the next morning, and feeling pressure not to slow down his friends.

The team now has pages of notes, fragments of quotes, highlighted frustrations, possible Job Success Criteria, identity jobs, and emotional reactions. Everything feels rich. Everything also feels slippery.

Discovery interviews generate more input than the team can hold in memory. If the team simply moves on to the next conversation, important context quickly disappears. Subtle meaning is lost. Exact customer language gets replaced by summaries. And interpretation begins drifting as the team starts remembering what they expected to hear rather than what was said.

This is why, as has been mentioned previously, a critical discipline of qualitative synthesis is immediate debriefing, and why it must happen after every single session, not just at the end of the full series.

Debriefing Protocol

The purpose of a debrief is to preserve the freshness of immediate reaction before subsequent sessions and the passage of time overwrites it. A practical debriefing protocol addresses six questions.

What surprised us?

Unexpected information matters. These are the moments where the customer said something the team did not anticipate, which means the data is extending beyond the team's initial ideas.

During Ryan's conversation, one surprise stood out clearly. The team had expected backpackers to focus primarily on weight and pack size. Instead, Ryan said: "I can deal with a little extra weight if I know I can get shelter fast when the weather turns." This directly challenges the team's prior assumption about what drives the market. It should be recorded immediately, before the next conversation begins to dilute its impact.

What problems or frictions did we hear?

Now the team identifies the concrete breakdowns the conversation revealed in the form of specific moments where the job-to-be-done became difficult and why.

From Ryan's story, the team records: pitching the tent is difficult on rocky terrain; wind complicates assembly; rain during setup can wet gear; fatigue makes setup feel harder. The team also notes that these problems often appear together. Ryan was tired, the terrain was rocky, and the weather was changing simultaneously. Context matters. A criterion that captures each problem in isolation may miss the compounding effect that makes the situation genuinely stressful.

What Job Success Criteria did we hear?

Ryan said, "It takes forever to get the tent up when the wind starts fighting you."

JSC: Minimize the time required to pitch the tent in adverse wind conditions.

Another statement: "Once rain starts, I want the inside protected as fast as possible."

JSC: Minimize the time the tent interior remains exposed to rain during setup.

The key discipline here is writing criteria in criterion format immediately, while the customer's language is still specific in the team's memory. A note that says "Ryan complained about setup time" has already lost the specificity that makes the criterion useful. A note that says "Minimize time required to pitch the tent in adverse wind conditions" has preserved it.

Which contexts mattered?

Ryan's frustrations were strongly shaped by context: alpine terrain, rocky ground, fatigue after hiking, and storms arriving late in the day. Without capturing these conditions, the team might interpret his complaints as universal when they are specific to a particular combination of circumstances. Context prevents false generalization and often reveals the conditions under which a criterion matters most, which is essential for both the criteria list and future conversations.

What should we probe in future conversations?

Discovery is iterative. The Debrief is the perfect time to identify gaps that future interviews should address. Ryan's conversation raises several issues that should be explored with future participants: what does "fast enough" setup mean in quantitative terms? Do solo backpackers experience different setup challenges from group backpackers? Are there other moments of social pressure beyond what Ryan described? How much extra weight would backpackers tolerate in exchange for faster, more reliable setup?

These questions should be captured immediately and evaluated in addition to the discussion guide before the next session begins. If the same new question arises from multiple consecutive sessions, it should be added to the guide.

Do we understand our notes?

The team should review their notes, refine the language, and check for mutual understanding. In particular, the team should evaluate all Job Success Criteria, making the statements as good as they can be. The notes should make sense to a colleague who didn't attend the interview.

Accumulating Job Success Criteria Across Sessions

As interviews accumulate, so does the list of Job Success Criteria. A project may generate hundreds of Job Success Criteria across a full set of qualitative sessions. This is normal.

Across several Big Sky conversations, the team records criteria such as:

- Minimize the time to pitch the tent in the wind
- Minimize the physical effort required to pitch the tent
- Minimize the likelihood of rain entering the shelter during setup
- Minimize the time to select a suitable campsite
- Minimize the likelihood that the tent loses structure overnight
- Minimize the time to repack a wet tent
- Minimize the time to remove stakes that are wedged in rocky ground
- Minimize the time to assemble poles in low light

Some of these will combine during synthesis. Some will be found to reflect the same underlying need expressed in different words. Some may move to the identity or emotional layer of the Jobs-to-be-Done Pyramid™. A few may be dropped entirely because they fall outside the scope of the Market Lens.

The goal is to ensure that every real need is somewhere on the list. Premature filtering at this stage risks losing a criterion that turns out to be one of the most important in the market.

What Comes Next

The team has now completed its discovery interviews. What began as a blank canvas has become something richer: a body of customer language, a set of Job Success Criteria in various states of refinement, identity and emotional jobs, contextual observations, and questions that opened up across sessions and are ready to be explored further.

The next task is to make sense of it. The raw output of qualitative discovery is valuable but unfinished: criteria that overlap, language that needs standardizing, patterns that appeared once and patterns that appeared across every session. Refining that material into a clean, survey-ready set of Job Success Criteria is the work that comes next, and it is where the full value of what the team collected begins to emerge.

Key Takeaways

- Preparation built the conditions for insight. Execution is what converts those conditions into actual learning. The shift that has to happen in the parking lot before every session, from expert to listener, from hypothesis-holder to curious investigator, is the orientation that makes every technique work.
- The selling instinct and the solving instinct are the two common ways professional backgrounds contaminate discovery conversations. Sales professionals reassure and advance toward a close; engineers and designers engage with the problem intellectually and suggest solutions. Both derail the research and should be named explicitly with the team before the first session.
- The debrief after each conversation is not optional. It is what separates research that can be synthesized from research that has to be reconstructed.
- Six questions govern every debrief: What surprised us? What frictions did we hear? What Job Success Criteria emerged? Which contexts mattered? What should we probe in future sessions? Do we understand our notes? Capture criteria in the proper format immediately, while the customer's language is still specific in the team's memory.
- During the accumulation phase, capture generously and filter nothing. A project may generate hundreds of Job Success Criteria across a full set of conversations. Some will merge during synthesis. Some will be dropped. A few will prove to be the most important criteria in the market. Premature filtering risks losing exactly those. The goal of this phase is completeness.

Where We Are in DISCOVER

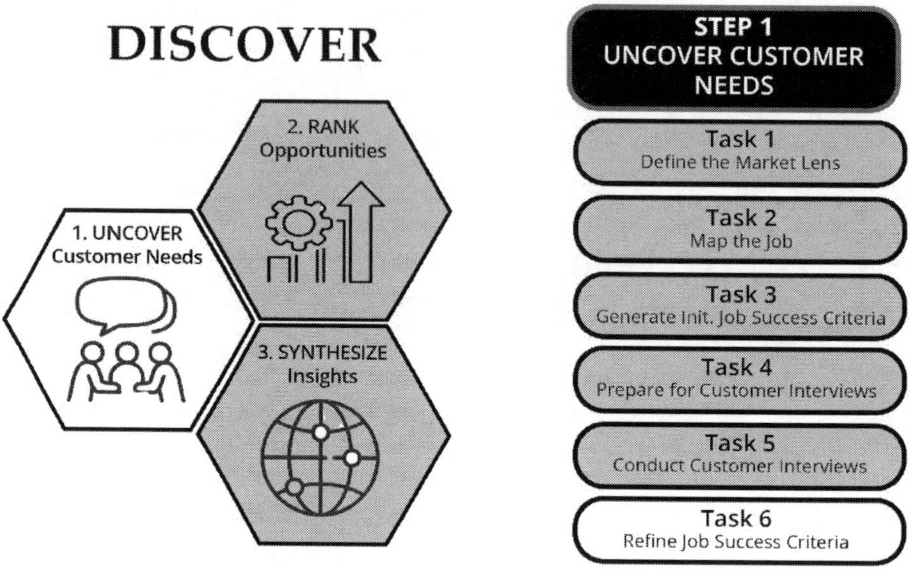

Step 1, Task 6: Refine Job Success Criteria

What this chapter helps you do

Review what you learned from customer interviews and turn the raw output into an organized set of Job Success Criteria.

What you will have by the end

A refined list of Job Success Criteria that is ready to be prioritized with customers.

Coming next

Step 2: RANK OPPORTUNITIES, beginning with Task 7: Design the Survey

Chapter 16: Task 6, Refine Job Success Criteria

Making Sense of Things

THE CONFERENCE ROOM WALL LOOKED LIKE A TORNADO had imploded a greeting card factory.

Sticky notes covered nearly every inch of the wall. Shelton stepped back and counted.

"One hundred eighty," he said.

Luis blinked. "Yeah..."

"All these Job Success Criteria," Shelton replied. "Or things that might be."

Tom laughed. "Well, at least we didn't miss anything."

Jenna studied the wall as she opened her laptop. "Hold on," she said. "How do we get ratings on 180 criteria?"

"And that's before we ask anything about who they are, what trips they take, or what gear they use," Shelton added.

Tom shook his head. "No one is answering a survey that long."

Shelton smiled. "Back up a second, guys. Remember our goal for this phase," he said. "The goal was to capture *everything*. We've been in divergence. Success is completeness. We have that." He gestured toward the wall. "Now, we need to make sense of it."

Luis crossed his arms. "Where do we start?"

Shelton turned to the whiteboard where their job map was still drawn in the corner. He drew eight columns, each representing a step from campsite selection through pack-out.

He began pulling notes from the wall and placing them under the relevant columns.

"There are multiple ways of doing this. This is one. Check this out," he said, placing three notes under the *Pitch the Tent* column.

- Minimize the time to establish protective shelter when weather conditions deteriorate.
- Minimize the amount of rain exposure inside the tent during shelter setup.
- Minimize the time to stake the tent on rocky terrain.

Luis nodded. "They're all about the same moment. Those are some of the Job Success Criteria that a customer uses to evaluate the job step, Pitch the Tent."

"Exactly," Shelton said. He moved another cluster of notes. "These others, they belong under *Break Camp*."

- Minimize the time to pack the tent.
- Minimize the time to remove tent stakes wedged in rocky soil.

Jenna stepped back. "So, we're affinity mapping."

Shelton smiled. "That's right. And an excellent way to do this is by job step."

Tom looked across the wall again. "Seeing it all here, this actually makes sense."

Shelton nodded. "We'll challenge our groups. Then get it right, and then move to see duplicates, tighten wording, and combine overlapping ideas."

Luis looked at the board. "How many are we trying to get down to?"

Shelton answered immediately. "No more than 75. But ideally, 40 to 50."

Jenna raised an eyebrow. "From 180?"

Shelton capped the marker. "Yep."

The Shift from Divergence to Convergence

This chapter marks a transition that runs through the entire Discovery Engine. Until now, the team has been expanding, generating Job Success Criteria, conducting conversations and capturing every customer need that surfaced, regardless of whether it seemed important. *That expansion was intentional, and it is now complete.* The divergence principle demands completeness before prioritization, and the team has honored it.

Now the mode shifts. The goal is no longer to capture everything. The goal is to organize, evaluate, and refine: to move from a large, messy, provisional list of Job Success Criteria to a structured, precise, survey-ready set that can be measured across the broader market.

In the first half of discovery, the team widens the lens. In the second half, it brings order to what it has learned.

This shift from divergence to convergence is an analytically demanding transition. It requires discernment about which criteria are distinct, which are redundant, which belong in the functional need set, and which jobs belong in the identity and emotional layers of the Jobs-to-be-Done Pyramid. It requires concentration, translating the raw language of customers into criteria that are specific enough to be surveyed reliably. And it requires discipline, resisting the temptation to over-consolidate, which produces criteria so broad they lose their analytical value, or to under-consolidate, which produces a survey too long for respondents to complete thoughtfully.

From Chaos to Structure: Affinity Mapping

When the conversations are complete and the Job Success Criteria list is as comprehensive as the team can make it, the synthesis process begins in earnest. A useful approach for organizing the raw list is affinity mapping. This is the process of grouping similar criteria to reveal patterns, reduce duplication, and prepare the set for quality evaluation.

Affinity mapping for a criteria set moves through five tasks.

Step 1 — Separate each criterion

Each criterion should exist on its own note: a sticky note, an index card, a row in a spreadsheet.

Step 2 — Group by job step

The team clusters statements that appear to express the same performance goal, organizing them by job step. This is the most natural grouping for a Jobs-to-be-Done-based discovery effort because the job map provides a ready-made structure that reflects how the customer experiences the job.

For the Big Sky team, the job map steps, Select a tent site, Retrieve the tent, Prepare the ground, Locate components, Pitch the tent, Monitor conditions, Adjust, Pack up, and so on, become the organizing columns. Each criterion is placed under the appropriate step. Once this has been done, patterns become visible that were invisible in the unorganized list.

Step 3 — De-duplicate

Within each group, the team identifies and removes straightforward duplicates. These are criteria that express the same need in different words with no meaningful distinction. For these, the team selects the clearest, most precise wording to represent that statement.

This step should be kept focused on obvious language-level redundancy. More complex consolidation decisions, where criteria share a consequence but differ in root cause, or where multiple specific criteria might be abstracted to a single broader one, are handled in the next section, where they can be evaluated with the full criteria set in view.

Step 4 — Refine the language

For each remaining criterion, the team evaluates the wording and rewrites where necessary. The goal is precision and clarity: a statement that any survey respondent could interpret consistently, without the benefit of the research context that produced it.

The team challenges each criterion with these questions:

- Is it as solution-free as possible?
- Is it as measurable as possible?
- Is it clear to someone outside the research team?
- Have we preserved the critical context or condition that makes this criterion meaningful?
- Would a member of this Market Lens, the Job Executor Persona, understand exactly what it states?

Step 5 — Get feedback

Before declaring victory, the team presents the organized criteria to others who are familiar with the market but were not involved in the research. The goal is a basic comprehension check.

- Do you understand this statement?
- What does it mean to you?

Ideally, this feedback comes from actual Job Executor Personas, in the Big Sky case, backpackers fitting the chosen profile. A criterion that confuses an outside reader will confuse a survey respondent. Better to discover that now than after the survey has been fielded.

Condensing the Set

One of the most demanding judgments in synthesis is deciding which criteria belong.

Are these the same need or different needs?

Two statements may use different words but describe the same performance goal, in which case they should be combined. Or they may appear similar on the surface but describe different dimensions of performance, in which case they should remain separate.

Consider these two Big Sky Success Criteria:

- Minimize time to pitch the tent
- Minimize the physical effort required to pitch the tent

These are different dimensions. One is speed. The other is effort. A design change that reduces time may not reduce effort, and vice versa. A backpacker who is strong and fit may rate the effort criterion as unimportant while rating the time criterion as critical.

They are different needs, and they should ideally be measured separately.

Now consider these three:

- Minimize the time to pitch the shelter when the weather changes
- Minimize the time to secure the shelter when pitched in the rain
- Minimize the time required to establish shelter when storms arrive

These are all describing similar performance goals in slightly different language. They can be combined into a single, precise statement:

- Minimize the time to establish protective shelter when weather conditions deteriorate.

The test for whether to combine or separate is: Would a survey respondent give meaningfully different importance and satisfaction ratings to each statement? If yes, keep them separate. If not, combine them.

A good criteria set is complete enough to trust and clear enough to measure.

When root causes differ, but the consequence is the same

A more nuanced situation arises when the team has multiple criteria that share a common consequence, but each points to a distinct root cause. Consider these three statements the Big Sky team encountered:

- Minimize the time to select a campsite due to the presence of dead trees
- Minimize the time to select a campsite due to the lack of flat ground

- Minimize the time to select a campsite due to competition with other backpackers

Each distinct root cause shares the same consequence: it takes longer to select a campsite. That common result is the basis for consolidation. When the criteria set needs to be reduced, and these distinctions are driving up the count, the team can drop the root cause qualifier and combine them into a single statement: *Minimize the time to select a campsite.*

If that criterion later emerges as important and underserved in the survey, the team can return to their discovery notes to investigate which root causes to address in product development.

This consolidation is a deliberate trade-off. The survey gains breadth. The team accepts that some root cause specificity is deferred rather than lost.

When specific criteria can be abstracted upward

This is similar to the varied root cause just mentioned, but can be more difficult to spot. It arises when several specific criteria all point to the same higher-level failure. In these cases, the team can apply the same "Explore Up" from the 3D Probing Model, asking what problem is created when each of these specific failures occurs.

Consider these three criteria:

- Minimize the likelihood that reapplied tent waterproofing fails
- Minimize the likelihood of puncturing the rainfly fabric during setup
- Minimize the likelihood of leaking due to UV exposure

Explore up: What problem is created when waterproofing fails, the tent is punctured, or UV exposure causes leaking? In each case, the answer is the same: the tent rainfly leaks. The team can abstract these three criteria into one: *Minimize the likelihood that the tent rainfly leaks.*

As with root cause consolidation, upward abstraction is a deliberate trade-off. The specific failure modes are no longer individually measurable in the survey. But the higher-level criterion is cleaner, more surveyable, and captures the performance standard the customer cares about. If it surfaces as a significant opportunity, the team can investigate the contributing failure modes in subsequent work.

A survey is a trade-off of breadth versus depth, with the limiting factor being a respondent's attention. The consolidation decisions made here determine where that trade-off lands.

When should the criteria be removed?

Not every criterion belongs in the set. Some statements fall outside the scope of the Product Job entirely. If a participant says, "I wish campsites were easier to reserve," that may be a real frustration, but it does not belong in the tent Product Job. It's a valid need, but it isn't a job that the project's sponsor, such as Big Sky Outdoors, is interested in addressing. That is a real need for a different study, with a different Market Lens.

What to Do with Identity and Emotional Jobs

Not every need surfaced in discovery is a functional Job Success Criterion. Customers also revealed identity and emotional jobs throughout the interviews: the desire to feel capable and prepared in the backcountry, the need to avoid embarrassment in front of more experienced companions, and the satisfaction of moving through a campsite with quiet efficiency. These are real needs. They shaped what participants said and how they said it. The question is what to do with them now.

The technically complete answer is that identity and emotional jobs can be cataloged according to their correct level within the Jobs-to-be-Done Pyramid, written using the syntax that level requires, and included in the survey alongside the functional criteria. When this is done, post-survey analysis can reveal how identity and emotional needs correlate with functional Job Success Criteria, which opens a richer view of how the customer's full motivation structure connects to specific performance gaps.

In practice, however, most teams leave identity and emotional jobs out of the survey. Survey space is the scarcest resource in the quantitative phase. Reducing 180 functional statements to a manageable set of 40 to 50 is already a demanding exercise in trade-offs. Adding identity and emotional jobs competes directly with functional criteria for the respondent's attention, and quite frankly, it's usually more straightforward to act upon the functional criteria.

Leaving them out of the survey does not mean losing them. The qualitative discovery notes remain available throughout the project. If a functional criterion surfaces as a top opportunity, the team can return to those notes and apply the same Explore Up logic used in the 3D Probing Model: asking what that functional failure means to the customer at the identity level, and what it costs them emotionally. That inquiry does not require survey data to be useful. It requires the qualitative notes to have been captured carefully, which the conversation process ensures.

The working recommendation is to catalog identity and emotional jobs during discovery interviews, retain them in the project record, and treat the survey as the primary measurement instrument for functional needs. The identity and emotional domains do not disappear; they remain available for later use.

However, if there is room in the survey to include a small subset of identity and emotional jobs, even 10–12, this can enable valuable downstream analysis, particularly the exploration of correlations between functional, identity, and emotional needs.

How many criteria should the final set contain?

Qualitative discovery may produce hundreds of Job Success Criteria. Survey-ready sets typically contain between 20 and 75 Job Success Criteria. The right number for a specific project depends on the complexity of the job and the breadth of the Market Lens. However, most projects target 40 to 50. Further, a study featuring a narrowly defined job with a tightly defined customer population can get by with fewer criteria than a broad job studied across diverse contexts.

The goal is comprehensive coverage without redundancy. Every major zone of the job map should be represented. Every dimension of performance that matters to the customer population (time, effort, reliability, output quality) should have at least one criterion in the set. No zone should contain multiple criteria that are essentially measuring the same thing.

For the Big Sky team, the final set contains forty-three criteria organized by job step. These were reduced from 180 statements through the affinity mapping and consolidation process. The wall that looked like a paper storm two days earlier now has a structure the team can work with and a foundation the survey can use.

Evaluating Each Criterion Against the Quality Standard

With the set organized and redundancy resolved, the team evaluates each remaining criterion against the quality standard. This evaluation should be systematic, working through the full set with the standard explicitly in hand.

A criterion meets the quality standard when it satisfies all of the following conditions:

It is solution-independent. It describes what successful performance looks like without specifying how that performance should be achieved. If the criterion names a product feature, design approach, or technology, it has crossed from problem space into solution space. However, as discussed in Chapter 8, there are times when elements of a technology, such as a guy line or a tent stake, can be mentioned. This is acceptable as long as it's a deliberate decision with the full knowledge that technology references tighten the project's scope. However, this decision can also make the results more actionable for an immediate product initiative.

It is measurable. It is specific enough that different respondents will interpret it consistently. "Improve the setup experience" is not measurable. "Minimize the time required to pitch the tent in adverse weather" is.

It is framed around minimizing failure rather than maximizing an abstract positive. Customers judge performance primarily by what goes wrong. "Minimize the likelihood of tent interior exposure to rain during setup" is framed correctly. "Maximize weather protection during setup" is not.

It follows the correct template: a direction of improvement, a performance metric, and, where useful, a context.

Preparing for Quantitative Validation

The refined criteria set is the bridge between qualitative discovery and quantitative measurement. Qualitative discovery expands the need set. Quantitative research prioritizes it. The survey phase will determine which needs matter most, which are currently underserved, and where innovation opportunity exists.

But a survey can only be as good as the qualitative groundwork supporting it. If the criteria are vague, redundant, or solution-loaded, the survey will produce weak results that are difficult to interpret and unreliable as a basis for prioritization.

The Team Reflects

Shelton stepped back from the whiteboard and looked at the clean list of 43 criteria. Two weeks of interviews. 18 customers. 180 sticky notes.

Now this.

Jenna studied the board. "It actually looks manageable," she said.

"That's the point," Shelton replied. "Manageable. But still complete. Every major thing we heard is somewhere in here. We haven't lost anything, or not much. We've just given it structure."

Tom nodded slowly. "Now we're actually ready to do the real research. Is that right?"

Shelton smiled. "We've been doing the research all along. But I get what you're saying. This is a major turning point in our project. It's time to prioritize this list."

What Comes Next

With the refined criteria set complete, the team has something they did not have when the interviews began: a structured, precise, survey-ready map of the customer's needs across the full scope of the job. The qualitative phase of discovery is complete.

The next step is to take that map to the broader market and to measure which needs matter most, which are currently underserved, and where the strongest opportunities for innovation actually exist. That measurement begins with designing the survey instrument.

Key Takeaways

- Discovery conversations generate large volumes of raw insight that must be organized and refined before they can guide strategy.
- The shift from conducting interviews to synthesizing them is a shift from divergence to convergence: From capturing everything to making sense of what was captured.
- Job Success Criteria should be captured generously during conversations and accumulated across the full series before any filtering begins.
- Affinity mapping organizes the raw criteria set by the job map step and clusters similar needs together, revealing patterns and preparing the set for refinement.
- Similar criteria should be combined carefully, using the test of whether survey respondents would rate them differently, without collapsing genuinely distinct dimensions into a single statement.
- When criteria share a common consequence but differ in root cause, they can be consolidated by removing the root cause qualifier, with the understanding that specificity is deferred, not lost.
- When multiple criteria point to the same higher-level failure, they can be abstracted upward into a single criterion using the same exploratory logic used in probing.
- The goal of the refined set is comprehensive coverage without redundancy: every major zone of the job map represented, every dimension of performance addressed, no criterion measuring the same thing as another.
- The survey can only reveal what the criteria set contains. Getting the set right is the most important preparation for the quantitative phase.

DISCOVER

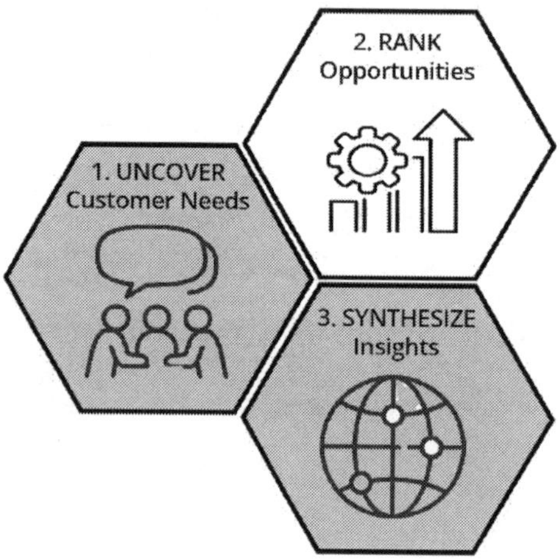

STEP 2
RANK OPPORTUNITIES

Task 7
Design the Survey

Task 8
Field the Survey

Task 9
Identify Opportunities

III. STEP 2: RANK OPPORTUNITIES

AS STEP 1 CONCLUDES, the Big Sky team has a complete list of Job Success Criteria. This is a major milestone, and from a time and effort perspective, the work is more than halfway completed, even though there are two more steps.

This is also the pivotal point in a major cognitive shift. From divergence to convergence. From exploring possibilities to narrowing them down. From "more is better" to making hard choices. From a conversational method to a controlled instrument that holds up to statistical scrutiny.

As the team begins Step 2 of DISCOVER, Rank Opportunities, the next tasks are:

Task 7: Design the Survey

Task 8: Field the Survey

Task 9: Identify Opportunities

It's time for the Big Sky team to embrace what comes next...

Where We Are in DISCOVER

Step 2, Task 7: Design the Survey

What this chapter helps you do

Design a survey that asks customers to rate the importance and satisfaction of the Job Success Criteria.

What you will have by the end

A survey instrument that is ready to test which customer needs are most important and least satisfied.

Coming next

Task 8: Field the Survey

Chapter 17: Task 7, Design the Survey

We've Been Building This All Along

THE MORNING FELT CALMER ON THIS DAY. The whiteboard looked very different from the way it did two days earlier.

The chaotic wall of sticky notes was gone. In its place was a clean list of 43 Job Success Criteria, organized within the job map.

Shelton looked at the board. "Okay," he said. "Now we build the survey."

Luis leaned back in his chair. "Where do we even start?"

Tom nodded. "Are we supposed to invent some kind of scoring system?"

Jenna picked up a marker. "We could ask people to rank them," she suggested.

Luis frowned. "43 rankings? That sounds miserable."

Tom looked at the list for a moment. "What if we asked people to make trade-offs? Like, which of these matters more than the others? Force them to choose."

Shelton tilted his head. "Say more."

"Well, in the real world, you can't have everything," Tom said. "A tent that sets up in two minutes probably weighs more than one that sets up in 20. One that handles rocky terrain might cost more than one that's more delicate. Customers make trade-offs when they buy. Shouldn't the survey reflect that?"

Shelton nodded slowly. "That's a reasonable instinct. And you're right that trade-offs are real." He paused. "But we're not there yet."

Tom looked up. "What do you mean?"

"We're still in problem space," Shelton said. "Our task right now is to understand how customers define excellence at this job-to-be-done. Not what they'd settle for. Not what they'd trade away. What they want, and no customer wants to make a trade-off."

Shelton turned to the board. "If we ask customers to make trade-offs now, we're asking them to do our job for us. We're assuming the constraints of the product before we even know what the market wants."

Luis crossed his arms. "So, the trade-offs come later?"

"When we get to designing product concepts, absolutely. That's where trade-offs live. But to see the market clearly, we need to know how customers rate each of these criteria on its own terms. Independently, without them second-guessing what's possible." Shelton picked up a marker. "If a backpacker needs fast setup and reliable staking on rocky ground, we need to know that both matter, even if today's products can't fully deliver both at once. That tension is the opportunity."

Jenna nodded. "I see. We're not asking what they'd compromise on. We're... we're trying to see their perfect, well, what they want, separated from what's possible, as measured across these Job Success Criteria."

"Exactly," Shelton said. He wrote two words on the board.

Importance. Satisfaction.

Tom looked up. "That's it?"

Shelton nodded. "Even better. I have good news. We don't have to create something new here. For each Job Success Criterion, we ask two questions, using a proven method." He pointed to one of the statements on the board.

Minimize the time required to establish protective shelter when weather conditions deteriorate.

"We ask backpackers how important that is, and how satisfied they are with their ability to accomplish it."

Luis nodded slowly. "Importance tells us if it matters."

"And satisfaction tells us how well the market is serving them," Jenna added.

Shelton wrote a scale beneath the two headings: 1, 2, 3, 4, 5.

"A 5-point scale," he said. "Simple and consistent."

Tom looked at the board again. "The survey is basically… this list?"

Shelton nodded. "That's the funny part." He gestured toward the wall. "You were thinking that designing the survey would be a whole new task. But we've actually been building it since the beginning of the project."

Luis looked back at the criteria list. "All those conversations… the probing… the cleanup…"

"That work wasn't just prep," Shelton said. "We were building the survey… all along."

The room went quiet as the team looked at the board. What had once been scattered stories from backpackers had turned into something precise: a structured way to measure what the market actually needed.

Shelton smiled. "It's time to see what matters."

The Survey's Role

By this point in the Discovery Engine, the Big Sky team has conducted customer interviews, refined a set of 180 Job Success Criteria to 43, and developed a clear picture of the friction points that exist within the shelter job.

What they do not yet know is which struggles matter most and which are already well addressed by existing solutions.

Not every need that surfaces in qualitative research represents an innovation opportunity. Some are widely felt but already well served. Customers mention them, but they rate existing solutions as performing adequately. Other needs are important and poorly served. Customers feel them acutely, and current products fall short. These are the opportunities. And the divergent phase, by its nature, doesn't try to distinguish the two.

A customer who describes difficulty pitching a tent in rocky terrain during a discovery interview is telling the team that this experience is real and memorable. They are not telling the team how important that difficulty is relative to 42 other difficulties, or how well existing tents address it compared to everything else on the list. That comparative measurement requires a different tool.

The survey is that tool. It takes the complete set of needs identified through qualitative research. It measures each one across two dimensions, importance and satisfaction, across a sufficiently large and representative sample of the target market. The result is a ranked order of customer needs: which matter most, which are best and worst served, and where the gaps between importance and satisfaction are largest. Those gaps are where opportunity lives.

The Logic of Opportunity Measurement

The survey measures two things for each Job Success Criterion: how much it matters to the customer, and how well current products address it.

Importance captures whether a need is consequential enough to drive product decisions. Satisfaction captures whether existing solutions are already meeting it. Neither score means much in isolation. Read together, they reveal where the market is underserved: needs that customers care about deeply and that current products have failed to address well.

Opportunity lives where important needs remain poorly served.

For the Big Sky team, the qualitative interviews suggest that needs related to setup speed in deteriorating weather and protection from rain during setup will show high importance and low satisfaction. But that prediction is still a guess. The survey will confirm some hypotheses, challenge others, and likely surface priorities that the interviews did not convey. The value of the quantitative phase is precisely that it replaces the team's intuitions about the market with evidence from the market. How to read and rank those results is the work of Chapter 19.

What Must Exist Before the Survey Can Be Designed

The survey design process assumes that four things are already in place. Attempting to design the survey without them produces an instrument that is either unfocused, incomplete, or measures the wrong population.

The first is the refined Job Success Criteria set. This is the backbone of the survey instrument. Every rating question in the survey flows directly from the criteria list. A survey designed without a well-refined criteria set will measure vague or redundant needs and produce results that are difficult to interpret.

The second is the Core Job Anchor from the Market Lens. The Core Job Anchor frames the survey for respondents. It tells them what context to have in mind when rating each criterion. Without this framing, different respondents will answer the same question with different mental models, producing ratings that reflect different experiences rather than a consistent measurement of the same need.

The third is the defined respondent population. This also flows from the Market Lens: the job executor, the use context, and the situational conditions that define the target customer. The respondent population definition becomes the basis for screening questions that will determine who qualifies for the survey.

The fourth is a clear understanding of the survey's purpose. The survey is a measurement instrument, not a discovery tool. Its purpose is to rank the importance and satisfaction of a pre-defined set of needs, not to generate new needs, test product concepts, or measure brand perception. Keeping this purpose clearly in view prevents the survey from accumulating sections that do not belong.

Organizing the Survey: A House with Four Rooms

A well-designed opportunity survey is not simply a list of rating questions. It is a structured journey. It moves the respondent naturally from entry to context to substance to close, with each section serving a function.

A useful way to think about this structure is to imagine the survey as a house. The respondent is a guest you are inviting in. You do not start them in the dining room. You welcome them at the front door, settle them in the living room, bring them to the table for the main course, and then walk them to the front porch before they leave. Each room has a purpose. Each room has a specific type of question.

The Front Door: Screening

The front door's role is simple: let the right respondents in and keep the wrong ones out. A well-designed survey protects its data quality early, long before any rating questions appear. Respondents who do not match the Market Lens will produce importance and satisfaction ratings that reflect a different customer's experience, contaminating the dataset in ways that are difficult to detect and expensive to correct.

The Front Door consists of screening questions that confirm the respondent belongs in the target population. These questions should be placed at the very beginning of the survey, before any substantive content. Respondents who do not qualify should be gracefully exited immediately and not allowed to complete questions whose responses will not be used.

Effective screening questions for the Front Door are behavioral rather than attitudinal. They ask what respondents have done, not how they see themselves. Typical Front Door questions cover job role or title, frequency of performing the relevant job, industry or environment, minimum experience thresholds, and usage recency. For surveys with constrained sample targets, quota checks can also be built into the Front Door to prevent over-representation from any single segment.

For the Big Sky survey, the Front Door might include questions such as:

- How many overnight backpacking trips have you taken in the past 12 months?
- Have you personally pitched and struck a backpacking tent on a multi-day trip in the past 12 months?
- What type of terrain do you most commonly backpack in?

Respondents who answer zero trips, who have not personally pitched a tent, or whose terrain profile falls entirely outside the Market Lens use context are exited before proceeding.

The Living Room: Context

Once respondents pass the Front Door, they move into the Living Room. This is a warm-up space designed to gather contextual information that will make the rating data interpretable later.

The Living Room is not the heavy part of the survey. It is a natural, low-effort section that helps respondents orient themselves to the topic while the team gathers the profiling variables needed for segmentation analysis. These are not questions meant for scoring. They produce the background information that allows the team to ask, after the analysis is complete, whether the opportunity rankings look different for experienced backpackers versus novices, for solo travelers versus group hikers, for users of different competitor products.

Typical Living Room questions cover industry or environment, job responsibilities or activity profile, tenure or experience level, frequency and context of use, current products or solutions used, and any demographic or firmographic variables relevant to the segmentation plan. For the Big Sky survey, this section might ask how long the respondent has been backpacking, whether they typically backpack solo or in groups, what tent brand they currently use, and how often they camp in adverse weather conditions.

Further, the Living Room should gather neutral background information without signaling what the survey considers important.

The Dining Room: Ratings

The Dining Room is the heart of the survey. This is where the need statements, that is, the Job Success Criteria, are presented and rated. Everything that came before was set up. Everything that follows is a wrap-up. The Dining Room produces the data the team will analyze most deeply.

The Dining Room contains the paired importance and satisfaction questions for each Job Success Criterion in the refined set, organized into two separate blocks. Importance questions appear in one block. Satisfaction questions appear in another. The importance block comes first.

[AUTHOR'S NOTE: Earlier survey formats, paper and PC-based, typically presented each Job Success Criterion once, with importance and satisfaction scored on the same line. This was efficient for respondents because they only needed to read the statement once. Smartphone screens cannot execute that layout well due to space, so modern surveys generally separate the importance and satisfaction sections, requiring respondents to encounter each criterion twice. If future survey technology can restore the single-presentation format while remaining mobile-friendly, that would be a meaningful improvement in respondent experience.]

If a job map was used in discovery, the Dining Room gains an additional layer of organization. Within each block, criteria are grouped by job step, and each group is introduced with a lead-in phrase drawn from that step. Respondents work through all criteria for one job step before moving to the next, following the natural sequence of the job. The satisfaction block then repeats the identical structure.

This organization serves two purposes. It reduces cognitive load by allowing respondents to orient to one part of their experience before moving to the next. And it produces data that is already structured by job step, making the analysis phase more efficient.

Each criterion within a group is rated on a five-point scale. The importance scale runs from Not important at all through Critically important. The satisfaction scale runs from Not satisfied at all through Fully satisfied. Every point on both scales is labeled, as shown below.

The importance scale:

1. Not important at all
2. Of limited importance
3. Moderately important
4. Important
5. Critically important

The satisfaction scale:

1. Not satisfied at all
2. Somewhat satisfied
3. Barely acceptable
4. Satisfied
5. Fully satisfied

Randomizing the order of criteria within each job step group further reduces bias, ensuring that criteria appearing early within a group do not systematically receive higher ratings than criteria appearing later.

If the project did not use a job map, each criterion is preceded by the job-to-be-done, such as "Backpacking with a tent," and all criteria appear in a single group within each block. If it did use a job map, the job step serves as the group lead-in, as shown in the example below, as applied to the Big Sky survey. Keep in mind that the importance scale is: 1 - Not important at all, 2 - Of limited importance, 3 - Moderately important, 4 – Important, and 5 - Critically important.

Importance Block

When selecting a tent site, how important is it to...

- Minimize the time to find a campsite that isn't unsafe due to the presence of dead trees
- Minimize the likelihood of selecting a site with insufficient flat ground for sleeping
- Minimize the time to identify a site with adequate wind protection

When retrieving the tent from the backpack, how important is it to...

- Minimize the likelihood of losing small components removed to access the tent
- Minimize the time to locate the tent among other packed gear
- Minimize the likelihood that tent components are damaged during retrieval

When pitching the tent, how important is it to...

- Minimize the time to establish protective shelter when weather conditions deteriorate
- Minimize the time to secure tent stakes in rocky terrain
- Minimize the likelihood of rain entering the shelter during setup

Satisfaction Block

Moving to the satisfaction block, keep in mind that the scale is: 1 - Not satisfied at all, 2 - Somewhat satisfied, 3 - Barely acceptable, 4 – Satisfied, and 5 - Fully satisfied.

When selecting a tent site, how satisfied are you with your ability to

- Minimize the time to find a campsite that isn't unsafe due to the presence of dead trees
- Minimize the likelihood of selecting a site with insufficient flat ground for sleeping
- Minimize the time to identify a site with adequate wind protection

When retrieving the tent from the backpack, how satisfied are you with your ability to...

- Minimize the likelihood of losing small components removed to access the tent

- Minimize the time to locate the tent among other packed gear
- Minimize the likelihood that tent components are damaged during retrieval

When pitching the tent, how satisfied are you with your ability to...

- Minimize the time to establish protective shelter when weather conditions deteriorate
- Minimize the time to secure tent stakes in rocky terrain
- Minimize the likelihood of rain entering the shelter during setup

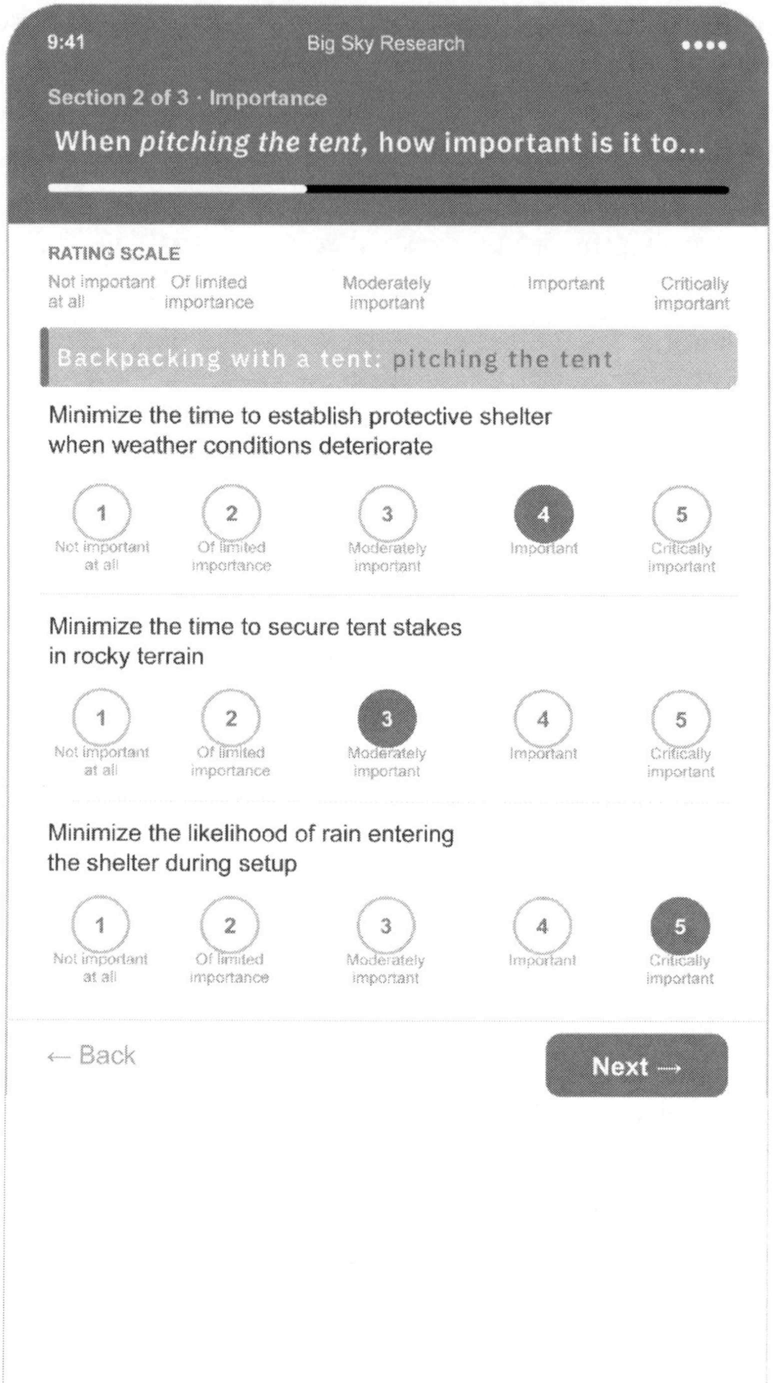
9:41
Big Sky Research
Section 2 of 3 · Importance
When pitching the tent, how important is it to...
RATING SCALE
Not important at all
Of limited importance
Moderately important
Important
Critically important
Backpacking with a tent: pitching the tent
Minimize the time to establish protective shelter when weather conditions deteriorate
1 Not important at all
2 Of limited importance
3 Moderately important
4 Important
5 Critically important
Minimize the time to secure tent stakes in rocky terrain
1 Not important at all
2 Of limited importance
3 Moderately important
4 Important
5 Critically important
Minimize the likelihood of rain entering the shelter during setup
1 Not important at all
2 Of limited importance
3 Moderately important
4 Important
5 Critically important
← Back
Next →

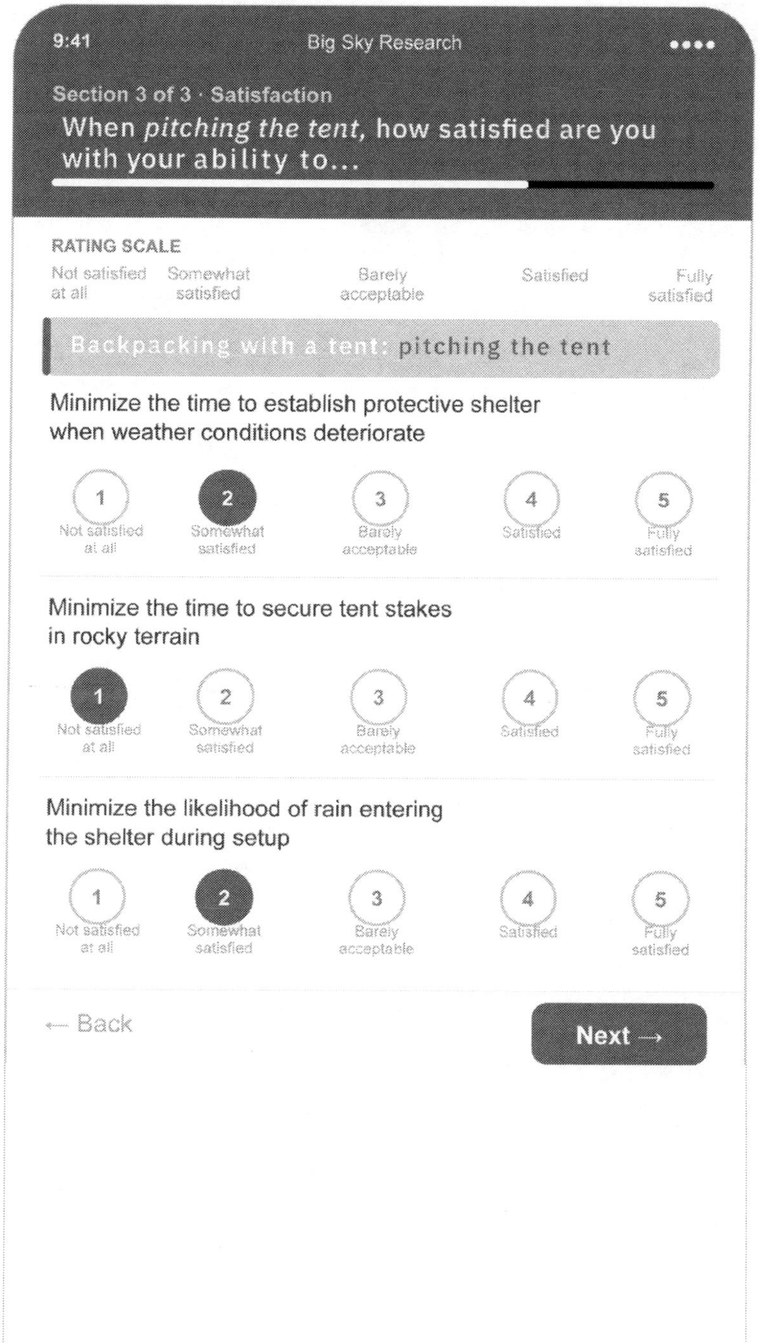
9:41
Big Sky Research
Section 3 of 3 · Satisfaction
When *pitching the tent,* how satisfied are you with your ability to...
RATING SCALE
Not satisfied at all
Somewhat satisfied
Barely acceptable
Satisfied
Fully satisfied
Backpacking with a tent: pitching the tent
Minimize the time to establish protective shelter when weather conditions deteriorate
1 Not satisfied at all
2 Somewhat satisfied
3 Barely acceptable
4 Satisfied
5 Fully satisfied
Minimize the time to secure tent stakes in rocky terrain
1 Not satisfied at all
2 Somewhat satisfied
3 Barely acceptable
4 Satisfied
5 Fully satisfied
Minimize the likelihood of rain entering the shelter during setup
1 Not satisfied at all
2 Somewhat satisfied
3 Barely acceptable
4 Satisfied
5 Fully satisfied
← Back
Next →

Using the same five-point structure for both scales allows direct comparison between importance and satisfaction scores, which is essential for calculating the opportunity gaps that drive prioritization.

Respondent fatigue is a real constraint in the Dining Room. A survey with 43 criteria and two questions per criterion produces 86 questions for ratings. Adding Front Door screening and Living Room profiling questions can push the total beyond 100. Much past that length, completion rates drop, and the quality of responses in the final third of the survey degrades as respondents rush or disengage. The practical guidance is to keep the core rating section to between 40 and 50 criteria, where possible. When the criteria set is larger, the team should consider reducing it further, splitting the survey into two instruments targeting different sections of the job map, or accepting the longer format and monitoring completion rates carefully.

The Front Porch: Wrap-up

Just as a gracious host does not send a guest directly from the dinner table to the front door, a well-designed survey does not end immediately after the rating questions. The Front Porch is a brief cool-down. It's a small number of final questions that close the survey naturally before the respondent steps out.

Closing questions are reflective, clarifying, and, if possible, optional for the respondent. Their purpose is to capture final insights that the structured rating questions may have missed, to offer respondents a space to flag anything that felt confusing or incomplete, and to handle any remaining objectives that do not belong in the Dining Room.

For example, "Is there anything about your experience that we didn't ask about that you think would be useful to understand?"

Adding clarifying branch logic for extreme ratings, for example, asking respondents who rated a criterion as extremely low in satisfaction to briefly explain why, can reveal additional insight depth. A brief post-survey satisfaction question, such as "How easy was this survey to complete?" with a scale from Very Easy to Very Difficult, provides a useful indicator about respondent experience that informs refinement. Contact information fields, if included, should generally be optional.

Before Fielding: Pilot the Survey

Before the survey is distributed to the full respondent population, it should be piloted with a small number of respondents, at least three to five, who match the Market Lens. The pilot is not a soft launch. It is a structured evaluation of whether the survey works as designed.

A good pilot reveals problems that are invisible in the design room: questions that respondents interpret differently than intended, criteria whose wording is confusing when read in a survey context rather than a workshop, scales that are being used in unexpected patterns, and length issues that the team underestimated. Respondents who complete the pilot should be asked what, if anything, was unclear, confusing, or missing. Their responses often surface the last round of improvements that the team could not have found on their own.

The investment in a pilot is a small insurance policy for quality before spending money on the full survey launch. A survey that was piloted and refined produces cleaner, more interpretable results than one fielded without that.final check.

What Comes Next

Some enjoy the detail of survey design while others find it tedious. There are indeed lots of rules and best practices. However, the reason is that once the survey has been fielded, it's a document that must work as a machine. It must walk the customer through the series of questions that will provide high data quality across a variety of reading levels, interests, etc.

For many practitioners, if the budget allows, it's often a good idea to use a professional market research firm to ensure that the survey is executed well.

Designing the survey is only the first step. The instrument now needs to reach the right people, a representative sample of the target market, and collect reliable data at a sufficient scale to support confident prioritization decisions.

The next chapter addresses how teams field the survey: how to construct the respondent sample, how to distribute the instrument, and how to monitor and protect data quality throughout the collection process.

Key Takeaways

- The survey translates the qualitative criteria set into a quantitative measurement instrument. It does not generate new needs; it measures the needs already identified.
- Opportunity emerges where importance is high, and satisfaction is low. The survey's purpose is to identify and rank those gaps across the full criteria set.
- A well-designed opportunity survey follows a four-room structure: the Front Door screens respondents, the Living Room gathers context, the Dining Room collects importance and satisfaction ratings, and the Front Porch closes with wrap-up questions.
- When a job map was used in discovery, criteria in the Dining Room are grouped by job step, with each group introduced by a lead-in phrase drawn from that step. This reduces respondent cognitive load and produces data that is already organized for analysis.
- Each Job Success Criterion becomes two rated items: one measuring importance, one measuring satisfaction. The job step serves as the lead-in for the group, and each item uses the criterion language precisely. Both scales use a consistent five-point, fully labeled structure.
- The Living Room gathers segmentation context. It should not prime respondents for the rating questions that follow.
- Survey length should be managed carefully. Respondent fatigue degrades data quality in the Dining Room, and the survey should be piloted with three to five respondents before fielding at scale.
- The quality of the survey results depends on the quality of the criteria set that precedes it. A well-designed survey built on a weak criterion set will produce precise measurements of the wrong things.

Where We Are in DISCOVER

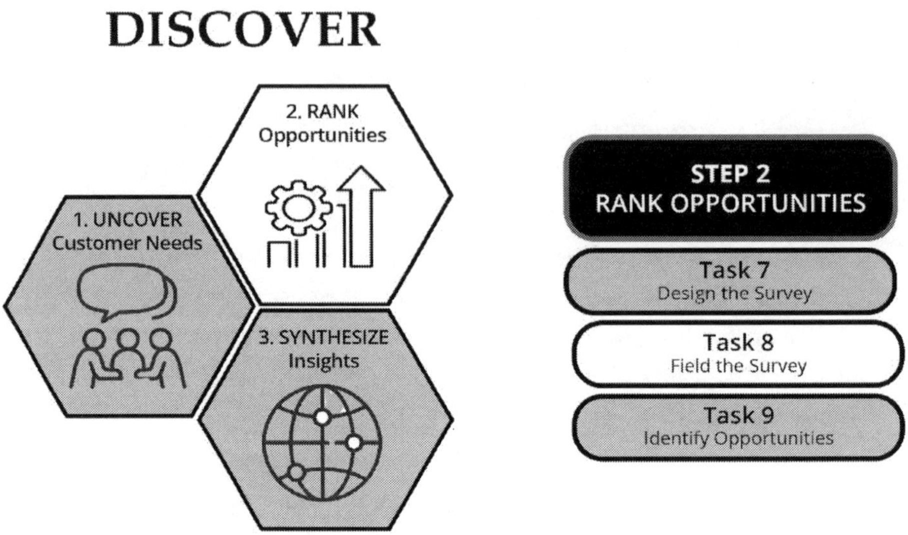

Step 2, Task 8: Field the Survey

What this chapter helps you do

Launch the survey, reach the right respondents, and collect reliable importance and satisfaction ratings for each Job Success Criterion.

What you will have by the end

A completed survey dataset that shows how customers rate the criteria you developed through discovery.

Coming next

Task 9: Identify Opportunities

Chapter 18: Task 8, Field the Survey

Representative and Relevant

LOCKED AND LOADED. The survey was ready.

Now the team had a new problem.

"Remind me again, who exactly should answer this?" Tom asked.

Jenna had a draft of the screener questions open on her laptop. "Well," she said, "during the interviews we tried to get a lot of variety. Different kinds of backpackers. Different trip styles. We even got a few just outside the Market Lens."

Shelton looked up. "And why did we do that?"

Tom answered first. "To uncover as many Job Success Criteria as possible, with as few interviews as possible."

"Exactly," Shelton said. "That was divergence." He paused. "But the goal is different now."

Luis leaned forward. "How?"

"We're not discovering criteria anymore," Shelton said, pointing at the survey draft. "We're measuring them. And to measure them reliably, we need people who tightly match our Market Lens."

Tom pointed to one of the screener response options. "What about car campers?"

Luis laughed. "They're out. It's not going to be the same if they can just choose to leave any minute. Or order a pizza."

Jenna scrolled further. "What about fastpackers? People doing 30-mile days?"

Shelton shook his head. "They're optimizing for distance and time. Crazy light kits, and they usually only eat while hiking. They are up before dawn and keep going late into the night. Without bad weather, they aren't even pitching a tent. Different context."

Jenna paused on another option. "What about thru-hikers?"

The room went quiet for a moment.

Tom tilted his head. "They still pitch tents. They deal with the same terrain and weather."

Jenna replied, "Yeah, they are very similar. Just longer trips."

Luis shrugged. "Much longer. I'm not sure about this. They're kind of a different world."

Shelton thought about it. "The job-to-be-done is the same," he said finally.

"Granted, the use context isn't completely identical. But everything else is very similar, plus they are extremely influential on what gear more casual backpackers buy. Understanding their priorities can give us a more complete picture of what it takes to win."

He wrote two words on the whiteboard.

Representative. Relevant.

"The goal isn't to include everyone," he said. "But it's also not to make the gate so tight that we miss adjacent insight. We want a sample that represents the market we care about, the people for whom these criteria are genuinely live questions."

Jenna opened the file of the screener draft. "For the first time," she said, "I can see how this will come together."

The Focus Shifts: From Design to Collection

The previous chapter addressed how to design the survey instrument, how to translate Job Success Criteria into paired importance and satisfaction questions, how to structure the response scale, and how to sequence and pilot the instrument. That work is complete.

This chapter addresses what comes next: getting the survey in front of the right people, collecting data of sufficient quality and scale to support confident prioritization decisions, and knowing when the collection process is complete.

The challenge here is different in character from the design challenge. Survey design is primarily an analytical problem. It requires judgment about question wording, scale construction, and instrument structure. Survey fielding is primarily a data quality problem. It requires discipline about who is included, how responses are collected, and how the integrity of the data is protected throughout the collection process.

Representative and Relevant: Setting the Gate

The Big Sky team's discussion about the variables of Representativeness and Relevance captures a genuine tension in survey sampling that practitioners must navigate.

Representative means the sample reflects the composition of the target market: the right mix of experience levels, trip styles, use contexts, and customer profiles that exist in the market the company serves. A representative sample produces results that can be generalized back to that market.

Relevant means the respondents have genuine experience with the job being measured. A respondent who has never pitched a tent in variable weather cannot reliably rate the importance of minimizing setup time in deteriorating conditions. They have no experiential reference point for the question. Relevance is the floor; representativeness is the target.

The tension arises at the edges of the Market Lens, such as thru-hikers who share some but not all of the target customer's characteristics. The practical resolution is to ask: do these respondents have enough experience with the core job, in sufficiently similar conditions, that their importance and satisfaction ratings would reflect genuine experience rather than speculation? If yes, they are relevant enough to include. If their experience is so different that their ratings would reflect a fundamentally different version of the job, they should be excluded.

For Big Sky, thru-hikers clear this bar in that they pitch tents in demanding conditions, and their experience with the shelter job is genuine, even if their priorities differ somewhat from those of weekend backpackers. Car campers and fast-packers do not clear it. Their shelter experience occurs in a context so different from the Market Lens that their ratings would introduce noise rather than useful data.

Setting the screening gate at the right level requires judgment, and that judgment should be documented. The team should be able to articulate why each respondent type was included or excluded, and that articulation should reference the Market Lens explicitly. Screening decisions carry financial consequences, and therefore should be documented in order to defend them if stakeholders question the results.

The Rules Have Changed: From Diversity to Representativeness

Before addressing the mechanics of fielding, the most important conceptual point of this chapter must be stated: the sampling logic that governed the qualitative phase is different from the sampling logic required here.

In Chapter 11, when the team was designing the qualitative sample, the governing principle was *diversity.* The goal of qualitative discovery was to uncover the full landscape of customer needs, to ensure that every important criterion, friction point, and success standard was somewhere on the list before measurement began. To achieve that completeness, the team sought variation: different experience levels, different trip styles, unusual use contexts, edge cases that might reveal needs the mainstream population would not surface. Representativeness still mattered, but the team intentionally sought diversity beyond the center of the target market.

That principle served its purpose. It produced a comprehensive criteria set. And yet, it is now the wrong principle to apply.

The survey's purpose is fundamentally different from the interview's purpose. The interview phase uncovered needs, and the survey measures them, specifically how widely they are shared across the target market and how well existing solutions address them. For that measurement to be reliable, the respondent population must mirror the target market. A sample that over-represents edge cases and extreme users, a successful strategy for qualitative discovery, will produce importance and satisfaction ratings that reflect those users' experiences, which may differ from the experiences of the mainstream market the company is actually trying to serve.

Consider what would happen if the Big Sky survey were fielded primarily to fast-packers, who are often looking to break speed records and go as far as they can as fast as they can. They would rate weight-related criteria as extremely important, which is accurate for them, but not representative of the weekend backpacker market that defines Big Sky's Market Lens. The survey would appear to confirm that weight is the dominant opportunity, which is exactly the hypothesis that the qualitative conversations challenged. The data would be real, but it would be measuring the wrong market.

The instincts developed during the qualitative phase are well-founded, but they are less applicable to the quantitative phase. The survey sample must be constructed on different principles than the qualitative sample, and the team must make that shift deliberately.

Qualitative research needs a wide range of voices. Quantitative research needs the right mix of them.

The governing principle for survey sampling is: the respondent population should mirror the target market defined by the Market Lens, not the full range of people who might conceivably answer the questions, but the specific customer the company is trying to understand and serve.

Screening for the True Job Executor

Before a single survey question is answered, the right respondents must be identified. This happens through a screener, a separate instrument used prior to the survey itself to qualify participants against the Market Lens. The screener and the survey are distinct tools. The screener determines who gets in. The survey measures what matters to those who do.

When a market research firm is engaged, the recruiter will typically guide the screener development process and may have established formats they prefer. Even so, the team should provide the recruiter with a clear description of the target customer drawn from the Market Lens, including the job executor profile, the use context, and any situational conditions that define who belongs in the sample. The recruiter translates that description into a workable screener. The team's job is to make sure the translation is accurate.

Whether built internally or in partnership with a recruiter, effective screeners share several characteristics.

They are behavioral rather than attitudinal. A respondent who answers "yes" to "Do you consider yourself an experienced backpacker?" may or may not match the Market Lens. A respondent who answers "four" to "How many overnight backpacking trips have you taken in the past 12 months?" almost certainly does. Behavioral screeners produce more reliable filtering than self-assessment screeners.

They are specific enough to enforce the lens without being so narrow that they exclude respondents who genuinely belong. Screening for "multi-day backpacking trips in alpine terrain" may inadvertently exclude weekend backpackers who primarily hike in forested or desert environments, which are legitimate use contexts within the Market Lens.

They are sequenced from least to most specific. Begin with broad qualifying questions that establish the respondent as a backpacker of any kind, then narrow toward the specific characteristics that define the target customer.

For the Big Sky survey, a screening sequence might look like this:

The first screen establishes basic participation: In the past 12 months, have you taken an overnight backpacking trip where you carried all your gear, including a tent? Respondents who answer no are exited immediately.

The second screen establishes trip frequency: How many overnight backpacking trips have you taken in the past 12 months? Respondents who answer zero are exited. Respondents who answer one or more continue.

The third screen establishes trip duration: What is the typical length of your backpacking trips? Respondents who primarily take single-night trips may or may not reflect the use context. The team should decide in advance whether to include or exclude them based on the Market Lens definition.

The fourth screen establishes tent use: On your most recent backpacking trip, did you personally pitch and strike a tent? Respondents who answer no, who may have shared a tent with someone else doing the pitching or used a shelter other than a tent, are excluded.

The fifth screen establishes weather and terrain exposure: In the past 12 months, have you pitched a tent in wind, rain, or changing weather conditions? This screen is particularly important for the Big Sky survey because many of the highest-priority criteria relate specifically to adverse conditions. A respondent who has only ever camped in ideal conditions cannot reliably rate those criteria.

Respondents who pass all screening questions are qualified for the survey. Those who do not should be thanked for their time with a brief explanation that the survey is designed for a specific type of backpacker, without revealing the criteria used to filter them out.

Building Quotas into the Sample

Passing the screener is a necessary condition for inclusion in the sample, but it is not sufficient on its own to guarantee a representative one. Some qualified respondents are simply easier to find than others, and without active management, the sample will drift toward whoever is most available.

For example, left to chance, an outdoor recreation survey will over-represent retired adults, who have more discretionary time for survey-taking, and under-represent younger working adults whose backpacking frequency may be just as high but whose availability for research participation is lower. The resulting sample may be technically qualified but systematically skewed toward one segment's priorities.

Quotas are the mechanism for preventing this drift. A quota sets a ceiling on how many respondents from a given demographic or behavioral segment can be included in the final sample, ensuring that no single group dominates the results. Once a quota is filled, additional respondents from that group are screened out even if they otherwise qualify.

For the Big Sky survey, relevant quota dimensions might include age range, trip frequency, solo versus group backpacking, and geographic region. The specific quotas should reflect the team's best estimate of the actual composition of the target market, not equal distribution across categories. If the market research firm has panel data on the backpacking population, that data can inform the quota targets directly.

Quota decisions involve a practical trade-off. Tighter quotas produce a more representative sample but take longer and cost more to fill. Looser quotas fill faster but may introduce imbalances that complicate the analysis. The team should discuss quota targets with the recruiter early in the process, since filling certain cells may require additional outreach, incentive adjustments, or extended fielding timelines.

Determining Sample Size

The right survey sample size for opportunity measurement is typically between 100 and 400 respondents. Within that range, the appropriate number for a specific project depends on several factors.

The complexity of the analysis drives the sample size upward. If the team intends to analyze results by subgroup, comparing importance and satisfaction ratings across experience levels, trip styles, or geographic regions, the sample must be large enough to support those subgroup analyses. A total sample of 150 respondents split across 4 subgroups produces cells of approximately 37 respondents each, which is too small for reliable subgroup comparison. If subgroup analysis is planned, the sample size should be designed to produce at least 75 to 100 respondents per meaningful subgroup.

The homogeneity of the target market affects reliability at a given sample size. A tightly defined market with relatively consistent customer profiles will produce stable results at smaller sample sizes. A diverse market with significant variation in customer experience and priorities requires a larger sample to produce results that reliably characterize the full population.

Budget and timeline constraints will drive the ultimate sample size. A smaller, well-targeted sample of 150 respondents who genuinely match the Market Lens will produce more reliable results than a larger sample of 400 that includes significant numbers of respondents who only partially match. When budget forces a choice between sample size and sample quality, quality should win.

For the Big Sky survey, a sample of 200 to 250 respondents who match the Market Lens is sufficient to produce reliable rankings of the 43 criteria and to support basic subgroup comparisons between solo and group backpackers, novice and experienced hikers, and users of different competitor products. A larger sample would increase statistical precision at the margins but is unlikely to change the ranking of the highest-importance, lowest-satisfaction criteria, which are the actionable outputs of the analysis.

Survey Distribution Methods

Reaching the right respondents requires choosing distribution channels that are likely to contain the target customer. Different channels offer different trade-offs between reach, targeting precision, cost, and data quality.

Research firms can guide the team through the process of building the screener, designing the survey, fielding the survey and analyzing the data. However, clever and motivated teams can find respondents on their own as well, such as the examples below.

Outdoor community forums and online communities — platforms like Reddit's backpacking communities, dedicated hiking forums, and gear review sites offer direct access to engaged, experienced backpackers who are likely to match the Market Lens. These communities tend to be self-selected for genuine outdoor interest, which means screening rates are often high. The limitation is that active forum participants may skew toward extremely experienced or opinionated users rather than the broader market, and recruiting from these channels carries risks if not done with care and transparency.

Gear review and trail communities — platforms built around outdoor activity tracking, gear ratings, and trip logging offer similar targeting advantages with slightly broader reach. Users of these platforms have demonstrated behavioral engagement with the category, which is a strong proxy for genuine job experience.

Backpacking and hiking groups — organized clubs, trail associations, and guided trip operators — provide access to backpackers whose participation is verified through membership or activity rather than self-report. These groups often require more logistical effort to access but produce high-quality, well-targeted samples.

Customer email lists — if the company has an existing customer database, surveying existing customers is fast and inexpensive. However, the limitation is that existing customers are not a representative sample of the target market. They have already been filtered by the decision to purchase from Big Sky, which means their preferences may differ systematically from the broader market. Existing customer surveys are useful for tracking satisfaction over time, but should not be the sole source for opportunity measurement.

Research panels — commercial panels maintained by survey research firms provide access to large, demographically profiled respondent pools with rapid turnaround. The advantage is scale and speed. The limitation is that panel respondents may be less engaged with the specific category than organic community members, and the screening burden falls entirely on the screening questions rather than on the channel's inherent targeting. Panel respondents who pass screening questions but are not genuinely experienced with the job may produce lower-quality data than community-sourced respondents.

For most opportunity surveys, a blended approach produces the best results: recruit primarily from channels that provide inherent targeting toward the Market Lens, supplement with panel respondents who pass rigorous screening, and monitor the data quality from each channel separately to identify any systematic differences. For teams with the budget and timeline to engage external support, a market research firm can manage the fielding process entirely, bringing panel access, quality controls, and sampling expertise that most product organizations do not maintain internally.

Monitoring Survey Quality

Data collection is not a passive process. Once the survey is in the field, the team should actively monitor the incoming responses for signs of quality problems and act on what they find before the field period closes.

Completion rate is the first indicator of survey health. If a significant proportion of respondents who begin the survey do not complete it, something is wrong: the survey may be too long, the questions may be confusing, or the respondent's experience may be frustrating. Completion rates below 70 to 75% warrant investigation. If the drop-off occurs consistently at a specific question or section, that is a sign that the question or section needs revision.

Response time is a proxy for response quality. Respondents who complete the survey significantly faster than the median time are likely not reading the questions carefully, selecting responses at random or following a pattern rather than engaging thoughtfully with each criterion. As a general guideline, responses completed in less than one-third of the median completion time should be flagged and reviewed before inclusion in the analysis.

Straight-lining is the pattern of selecting the same response for every question. It is one of the most common forms of low-effort responding. A respondent who rates every criterion as a 4 on both importance and satisfaction has not provided useful data. Straight-lined responses should be identified and removed from the dataset. Most survey platforms can flag these patterns automatically.

Screening validation is an underestimated quality check. Even with well-designed screening questions, some respondents who should not qualify will pass the screens, either because they misread a question, because they gave a socially desirable answer rather than an honest one, or because the screening questions did not capture every relevant dimension of qualification. Including one or two validation questions embedded in the core survey, behavioral questions that a genuine backpacker would answer consistently with their screener responses, allows the team to identify and remove respondents whose answers are internally inconsistent.

Sample composition should be monitored throughout the field period against the quota targets established before fielding began. If a particular quota cell is filling faster than others, recruitment effort should be redirected toward the cells that are lagging. Waiting until fielding is complete to discover that retired adults represent 70% of the sample, or that responses are clustering around a single online community with its own user culture, leaves the team with results that may reflect a narrow slice of the market rather than its full range.

Monitoring by quota cell also helps catch channel-specific bias. If a disproportionate share of respondents is coming from a single source, such as a brand's existing customer list, a specific outdoor forum, or a single panel provider, the team should evaluate whether that channel is introducing a systematic skew and adjust accordingly. The goal is not perfect balance across every dimension, but a sample whose composition the team can defend when presenting the results.

Closing the Field Period

Knowing when to stop collecting responses is a judgment call that balances statistical sufficiency against practical constraints. The right starting point is the sample size target established before fielding began, since that target was set with specific analytical goals in mind, not just overall headcount.

If the survey was designed to compare opportunity rankings across subgroups, such as novice versus experienced backpackers, solo versus group hikers, or users of different competitor products, the sample size requirement is driven by those subgroup comparisons, not just the total. A sample of 200 respondents may be sufficient to rank criteria across the full market, but too thin to support reliable comparisons between two subgroups of 40 each. When subgroup analysis is a primary objective, the minimum threshold for each cell must be met before the field period can close, regardless of whether the overall sample target has been reached.

The primary metric for closure beyond hitting targets is sample stability, the point at which adding more responses stops meaningfully changing the rankings of the top criteria. In practice, this means monitoring importance and satisfaction rankings as responses accumulate and watching for the point at which the top 10 to 15 criteria have stabilized in their relative positions. Once the team can predict with confidence which criteria will rank highest regardless of additional responses, the sample is sufficient for its primary analytical purpose.

A second metric is whether quota targets have been met across the key subgroups defined before fielding. If certain cells remain underrepresented relative to their targets, extending the field period to recruit from those segments is warranted, even if the overall sample size looks adequate on paper.

The field period should have a defined maximum duration regardless of whether all sample goals are fully met, typically three to six weeks for most surveys. Surveys that remain open indefinitely can attract respondents who are systematically different from those who responded early, as the pool of willing participants in any given channel becomes exhausted. The remaining respondents tend to be less engaged with the category.

When the field period closes, the team should document the final sample composition before beginning the analysis: the total number of qualified respondents, the distribution across quota dimensions, whether all subgroup thresholds were met, and any known limitations of the sample. This documentation becomes essential context for interpreting the results and for communicating confidence levels to stakeholders.

Working with a Market Research Firm

Many product teams will choose to engage an external market research firm to execute the survey fielding. This is entirely appropriate. Fielding a quantitative opportunity survey well requires expertise in panel management, data quality protocols, and statistical sampling that most product organizations do not maintain internally. The decision to outsource execution is often the right call.

What matters is how the handoff is managed. A research firm can execute flawlessly against a poorly specified brief and return data that is useless for opportunity analysis. The product team's job is not to become survey methodologists. It is to specify the research clearly enough that a capable firm can execute it correctly. Several practices, as follows, protect the quality of the engagement.

Brief the firm on the methodology, not just the instrument. Most research firms are experienced with customer satisfaction surveys, brand tracking studies, and concept tests. Opportunity measurement using Job Success Criteria is a specific methodology with specific requirements, particularly the importance versus satisfaction paired structure, the solution-independent question language, and the need for a screener that enforces the Market Lens rather than simply demographic criteria.

The firm needs to understand why the survey is structured the way it is, not just what it contains. A firm that treats the importance and satisfaction sections as interchangeable, or that suggests rewriting criteria language for "clarity" without understanding the methodological implications, puts the data quality at risk.

Specify the screener criteria precisely and in behavioral terms. Do not leave screener design to the firm's discretion. Provide the specific screening questions, the specific qualifying criteria for each, and the explicit logic for inclusion and exclusion. Many research firms default to demographic screeners such as age, income and outdoor activity interest level, which do not reliably produce respondents with genuine experience performing the specific job. The screener must be behavioral, as described in the previous section, and the firm must understand why.

Ask about panel quality and respondent source. Research panels vary significantly in quality. Some panels are maintained with rigorous participation standards, regular fraud detection, and active management of over-surveyed respondents. Others are assembled opportunistically and contain significant proportions of professional survey-takers who complete surveys at high volume for compensation without genuine engagement.

Ask the firm specifically: how is their panel maintained, how do they detect and remove fraudulent or low-effort responses, and what is the average completion rate for surveys of similar length in the target category? A firm that cannot answer these questions clearly is not a firm whose panel quality can be trusted.

Negotiate data deliverables, not just results. The firm's standard deliverable may be a summary report or a top-line results deck. What the team actually needs is the cleaned, de-identified response-level dataset, including the raw data, completion times, screening responses, and individual criterion ratings for each respondent. This dataset is what allows the team to run their own opportunity analysis, conduct subgroup comparisons, and verify the quality of the data independently. Insist on receiving it as part of the deliverable, and specify the format, typically a flat CSV or Excel file, in the research brief.

Retain review rights before the field period closes. Negotiate the right to review a sample of early responses, typically after the first 20 to 30 qualified completes, before the full field period runs. This early review allows the team to catch problems with question interpretation, screening failures, or quality issues before they affect the full dataset. Problems identified in 25 responses can be corrected. Problems identified at 300 responses cannot.

A well-briefed research firm is a genuine asset. The goal is not to manage them defensively but to give them what they need to execute the research correctly, which means investing the time to specify the brief as precisely as the survey instrument itself.

What Comes Next

With the survey closed and the data collected, the team has something it did not have before: market-level evidence about which needs matter most and which are least well served by existing solutions. The qualitative phase revealed the landscape of customer needs. The survey has measured it.

The next step is to make sense of what the data is saying, to move from a spreadsheet of importance and satisfaction scores to a ranked map of innovation opportunity. That analysis, and the strategic implications it reveals, is the subject of the next chapter.

Key Takeaways

- The shift from qualitative to quantitative sampling is one of the most important transitions in the Discovery Engine. Qualitative sampling seeks diversity. Quantitative sampling seeks representativeness. These are opposite instincts, and the switch must be made deliberately.
- Respondents must be both representative of the target market and genuinely relevant to the job, meaning they have real experience with the job in conditions similar to those defined by the Market Lens.
- Screening questions should be behavioral rather than attitudinal, sequenced from broad to specific, and tight enough to protect data quality without excluding legitimate respondents.
- Survey sample size typically ranges from 100 to 400 respondents. The right number depends on the complexity of the planned analysis, the homogeneity of the target market, and budget constraints. Quality of targeting matters more than the size of the sample.
- Distribution channel choices should be driven by where the target customer actually exists. Channels with inherent targeting toward the Market Lens produce better data than generic panels relying entirely on screening questions.
- Active quality monitoring throughout the field period — tracking completion rates, response times, straight-lining patterns, and screening validation — protects the integrity of the dataset.
- Quota targets should be set before fielding begins and monitored actively throughout the field period. Without quotas, the sample will drift toward whoever is most available, which may not reflect the composition of the target market. Subgroup quota cells must each meet minimum thresholds if subgroup comparisons are planned.

- The field period closes when the sample has reached sufficient size, the top criteria rankings have stabilized, quotas have been met, and the sample composition adequately represents the target market.
- A well-fielded survey built on a strong criteria set and a representative sample is what allows the next step, identifying opportunities, to produce results the team can act on with confidence.

Where We Are in DISCOVER

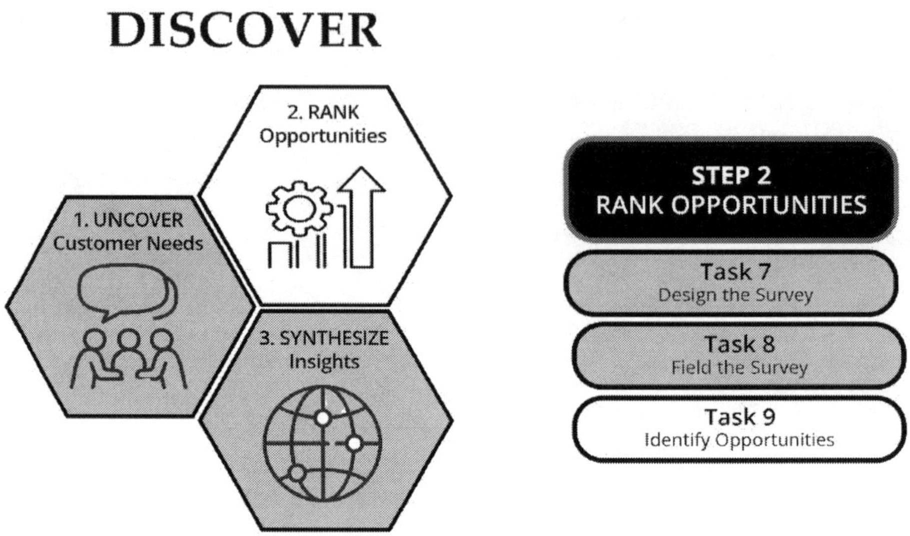

Step 2, Task 9: Identify Opportunities

What this chapter helps you do

Analyze the survey results to identify which Job Success Criteria are most important and least well satisfied.

What you will have by the end

A prioritized set of customer needs that reveals where the strongest product opportunities are likely to exist.

Coming next

Step 3: SYNTHESIZE INSIGHTS, beginning with Task 10: Scan for Signals

Chapter 19: Task 9, Identify Opportunities

The Market Speaks

JENNA SMILED AS SHE SET HER COFFEE ON THE TABLE. The team gathered around the screen.

Tom had just finished importing the survey results. "Alright," he said. "We've got responses from 612 backpackers."

Luis leaned forward. "Wow. What do we do first?"

Shelton pointed at the spreadsheet. "Start with the Opportunity Scores. Importance and satisfaction — Top-2 Box."

Tom sorted the table. Rows of numbers filled the screen.

Jenna scanned the list. "Wait," she said. "That can't be right." She pointed to one of the criteria near the top of the list.

Minimize the packed size of the tent.

"Importance is lower than I expected," she said.

Tom nodded. "Same with weight."

Luis frowned. "That's like... the whole industry narrative."

Shelton smiled slightly. "Maybe not our market's narrative."

Jenna scrolled further down the list. "Okay. Here's something interesting." She read aloud.

Minimize the time required to establish protective shelter when weather conditions deteriorate.
Importance: 8.4. Satisfaction: 4.1.

Luis sat up straight. "That's a massive gap."

Shelton nodded. "That's what we're looking for."

Tom pointed to another row.

Minimize the amount of rain exposure inside the tent during setup.
Importance: 8.1. Satisfaction: 4.4.

"And here's another one," he said.

Jenna leaned closer. "What about the rocky ground issue?"

Tom searched the list. "There it is."

Minimize the time to stake a tent on rocky terrain.
Importance: 7.8. Satisfaction: 3.9.

Luis leaned back in his chair. "The interviews were pointing us in the right direction."

"They usually do. But the survey is showing us something more precise," Shelton said. "We're not just seeing problems. We're seeing which problems matter most, and where the market is most underserved."

He paused, looking at the screen.

"The opportunity isn't making tents lighter. It's helping backpackers establish shelter quickly when conditions aren't perfect."

The room went quiet as the team studied the data.

For the first time, the team could hear the market clearly. And what it was saying was not what they had assumed from the start.

From Data to Insight

Six hundred twelve responses have come in, each containing importance and satisfaction ratings for 43 Job Success Criteria. The raw dataset is a grid of numbers. The team's task is to transform that grid into a ranked map of innovation opportunities.

This transformation is not primarily a statistical challenge. The analysis is accessible to any practitioner who understands what importance and satisfaction scores represent and how to read them together. This chapter provides a practical guide to applying that logic.

The Measurement System: Top-2 Box on a 0-10 Scale

Before examining the analytical tools, the measurement system that powers them needs to be clearly established.

Throughout this chapter, *Importance* and *Satisfaction* are expressed as Top-2 Box scores on a 0-10 scale. This is the convention used by Tony Ulwick in his Outcome-Driven Innovation methodology.

Top-2 Box measures the proportion of respondents who gave a criterion one of the two highest ratings on an importance or satisfaction scale. On a 5-point importance scale, Top-2 Box captures the percentage of respondents who rated the criterion as either "Important" (4) or "Critically important" (5). On a 5-point satisfaction scale, it captures the percentage who rated existing solutions as either "Satisfied" (4) or "Fully satisfied" (5).

Converting these percentages to a 0-10 scale is straightforward: divide by 10. A criterion where 84% of respondents rated importance as 4 or 5 has a Top-2 Box importance score of 8.4. A criterion where 41% of respondents rated satisfaction as 4 or 5 has a Top-2 Box satisfaction score of 4.1.

All importance and satisfaction scores in this chapter are Top-2 Box scores on a 0-10 scale.

Reading Importance and Satisfaction Together

The foundation of opportunity analysis is the relationship between Importance and Satisfaction. A high Importance score tells the team that a large proportion of customers care intensely about the criterion. If customers also provide a high Satisfaction rating on that same need, it is well served. The market has been heard, products have responded, and customers are not seeking improvement.

A low Satisfaction score tells the team that customers are unhappy with the performance that current products provide. A low Satisfaction score alone does not define an opportunity either. Solving a problem that customers are not invested in will not produce results. Opportunity emerges where Importance is high, and Satisfaction is low. That's where innovation creates competitive advantage.

For Big Sky, the data makes this logic concrete. *Minimize the packed size of the tent* has a modest importance score. Customers care about it, but not as much as the industry narrative suggests, and Satisfaction is reasonably high. The gap is small, and the upside for innovation is limited.

Opportunity appears when customers care deeply and current solutions fall short.

But *Minimize the time required to establish protective shelter when weather conditions deteriorate* has an Importance score of 8.4 and a Satisfaction score of 4.1, representing a gap of 4.3 points on the 0–10 scale. Over 80% of customers find it Important, while less than half feel current tents address it well. The gap is real, and the market is telling them where to look.

Why Top-2 Box Captures What Averages Miss

The Top-2 Box approach captures intensity rather than averaging across the full scale, including lukewarm and indifferent ratings.

A criterion where half the respondents rate Importance as a 5.0 and half rate it as a 1.0 would produce a mean of 3.0, which might suggest moderate importance when the reality is a deeply polarized market. Top-2 Box would show 5.0, reflecting that exactly half the market cares intensely, which is a very different strategic picture.

The Opportunity Matrix

Plotting all 43 criteria on a two-dimensional matrix, with Importance on one axis and Satisfaction on the other, provides a visual map of the full opportunity landscape. This matrix reveals not just the highest-priority opportunities but the strategic context in which each criterion exists.

The matrix produces four quadrants, and each carries a distinct implication for innovation investment. This view, as presented and named, is an artifact of Outcome-Driven Innovation within Tony Ulwick's process.

Underserved: High Importance, Low Satisfaction

This is where the strongest innovation opportunities live. Criteria in this quadrant represent needs that customers care deeply about and desire improvement. Increasing performance here creates value, and the data support investing in features that address them even when doing so increases product cost.

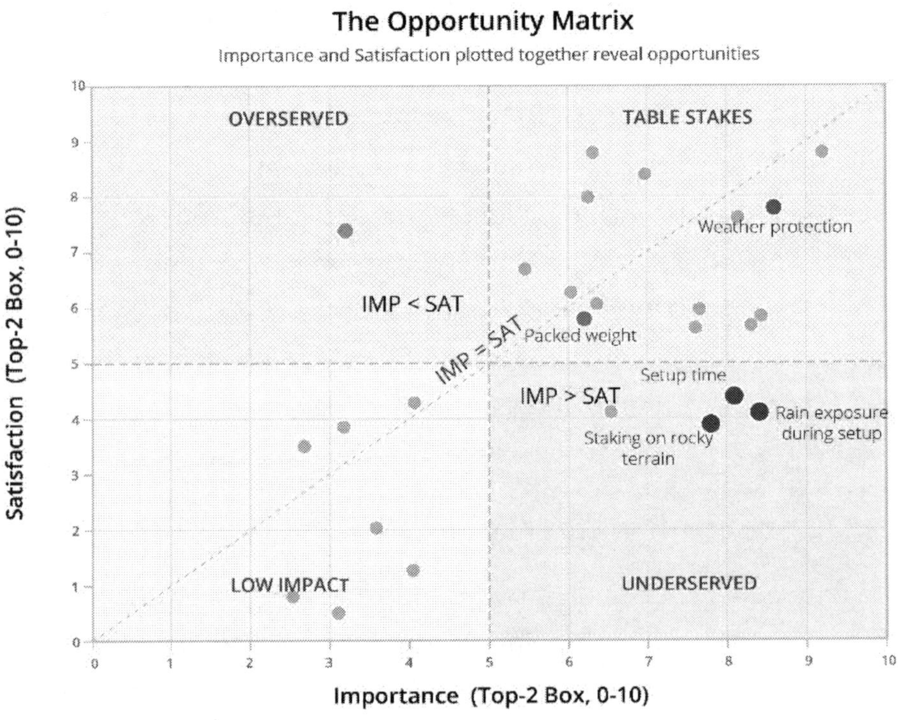

For Big Sky, the shelter setup criteria cluster here.

Minimize the time to establish protective shelter when weather conditions deteriorate scored 8.4 on importance and 4.1 on satisfaction.

Minimize the likelihood of rain exposure inside the tent during setup scored 8.1 and 4.4.

Minimize the time to stake the tent on rocky terrain scored 7.8 and 3.9.

Each of these represents a need the market cares about and that existing products do not address well.

Table Stakes: High Importance, High Satisfaction

These are needs that matter greatly to customers, but where current products perform well.

Every competitive product must perform decently here to remain in consideration. However, improving beyond current satisfaction levels will produce diminishing returns. Customers are already well served, and marginal improvement will not drive product success.

These criteria are not typically opportunities. They are requirements. Performance here must be maintained, and improvement is only warranted if it carries no cost penalty. For Big Sky, basic weather protection when the tent is properly pitched in normal conditions likely falls into this category.

However, if a supplier offers a new fabric with higher weather protection at the same cost, it's probably a good idea. But the team should resist the temptation to invest significant effort in improving performance against these criteria, because any increase in cost is likely to reduce the product's value.

Low Impact: Low Importance, Low Satisfaction

This quadrant offers limited opportunity for innovation and is best suited for opportunistic investments.

Even though current products do not serve these needs well, customers do not value them highly. Since Importance is low, improving Satisfaction will not create meaningful value. These criteria can be deprioritized at the market level without strategic risk, though segment-level analysis may reveal pockets where Importance is higher than the aggregate.

There may be innovation opportunities when performance can be increased at minimal cost, since, as opposed to Table Stakes, there is headroom for improvement.

Disruption Targets: Low Importance, High Satisfaction

This quadrant contains criteria that current products address well but that customers do not highly value. It is worth examining carefully because it often reveals where the industry has over-invested in performance areas that do not drive customer decisions.

This creates a strategic opportunity that many teams overlook: reducing performance slightly if it enables a greater reduction in cost. This is sometimes referred to as the "less for less" strategy.

For Big Sky, "Minimize the time to connect tent poles during setup" might fall here. Current designs have largely solved this through pre-attached, color-coded systems, and satisfaction ratings reflect that. Customers can get the poles together without much difficulty. But when weighed against shelter speed in deteriorating weather and protection from rain during setup, this criterion does not rank as important. The industry invested heavily in solving it, and customers recognize that. But further improvement does not increase product value.

The strategic implication is the inverse of the Underserved quadrant. If performance in this zone can be reduced, and that reduction enables a meaningful decrease in cost, the trade-off improves overall value, even though the product performs less well on that dimension. This is why the quadrant is called Disruption Targets. It is where reducing performance can be a value-creating choice.

Thoughts on the Opportunity Matrix

The matrix does not tell the team what to build. It tells them where investment creates value, where it merely maintains position, and where it may be wasted entirely. That clarity is the foundation for future strategy decisions.

Ranking Criteria: The Ulwick Opportunity Algorithm

The opportunity matrix provides a visual picture of the landscape. For a precise, priority order, the team needs a calculated Opportunity Score for each criterion.

Tony Ulwick developed the standard approach as part of his Outcome-Driven Innovation methodology. The Ulwick Opportunity Algorithm calculates an Opportunity Score for each criterion as follows:

Opportunity Score = Importance + Maximum of (Importance - Satisfaction, 0)

The formula builds on the importance and satisfaction relationship introduced earlier. Importance sets the baseline, and the gap between importance and satisfaction increases the score when it exists.

When satisfaction falls below importance, a gap exists. The larger the gap, the higher the Opportunity Score, reflecting the magnitude of the unmet need.

With a 0-10 scale for both importance and satisfaction, this means that the maximum possible Opportunity Score is 20: a criterion where 100% of respondents rate importance as 4 or 5 (score of 10.0) and 0% rate satisfaction as 4 or 5 (score of 0.0) would produce 10.0 + (10.0 - 0.0) = 20.0. In practice, scores under eight represent limited opportunities, those above 10 represent significant opportunities, and those above 15 represent extreme opportunities. These thresholds are not fixed rules. However, clearly, the higher the score, the stronger the evidence of a substantial market opportunity.

Applied to the Big Sky criteria, the formula produces the following results:

Minimize the time to establish protective shelter when weather conditions deteriorate — Importance 8.4, Satisfaction 4.1

Opportunity Score:
= 8.4 + (8.4 - 4.1)
= 8.4 + 4.3
= 12.7

Minimize the likelihood of rain exposure inside the tent during setup — Importance 8.1, Satisfaction 4.4

Opportunity Score:
= 8.1 + (8.1 - 4.4)
= 8.1 + 3.7
= 11.8

Minimize the time to stake the tent on rocky terrain — Importance 7.8, Satisfaction 3.9

Opportunity Score:
= 7.8 + (7.8 - 3.9)
= 7.8 + 3.9
= 11.7

Now compare these to a weight-related criterion:

Minimize total packed weight of the tent system: Importance 6.2, Satisfaction 5.8

Opportunity Score:
= 6.2 + (6.2 - 5.8)
= 6.2 + 0.4
= 6.6

[AUTHOR'S NOTE: An astute observer will recognize that "pack weight" is clearly a product attribute. Have we violated our agreement to remain in problem space? Yes, but deliberately. Sometimes, when the linkage between product attributes and their benefits is exceedingly obvious and uncontroversial, and since this study's objectives include Product Jobs, we may consciously make this decision. Jobs-to-be-Done gives the guiding principles, but we value actionable insights above methodological purity.]

The gap between importance and satisfaction is small because satisfaction is already reasonably close to importance. The Opportunity Score correctly reflects that this is not where the most significant unmet need exists, not because weight does not matter, but because the market is already reasonably served on this dimension.

The ranked list produced by the opportunity algorithm gives the team a clear, defensible priority order for all 43 criteria. The top-ranked criteria are where the most significant unmet needs exist. These are the criteria around which product development, messaging, and positioning decisions should be organized.

The Full Picture

The full picture that emerges for Big Sky is striking. The criteria the industry has historically emphasized, weight, packed size, and structural specifications, are clustered in Table Stakes. They matter, but they are reasonably well served.

The Underserved quadrant, where larger opportunities lie, is populated almost entirely by criteria related to setup speed and protection in adverse conditions. This is the market speaking clearly. And it is saying something the industry has not fully heard.

Interpreting Results

Begin with the market-level scores before examining differences across segments.

The full-sample rankings establish the baseline by showing which criteria are most important, which are least well served, and where the largest opportunity gaps exist across the market. This is the foundation that segment-level analysis builds on, not the other way around.

With the baseline established, read the ranked list for themes. What patterns are emerging among the higher-opportunity criteria? If the themes are not immediately apparent, return to the 3D Probing Model. Explore Up by asking, What do these ultimately help a customer accomplish? Explore Down by asking, Are a subset of these downstream of a common constraint or root cause? Explore Across by asking, Is there a common context driving this need?

Then use the Jobs-to-be-Done Pyramid to look for patterns. Is there a commonality in where these fall within the levels of the Pyramid? For example, if they fall within Product Jobs, are they concentrated in one of the five subjobs: Acquisition, Preparation, Usage, Maintenance, or Disposal?

Then reference the job map. Are they concentrated in a specific job step or group of steps? At this point, all the tools of Prism help the team step back and read the pattern across the high-opportunity criteria.

Next, once the market-level picture is clear, the team should run the opportunity analysis separately for the key segments defined by the Market Lens and compare those rankings to the baseline.

Market-level priorities can conceal important differences. A criterion that ranks as a moderate opportunity across the full sample may emerge as the highest priority within a specific segment, such as experienced alpine backpackers, solo travelers, or users of a specific competitor's product. Conversely, a criterion that ranks highly overall may matter much less to the segment the company most wants to win.

Segments that tell a significantly different story from the market-level baseline deserve explicit attention in the strategy conversation. But that story only becomes meaningful once the baseline has been established.

This sequence matters. Without a clear baseline, segment differences can be misread or overemphasized. With it, they become a source of strategic insight.

Caution with Small Score Differences

Do not over-interpret small differences in scores. Survey data contains measurement error. The difference between an Opportunity Score of 12.7 and 11.8 may reflect sampling variation as much as a true difference in market priority.

A practical approach is to treat the top-ranked criteria as a cluster rather than as a precise rank order. Think of this less like a leaderboard and more like a tiered grouping. Within a cluster of similarly high-scoring criteria, small differences in rank should not drive disproportionate differences in strategy. The boundary between tiers matters more than the precise position within a tier.

What Comes Next

The opportunity analysis has produced something the team did not have at the start of the project: a ranked, evidence-based map of where the weekend backpacker market most needs improvement. The qualitative conversations revealed the landscape of needs. The survey measured them. The opportunity algorithm has ranked them.

The next step is Step 3: Synthesize Insights, in which the final tool from this book, The Signal Translator™, gives teams the ability to decode market insights with more confidence than any single study can deliver.

Key Takeaways

- Opportunity analysis transforms raw survey data into a ranked map of unmet customer needs, identifying where the market most needs improvement and where existing solutions fall furthest short.
- Importance and satisfaction are expressed as Top-2 Box scores on a 0-10 scale: a score of 8.4 means 84% of respondents rated that criterion as Important or Critically Important. This convention is consistent with Tony Ulwick's Outcome-Driven Innovation methodology.
- Top-2 Box captures the intensity of customer feeling rather than averaging across all responses. It separates criteria where the market is uniformly lukewarm from criteria where a large proportion of customers feel strongly — a distinction that mean scores can obscure.
- Importance and satisfaction must always be read together. High importance establishes that a criterion matters. Low satisfaction establishes that the market is poorly served. The gap between them defines the opportunity.
- The Opportunity Matrix organizes all criteria into four quadrants: Underserved: high importance/low satisfaction (strongest opportunities), Table Stakes: high importance/high satisfaction, Low Impact: low importance/low satisfaction, and Disruption Targets: low importance/high satisfaction.
- The Ulwick Opportunity Algorithm — Opportunity Score = Importance + Maximum of (Importance minus Satisfaction, 0) — provides a precise, defensible ranking of all criteria by unmet need. Scores above 10 on a 0-20 scale represent strong opportunities. Scores below 8 represent a limited opportunity.

- Small differences in Opportunity Scores may reflect measurement error rather than genuine market differences. Treat the top-ranked criteria as a cluster, not a precise rank order.
- Segment-level analysis may reveal significantly different opportunity rankings for specific customer subgroups. Always establish the market-level baseline first, then run the analysis by segment and compare the rankings against that baseline.
- The opportunity rankings are an essential input to strategy, not a substitute for it. Strategic fit, capability assessment, and competitive context all bear on how the opportunities are ultimately pursued.

The Big Sky Team Looks Back, Looks Ahead

The Big Sky team had their ranked data. The top opportunities were clear, the gaps were real, and the study had been executed with care. By any reasonable standard, they were ready to move.

But Shelton paused.

A single study, however well designed, is still one view of a complex market. Before findings become strategy, they need to be tested against the other evidence the organization already holds — the support tickets, the retailer observations, the prior research, and the competitive signals. Each of those sources sees the market differently. When they point in the same direction, the finding is robust. When they diverge, there is something worth investigating before acting.

That is what Step 3, Synthesize Insights, is for.

DISCOVER

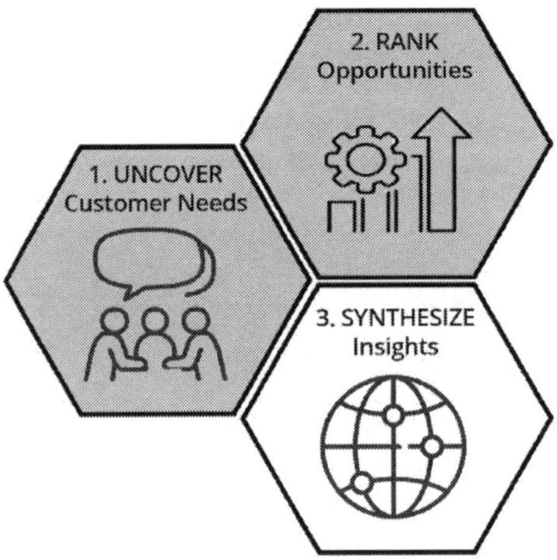

STEP 3
SYNTHESIZE INSIGHTS

Task 10
Scan for Signals

Task 11
Build the Signal Translator

Task 12
Maintain the Signal Translator

IV. STEP 3: SYNTHESIZE INSIGHTS

Most innovation "discovery" methods stop at this point. Having completed a study, teams move forward with developing new products. Marketing groups start writing new copy. M&A teams search for targets.

This is better than performing those activities without the benefit of research. However, there's another step to build a living insight system.

A company has lots of data: older research projects, secondary research, and a mountain of internal information as well. The true power comes from synthesis, so that the noise fades away and the truth can be heard with the clarity of a harmonized chord.

In Step 3, DISCOVER makes this transition. The output of that transition is the Signal Translator: a synthesis framework that maps every opportunity against multiple independent signal sources, normalizes them into a shared structure, and produces the kind of cross-validated confidence that a single study cannot. It is what the entire DISCOVER process has been building toward.

Where We Are in DISCOVER

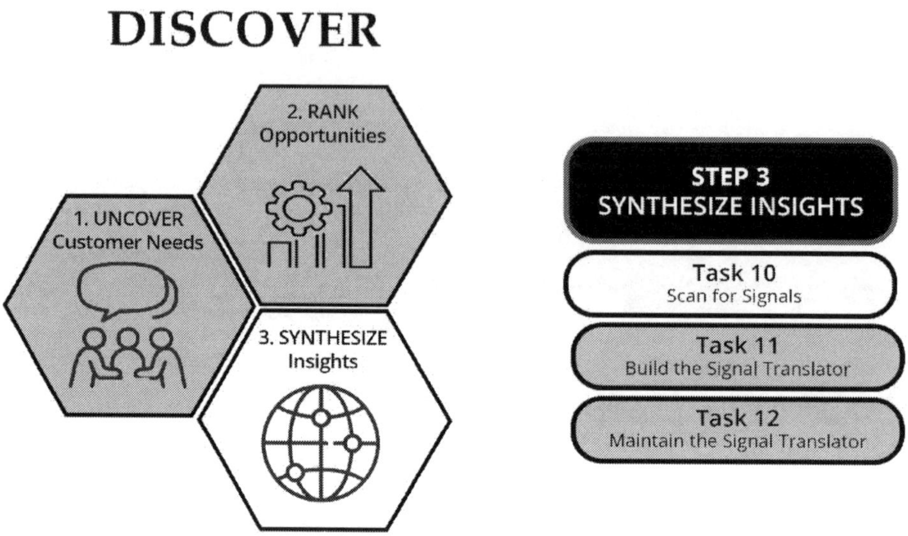

Step 3, Task 10: Scan for Signals

What this chapter helps you do

Understand how triangulation helps turn scattered customer input into stronger evidence.

What you will have by the end

A clearer view of the insight sources that can strengthen, challenge, or add context to what you learned from interviews and surveys.

Coming next

Task 11: Build the Signal Translator

Chapter 20: Task 10, Scan for Signals

More Than One Satellite

THE WHITE LIGHT FROM THE PROJECTOR ECLIPSED THE CONFERENCE ROOM. A spreadsheet, filling the screen, reflected columns of numbers stretched across the display. Importance. Satisfaction. Opportunity Scores.

Tom leaned back in his chair. "Well," he said, "that seems pretty clear."

Luis nodded. "Yeah. We design the tent around faster setup and storm protection. The data is right there."

Jenna pointed at the top rows. "These three criteria have massive gaps. Minimize the time to establish protective shelter when weather conditions deteriorate. Minimize the likelihood of rain exposure inside the tent during setup. Minimize the time to stake the tent on rocky terrain." She looked up. "We've got our answer."

Shelton was looking at the screen quietly.

Tom noticed. "What is it?"

Shelton turned toward the group. "How confident are we that this survey tells the whole story?"

Luis shrugged. “612 respondents. Strong sampling. We followed the process.”

“It is a strong study,” Shelton said. He paused. “But we can do better.”

The room went quiet.

Jenna leaned forward. “What do you mean?”

Shelton walked to the whiteboard. “Think about how science handles the pursuit of knowledge. One study produces a finding. Researchers don’t just stop there. When something matters, they look for corroboration. They pull together multiple studies, translate them into a common form, and look where they converge. It’s called a meta-analysis. A study of studies.” He uncapped a marker. “And we have more than one study.”

Luis asked, “We do?”

Shelton replied, “We do.”

Tom raised a finger and said, “Retailer feedback. The buyers we work with constantly mention weather setup.”

Shelton said, “Yes.”

Luis added: “Customer support tickets. A lot of them are about staking problems and setup confusion.”

Shelton agreed, “That’s right.”

Jenna looked up from her laptop. “We also have warranty data.”

“And last year’s campsite frustration research,” Shelton said. “And the win/loss analysis from the sales team.”

He wrote the list on the board.

Discovery interviews. Surveys. Retailer feedback. Customer support. Warranty claims. Product reviews. Prior research.

He stepped back. “Each of these sees the market a little differently.”

Jenna nodded slowly. "So, the survey isn't the answer. Or at least, not the only one."

"It's one excellent signal," Shelton said. "But we haven't checked what the others say."

Tom looked at the board. "And if they agree..."

Shelton finished the thought. "Then we're not trusting one well-executed study. We're trusting a body of evidence. That's a different thing entirely."

One Signal Is Good. More Is Better.

A 612-respondent survey with rigorous sampling, carefully constructed Job Success Criteria, and properly calculated Opportunity Scores is a serious piece of research. The conclusions it suggests deserve to be taken seriously.

The question isn't whether the study is good. It is. The question is whether we can do better. And almost always, we can.

Every study is a snapshot. It captures what a defined group of respondents reported about their needs, at a specific moment, using a specific method. The method has strengths. It also has limits.

A survey reveals the distribution and intensity of unmet needs across a population. It cannot capture the moment Ryan Carter described when the rain started before his tent was pitched. Qualitative research captures that kind of depth.

Internal data tells a different story still. Support tickets reflect needs serious enough to prompt a customer to seek help. That's a different perspective than a survey respondent selecting an importance rating. Warranty claims reflect what actually fails under real-world conditions. Win/loss analyses, when done well, capture why the market chose or rejected the product at the moment of decision. Each of these sources was created for a different purpose, and each carries its own structural bias as a result.

None of this is a flaw. It is simply how evidence works. No single source sees the whole market. The solution is not a perfect method. It is multiple imperfect methods whose blind spots do not overlap.

What Science Already Knows

Every field where getting close to the truth matters has arrived at the same conclusion.

In medicine, a single clinical trial is rarely sufficient to establish a treatment protocol. Researchers conduct meta-analyses, pulling together findings from multiple studies, translating them into a common form, and identifying where they converge. The same principle operates in social science, behavioral economics, and epidemiology. In criminal law, a prosecution built on a single piece of evidence is a weak prosecution. Both the prosecution and the defense know this. The strength of a case is the strength of the convergent body of evidence, not only the strength of the single best exhibit.

When the stakes are high and uncertainty is real, you need more evidence, properly synthesized. One source can suggest a finding. Multiple sources pointing to the same conclusion reveal something much closer to a reliable conclusion.

Most product teams, regardless of what research approach they use, treat a study as *the answer* and move on. This is understandable. A strong survey result projected on a conference room screen feels conclusive. But it leaves the team exposed to whatever biases and errors are inherent to that single method. And it ignores a body of potentially relevant evidence sitting on company servers that nobody thought to connect.

Building a meta-analysis into the Discovery process is uncommon in product management. *But it doesn't need to be.*

The Real Problem: Fragmentation

Here's what makes this harder than it should be. Most organizations already possess far more relevant signals than they realize. The problem is not that the signals do not exist. It is that they live in different places, owned by different functions, formatted in different ways, and never brought together in a form that allows comparison.

The discovery interview transcripts are in a research folder maintained by the product team. The support ticket data is in a platform managed by the support organization. The sales notes are scattered across a CRM that the product team has read-only access to at best. The warranty claims are summarized quarterly by an operations team that does not typically share them with product or marketing. The retailer feedback exists in email threads and call notes that no one has systematically organized. The competitive reviews are bookmarked in someone's browser.

> *One signal can suggest a path; many aligned signals give the team confidence to follow it.*

Each of these sources contains real intelligence about the market. None of it is connected. The product team making strategy decisions may know that some of these sources exist, but pulling them together requires effort that is easy to defer when a survey result feels conclusive enough.

This is how organizations end up making strategic decisions based on one study. Not because they lack the signals, but because no one has built the practice of connecting them.

Recognizing fragmentation as the real problem changes what the solution needs to look like. The answer is not simply more research, although that can be part of it. A faster path is to systematically gather the signals that already exist, translate them into a comparable form, and identify where they converge. That translation is the focus of the next chapter. Before it can happen, however, the signals must first be identified.

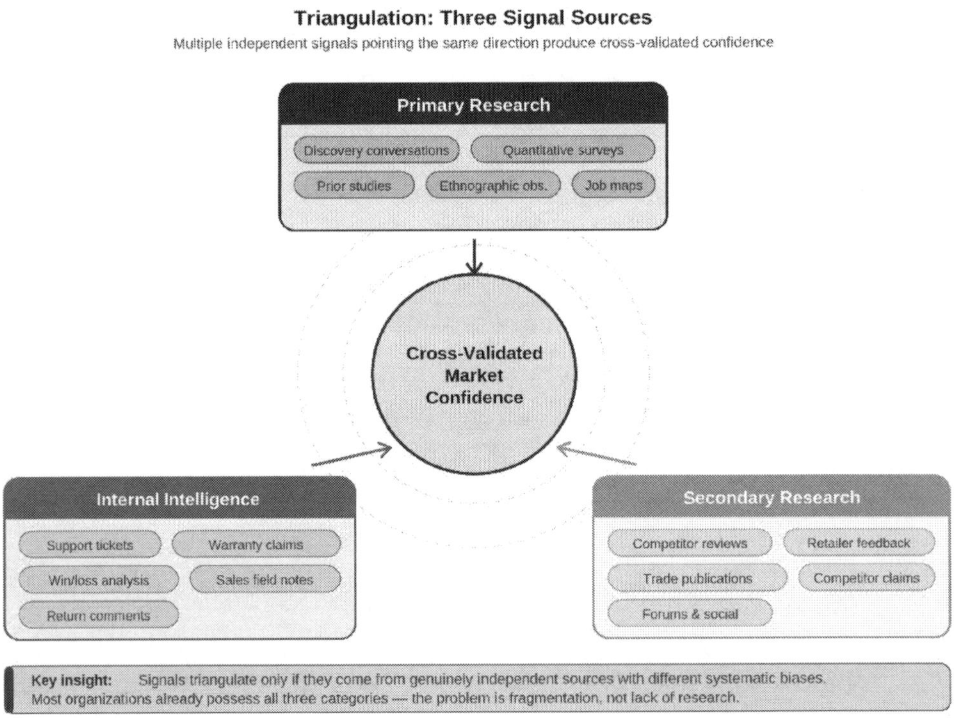

The Scan

The scan is a structured pass through what the organization already knows. The team is answering one question: what do we already have?

The scan covers three categories of sources. Primary research includes everything the organization has conducted directly with customers: the current survey, the discovery interviews, any prior qualitative studies, ethnographic observations and usability sessions. These are the highest-quality sources because they capture the customer experience directly. Their limitation is that each ages, and each is vulnerable to the methodological constraints of the approach used.

Internal intelligence includes data generated by the organization's own operations: support tickets, warranty claims, win/loss analyses, return comments and sales field notes. This captures real customer behavior rather than reported preferences, which gives it a different and complementary kind of validity. But each source was originally built for a purpose other than market insight, which shapes what it can and cannot see.

Secondary research includes publicly available information about the market and competitive landscape: competitor product reviews, trade publication roundups, category trend reports, competitor marketing language and community forums. This reveals how the broader market is moving and how competitors are interpreting customer needs. What it lacks is direct customer voice and the job-level specificity that primary research provides.

For each source the team identifies, one question matters: does this source have anything to say about the job-to-be-done and the criteria that were evaluated within the survey? Not every source will speak to every criterion, and that is expected. A source without data on a particular criterion simply has nothing to contribute for that row.

The output of the scan is not a finished analysis. It is a map of what exists. That provides input to the Signal Translator, the tool that will normalize and synthesize what the scan has surfaced.

What Comes Next

The scan produces something the team did not have before: a clear view of what evidence exists and where it lives. The organization's signals are no longer hidden across systems and functions. They are visible, named, and connected to the Job Success Criteria that define the market.

That visibility is necessary, but it is not yet useful. At this point, the team has an inventory, not an analysis. The signals still exist in their native forms, shaped by the methods that produced them. A survey expresses itself in scores. Support data appears as counts and categories. Retailer feedback lives in unstructured notes. Each source contains real insight, but none can yet be placed side by side in a way that supports decision-making.

The challenge now is practical. How do you take these fundamentally different forms of evidence and make them comparable?

That requires more than collecting inputs. It requires a structure for translating them. The next chapter introduces that structure. It moves from identifying signals to operationalizing them, showing how to build the Signal Translator and turn a fragmented set of inputs into a unified, decision-ready view of the market.

Key Takeaways

- A strong study is valuable. More evidence is better. A well-executed survey produces a finding worth taking seriously. It does not produce certainty. Additional signals from different sources reduce residual uncertainty further, and those signals often already exist inside the organization.
- Every method has structural blind spots. Qualitative research sees depth, not scale. Quantitative research sees scale, not context. Internal data sees behavior, not intent. Secondary research sees category movement, not specific customer needs. These are not failures. They are inherent to each method, and they define what multiple sources can together accomplish that none can alone.
- Science and law have already solved this problem. When a single study leaves residual uncertainty and the stakes are high, the answer is a meta-analysis: multiple independent sources, properly synthesized. Product strategy has the same stakes. Building this practice into the Discovery process is uncommon. It shouldn't be.
- Most product teams treat the study as the answer. This leaves them exposed to whatever biases and errors are inherent to a single method, and it ignores evidence already sitting in the organization that could strengthen or challenge the finding.
- Fragmentation is the real enemy. The signals exist. They live in different places, owned by different functions, and are never synthesized. The solution is not more research. It is a systematic way to connect what already exists.
- The scan is an inventory, not an analysis. Before signals can be synthesized, they have to be found. The scan is a pass through primary research, internal intelligence, and secondary research.

Where We Are in DISCOVER

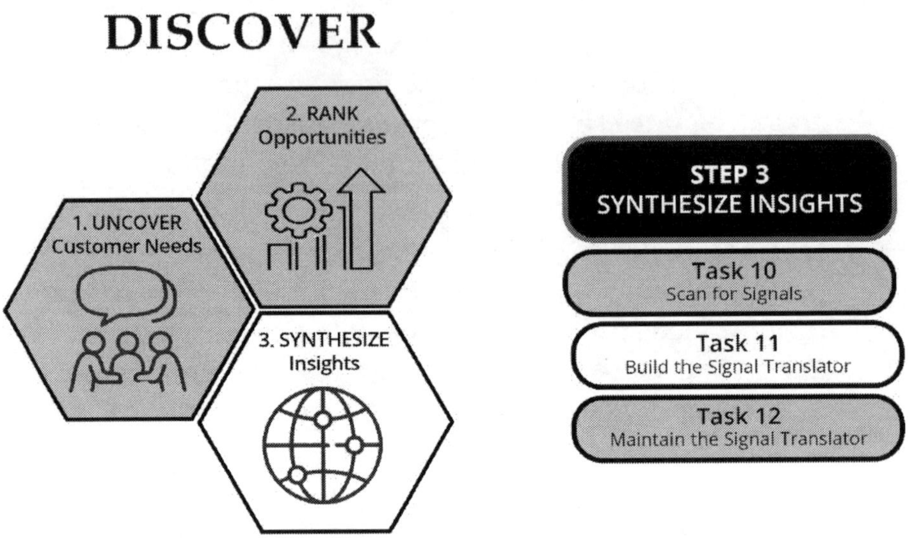

Step 3, Task 11: Build the Signal Translator

What this chapter helps you to do

Organize interviews, surveys, and other customer insight sources into a system for analysis.

What you will have by the end

A working Signal Translator that helps you synthesize multiple sources of customer knowledge into opportunity patterns.

Coming next

Task 12: Maintain the Signal Translator

Chapter 21: Task 11, Build the Signal Translator

Everything Speaks a Different Language

THE TEAM FOUND MORE POSSIBILITIES than they could have imagined just days earlier. The whiteboard still held Shelton's list from the afternoon before.

Discovery interviews. Surveys. Retailer feedback. Customer support. Warranty claims. Product reviews. Prior research.

Tom looked at it. "So now we just compare them?"

Luis shook his head slowly. "That's harder than it sounds."

Jenna pulled up the survey output on her laptop. "The survey gives us numbers. Opportunity Scores. Importance ratings. Satisfaction gaps." She turned the screen toward the group. "What does support give us?"

Luis opened another window. "Issue categories and ticket counts. The top category this quarter is setup difficulty in adverse conditions. 147 tickets."

Tom had the retailer notes open on his tablet. "Retailer feedback isn't even structured. It's call notes. 'Customers keep asking about how to re-waterproof their tent.' Others, for years, have complained about the stretch cords inside the pole systems losing their stretchiness. What are we supposed to do with that? No numbers or anything with those."

Jenna scrolled further. "And PCT hiker interviews from their trail-days event. Themes were coded as high, medium, or low. No scores at all."

The room was quiet for a moment.

"So we have lots of sources," Shelton said, "each telling us something real, and no way to put them side by side."

"An Opportunity Score of 12.7, a ticket count of 847, and a call note," Luis said. "Those aren't the same kind of thing."

"No," Shelton said. "They're not. Which means before we can compare them, we have to translate them." He uncapped a marker and drew a large grid on the whiteboard. Across the top, he wrote the sources. On the left side, he created a column heading: Job Success Criteria.

Tom watched the grid take shape. "Each criterion gets scored from every source?"

"Once we normalize them onto a common scale," Shelton said. "Then yes. Everything speaks the same language."

Jenna leaned forward. "That's what researchers do when they combine studies from different labs. They translate the results into a common metric first."

"Exactly," Shelton said. He wrote two words at the top of the board: Meta-Analysis. Then, below them, two more words.

Signal Translator.

"This," he said, tapping the grid, "is what we've been building toward since the start."

The Translation Problem

A set of signals is a valuable asset. The problem is that the signals cannot be compared directly in their natural state.

An Opportunity Score is a calculated value derived from paired importance and satisfaction ratings across hundreds of respondents. A support ticket count is the frequency of reported incidents over a defined time period. Retailer field notes are a set of qualitative observations captured from sales calls. A discovery interview theme coded as high-frequency is a judgment about how often a pattern appeared across sessions. These are not different measurements of the same thing. They are different things entirely, produced by different methods, scaled differently, and reflecting different aspects of customer reality.

Placing them side by side without a translation layer does not produce an analysis. It produces a list. The team may notice that multiple sources seem to point toward the same criteria. However, they cannot answer the question that matters: how well-supported is the finding across the full body of evidence? Is the support ticket data confirming the survey finding strongly or weakly? Is the retailer feedback adding meaningfully to the picture, or does it reflect too small a sample to carry real weight?

Direct comparison fails because each format reflects the nature of the source that produced it. None of those sources was designed to be compared to the others. Doing so without a translation layer creates the appearance of convergence without the substance of it.

However, the translation layer that makes genuine comparison possible already exists. It was built during the first tasks of the Discovery Engine.

Job Success Criteria as the Common Language

At the center of the Jobs-to-be-Done framework is a straightforward premise: customers hire products to perform a job, and they evaluate how well that job is performed using a consistent set of standards. Those standards are Job Success Criteria. They describe, in precise and measurable language, what excellent performance looks like from the customer's perspective.

This is what makes Job Success Criteria the right backbone for a meta-analysis in product management. Every signal from every source, regardless of format, can be mapped to a Job Success Criterion. A support ticket about stakes not holding in rocky ground maps to a criterion about staking reliability. A retailer's note about customers asking for faster setup in bad weather maps to a criterion about setup time in deteriorating conditions. A product review praising a competitor's storm door design maps to a criterion about rain exposure during setup. The criterion is the translation unit.

The Signal Translator turns scattered evidence into a machine for decision-making.

It is the common denominator that allows fundamentally different types of evidence to be placed in the same row of the same grid and assessed as evidence about the same underlying customer need.

Triangulation in product development is not about combining data. It is about translating data into a shared language first. Job Success Criteria provide that language.

The Jobs-to-be-Done Pyramid as Classification Structure

For a more robust Signal Translator, the Jobs-to-be-Done Pyramid can be used to further classify categories of customer objectives.

Not all signals refer to the same level of customer motivation. Support tickets and warranty claims tend to reflect Product Job failures, specific operational breakdowns at the product level. Survey data about importance and satisfaction tends to reflect Core Job performance, and how well the product enables the customer to accomplish their primary goal.

For the more ambitious, Identity and Emotional Jobs can be captured and compared to various signals using the Jobs-to-be-Done Pyramid classification system, but that would be a post-MVP (post "Minimum Viable Product") activity. In other words, it's more important to build the Signal Translator to understand customer priorities for functional needs first.

What the Signal Translator Is

The Signal Translator is a tool. It is the artifact that the meta-analysis process produces.

In structure, it is a grid. Each row is a Job Success Criterion. Each column is a signal source. Each cell contains a normalized score representing how strongly that source indicates that the criterion is important and underserved. The grid allows the team to look across each row and see, at a glance, which criteria are supported by multiple strong signals and which rest primarily on a single source.

It does not generate new insight per se. It produces stronger clarity about what is already present within existing insight. The survey has already identified the top opportunities. The Signal Translator validates that map against everything else the organization knows and shows where the evidence is aligned and where it is thin.

It is worth being explicit about what is unusual here. Most product teams, regardless of research approach, stop at a single study. The survey, the customer interview series, the focus group, the win/loss analysis, whichever method the team used, becomes the answer. That is understandable. A strong finding is compelling. But it is also a bet that the method captured reality without significant distortion.

The Signal Translator provides better information for a better bet. It is standard practice in science and law that when the stakes are high, you seek more evidence, synthesize it, and build confidence where independent sources point to the same conclusion. In product management, this practice is rare. The Signal Translator is the tool that enables this to work.

Normalization: Making Unlike Things Comparable

The mechanics of the Signal Translator begin with normalization: the process of converting each source's signals into a consistent scale so that unlike formats can be placed side by side meaningfully.

The goal is comparability, not false precision. The team is not producing mathematically exact measurements from qualitative sources. They are creating a consistent language that allows signals of different types to be assessed against the same scale, without one type dominating or disappearing simply because of the format in which it was produced.

Here is one way to create a scoring and normalization scheme:

Use a 1-to-100 scale with defined anchor tiers, calibrated against ODI Opportunity Scores so that the tiers carry consistent meaning across sources.

The score represents the degree to which that source indicates the criterion is an underserved market opportunity: important to customers and poorly served by current solutions.

We could use five grades, scored from A, B, C, D, and F.

A score in the 81-to-100 range, for an A, indicates the source strongly suggests the criterion is an extreme opportunity: active frustration, frequent workarounds, a gap customers feel acutely, painfully, and often. These would correspond to an Opportunity Score of 15 or greater.

The 61-to-80 range, for a B, indicates a high opportunity: the gap is real and influences decisions. These are substantial problems, but without the height of frustration delivered in an A. These would correspond to an Opportunity Score of 12-15.

The 41-to-60 range, for a C, indicates a moderate opportunity: the market is partially served, and some customers feel the gap, while others are reasonably satisfied. Many customers have found workarounds and have addressed the issue on their own. These would correspond to an Opportunity Score of 9-11.9.

The 21-to-40 range, for a D, indicates a low opportunity: current solutions are largely meeting the need. These would correspond to an Opportunity Score of 6-8.9.

A score of 1-to-20, for an F, indicates no meaningful opportunity, or that the criterion is overserved. Investment here risks over-engineering something the market does not value enough to drive decisions. These correspond to an Opportunity Score of less than 6.

Unscored criteria are a separate matter entirely. Many sources will not address certain criteria. They were scoped differently, generated by a different customer interaction, or focused on a different aspect of the job-to-be-done. A criterion that goes unscored in a particular column is not a low-opportunity indicator. It is the absence of data. The cell stays empty.

How a scorer gets to a number depends on what the source actually is. For data sources that are already numerical, such as survey Opportunity Scores, support ticket counts, and warranty claim frequencies, the conversion to the 1-to-100 scale can be done with a straightforward formula. Define the conversion logic once, apply it consistently, and the scores follow automatically without any subjective judgment required.

For qualitative sources, or any source with a small sample size, there is no formula. A handful of retailer call notes, a win/loss summary from six conversations, or a set of discovery interview themes requires a different approach. These require the scorer to read the evidence and assign a number based on the anchor tier descriptions.

These definitions must be written down and agreed upon before scoring begins, and they must be applied consistently within each source. Whatever logic produces a high score for one criterion in the support ticket column must be applied the same way to every other criterion in that column. This discipline is what separates a genuine synthesis from a scorecard that simply reflects the team's existing beliefs.

Not every source will have data on every criterion. Some sources were simply not scoped to certain needs. Where a source has nothing to say about a criterion, the cell stays empty. The criterion's combined signal strength is built from the sources that speak to it, and the confidence behind it reflects how many independent sources are contributing.

The Signal Translator™

Job Success Criteria x Signal Sources x Normalized to a 1-100 scale

Job Success Criteria Tent - Weekend Backpackers	Survey	Win/Loss Study	Cust Support	Retailer Feedback	Product Reviews	Warranty Data	Qual Study	Average
Minimize the time to establish shelter when weather deteriorates	95	98	80	79	67	62	61	77
Minimize the amount of rain exposure inside tent during setup	90	85	65	80	83	60	44	72
Minimize the time to stake the tent on rocky terrain	85	64	85	65	65	83	38	69
Minimize the time to pack up the tent	52	25	30	60	61	52	49	47
Minimize the amount of condensation that collects in the tent overnight	55	23	26	33	55	34	48	39

Scoring and Weighting

With quantitative and qualitative signals translated into a 1-to-100 score, they can be averaged into an overall score. The process of averaging also handles the reality that different criteria will have different numbers of direct signals.

However, with the differences in the number of sources, it can be useful to weight the sources. If one source was fielded with rigorous controls and another was gathered informally from a handful of conversations, there is a reasonable argument for treating them differently.

Signal Translator: Scoring Reference

Range	Interpretation	ODI Opportunity Score
81–100	**Extreme Opportunity** The criterion is highly important to customers, and current solutions are failing to address it in a meaningful way. Evidence of active frustration, frequent workarounds, or significant unmet need. Customers feel the gap acutely. This is where markets are most vulnerable to disruption and where well-targeted solutions earn the strongest response.	>15
61–80	**High Opportunity** The criterion matters significantly to customers, and existing solutions are falling short, though not as dramatically as the top tier. Customers notice the gap, and it influences decisions, but they may have found partial workarounds or accepted some degree of underservice. A clear target for differentiation.	12–15
41–60	**Moderate Opportunity** The criterion is real, but the market is partially served. Some customers feel the gap; others are reasonably satisfied. Investment here may improve the product without producing a decisive competitive advantage. Worth monitoring, but unlikely to be a primary strategic driver.	10–11.9
21–40	**Low Opportunity** Current solutions largely meet this need. Customers may care about the criterion, but are not experiencing significant failure. Improving performance here is unlikely to move purchase decisions in a meaningful way.	7–9.9
1–20	**No Opportunity / Overserved** The criterion is well-addressed by current solutions, or customers do not weigh it heavily enough to create a gap worth closing. Investment here risks over-engineering a dimension of performance that the market does not value at a level that drives decisions.	<7

But weighting introduces a risk: the tendency for decisions to be influenced, consciously or not, by the conclusion the team or its stakeholders prefer. A team already committed to a product direction will often find reasons to weight the sources that support that direction and discount the ones that challenge it. Weighting usually makes sense, but it should be performed with caution and with a clear intention not to use it to drive a desired conclusion.

What This Unlocks

Without a structure like the Signal Translator, teams default to whichever signal source is most available. Survey data, because it is numerical, tends to dominate. Qualitative signals get acknowledged in presentations and quietly set aside when actual decisions get made. Internal data gets reviewed in isolation by the functions that own it and rarely reaches the product strategy conversation at all.

With the Signal Translator, something different becomes possible. The survey finding that setup time in deteriorating weather is a top priority becomes substantially more actionable when multiple independent sources point to the same conclusion. The team's confidence is no longer resting on a single instrument and its inherent limitations. It is grounded in the kind of cross-validated evidence that characterizes the strongest strategic decisions.

Once the Signal Translator has been used to develop a product strategy, it can be tempting to think the work is done. In reality, the team is on the precipice of building a living insight system to continue for many years to come. That is the topic of the next and final chapter.

What Comes Next

The Signal Translator brings the Discovery Engine to a meaningful point of completion. The team now has a unified view of customer needs, grounded in multiple sources and translated into a common language. What began as scattered signals is now a coherent, evidence-based picture of where the market is underserved.

At this stage, it is natural to think the work is finished. In one sense, it is. The highest-priority Job Success Criteria are clear, the opportunity landscape is defined, and the evidence holds together across sources.

But this moment also marks the beginning of something more powerful. The Signal Translator is not just a synthesis of past work. It is a structure that can absorb new evidence over time. Each additional research activity, whether a new survey, another round of interviews, or fresh support and field data, does not replace what came before. It strengthens it. As more signals are added, patterns become clearer, weak signals either fade or gain support, and confidence in the opportunity map increases.

This is the shift from a one-time insight to a compounding system. The value does not come only from preserving accuracy as the market changes. It comes from building a deeper, more resilient understanding with each new source of evidence. Over time, the Signal Translator becomes not just a snapshot of the market, but a progressively sharper lens on it.

The next chapter moves from constructing the Signal Translator to maintaining and evolving it as a living system, one that grows more valuable with every new signal the organization captures.

Key Takeaways

- Direct comparison of disparate signals fails without a translation layer. An Opportunity Score, a ticket count, and a field sales note are not the same kind of thing. Placing them side by side without normalization creates the appearance of analysis, not the substance of it.
- Job Success Criteria are the common language that makes synthesis possible. Every signal from every source can be mapped to a criterion regardless of format. The JSC is the translation unit: the row in the grid that absorbs fundamentally different types of evidence about the same underlying customer need.
- The Signal Translator is a tool. It is the artifact the meta-analysis process produces: a grid of Job Success Criteria, signal sources, and normalized scores. It produces stronger confidence in existing insight.
- Not every source speaks to every criterion. Confidence is built from the sources that do contribute, and the number of contributing sources is itself information about how strongly a criterion is supported.
- Most product teams stop at a single study. The Signal Translator is what the Discovery Engine does instead: it validates the primary research finding against the full body of evidence the organization already has.

Where We Are in DISCOVER

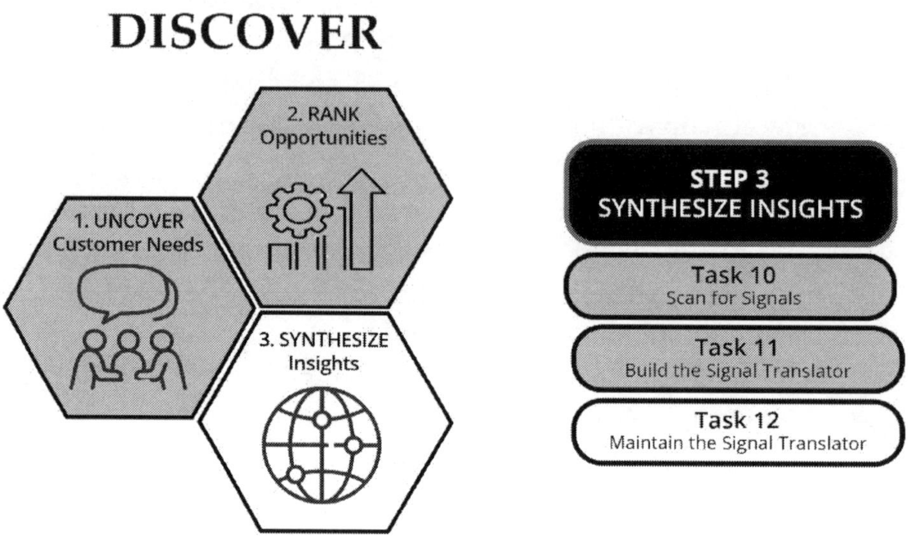

Step 3, Task 12: Maintain the Signal Translator

What this chapter helps you do

Keep the Signal Translator current as new customer knowledge emerges, so discovery becomes a living system rather than a one-time project.

What you will have by the end

A practical approach for updating, challenging, and improving the customer insight system over time.

Coming next

Epilogue: A look ahead to STRATEGIZE, Book 2 of the Prismatic Product System.

Chapter 22: Task 12, Maintain the Signal Translator

Celebration

THE FIRST PRODUCTION RUN HAD SOLD OUT IN THREE WEEKS. Retailers were asking for more. The field reps who had spent months collecting backpacker feedback were now fielding calls from buyers who wanted to know when the next shipment was arriving.

Tom lifted his glass. “To the fastest-selling tent Big Sky has ever launched.”

The group laughed and clinked glasses.

Luis looked over at Shelton. “Not bad for a project that started with sticky notes and coffee-shop conversations.”

Jenna smiled. “And a wall of 180 criteria.”

The team laughed again. For a moment, the room settled into the comfortable quiet of a job well done.

Then Tom asked the question.

"So… what's next?"

Luis shrugged. "Another DISCOVER project?"

Shelton nodded slowly. "Probably." He glanced at the laptop sitting open on the table. The Signal Translator was still on the screen. Rows of Job Success Criteria. Columns of signal sources. Survey scores. Conversation signals. Support data. Retailer feedback.

Jenna looked at it. "Do we start over next time?"

Shelton shook his head. He turned the laptop slightly so everyone could see. "This doesn't go away."

Luis frowned slightly. "But the market changes."

"It does," Shelton said. "But the Signal Translator grows with it." He leaned back in his chair. "When we run another study, we add a column. When support trends shift, we update the scores. When a competitor makes a move that changes customer expectations, we record it."

Tom tilted his head. "But won't old studies distort the picture? If we keep the original survey data in there, won't it pull the scores toward what was true two years ago?"

Shelton smiled. He grabbed a napkin and sketched a small diagram. "In forecasting models, evidence can be weighted over time. Recent signals get more weight. Older signals fade gradually, but they don't disappear. Their influence on the current picture should decrease as time passes."

Jenna leaned forward. "So stable problems stay visible."

"And emerging problems appear faster," Shelton said. "The system keeps us grounded in what has always been hard, while still responding when something genuinely changes."

Luis looked back at the screen. "That's a relief. We're not starting over every time."

"We're building," Shelton said. "Every study, every quarter of support data, every round of retailer feedback. It all goes in. Over time, the picture gets clearer. The noise fades away. And the next time will be easier than the first. This becomes a customer cipher. A tool that can decode the mysteries of our markets with increasing accuracy. And better certainty as we go."

The group sat quietly for a moment.

Then Jenna smiled. "You know what we actually built?" She raised her glass slightly. "A system that will still be helping Big Sky understand its market long after we've all moved on."

Luis laughed. "That's a little strange to think about."

"But it's also the point," Shelton said.

Tom lifted his glass. "To the next tent."

Jenna shook her head. "No." She smiled. "To the system that will help build all of them."

The team raised their glasses.

The Problem With Finishing

There is a moment in every research project that feels like completion. The study is done. The findings are presented. The team aligns around the opportunities. Decisions get made. The work moves forward.

That moment is real and worth celebrating. What happens after it is what separates organizations that build durable strategic clarity from those that build only temporary alignment.

In most organizations, the research that produced the alignment gets filed. The slide deck goes into a shared drive. The survey data lives in a folder that gradually becomes harder to find. The Signal Translator, if one were built, sits in a spreadsheet that no one updates because the project that motivated it is over. Twelve months later, when a new product decision requires market understanding, someone pulls out the old research and asks whether it is still current. Often it is not, but the team uses it anyway, because starting over is expensive and time-consuming, and the old data feels close enough.

This is how organizations make strategic decisions based on aging insight, not through negligence or bad intentions, but through a structural failure to treat discovery as an ongoing practice rather than a periodic project. The research was excellent when it was conducted. The market has moved since then. And the gap between what the data shows and what the market currently needs has been growing quietly ever since.

The cost is not just outdated data. It is also the repeated cost of starting over. It is the cost of rebuilding from scratch every few years, which could instead have been maintained and compounded continuously.

The antidote to this failure is not only more research. It is a different relationship with research, one in which discovery is not an event that produces a deliverable, but a practice that produces a continuously updated knowledge base.

The Hidden Advantage: It Gets Easier Over Time

The first Signal Translator is the hardest thing the team will build. It requires a Market Lens, a job map, a full set of discovery interviews, a refined criteria set, a fielded survey, and the painstaking work of normalizing signals from multiple sources onto a common scale.

Every update after the initial build is fundamentally different in character. The framework becomes something new: a continuous

Signal Translator, a self-correcting system that can decode the opportunities within any market with increasing confidence.

This is the compounding dynamic that Shelton described at the celebration. The first Signal Translator is a project. Every update after that is leverage.

A living insight system becomes more valuable each time the market teaches it something new.

Maintaining a Signal Translator over time does not eliminate the need for meaningful discovery work. New Market Lenses, new questions, and new contexts still require depth. But each additional input builds on what already exists, reducing the need to start from scratch and allowing the system to grow in value with every cycle.

The compounding effect extends to organizational learning as well. A team that has maintained a living Signal Translator for several cycles develops an increasingly refined sense of which signals are reliable, which sources tend to lead or lag the market, and which criteria have proven to be genuinely durable versus situationally significant. That calibration is itself a form of competitive knowledge, and it is only available to teams that have stayed with the system long enough to not just build it, but to maintain it.

Organizations that treat every discovery effort as a fresh start from zero do not accumulate this kind of knowledge. They reset it. The Signal Translator, maintained over time, is the mechanism that turns individual research efforts into an organizational capability that grows more powerful with each iteration.

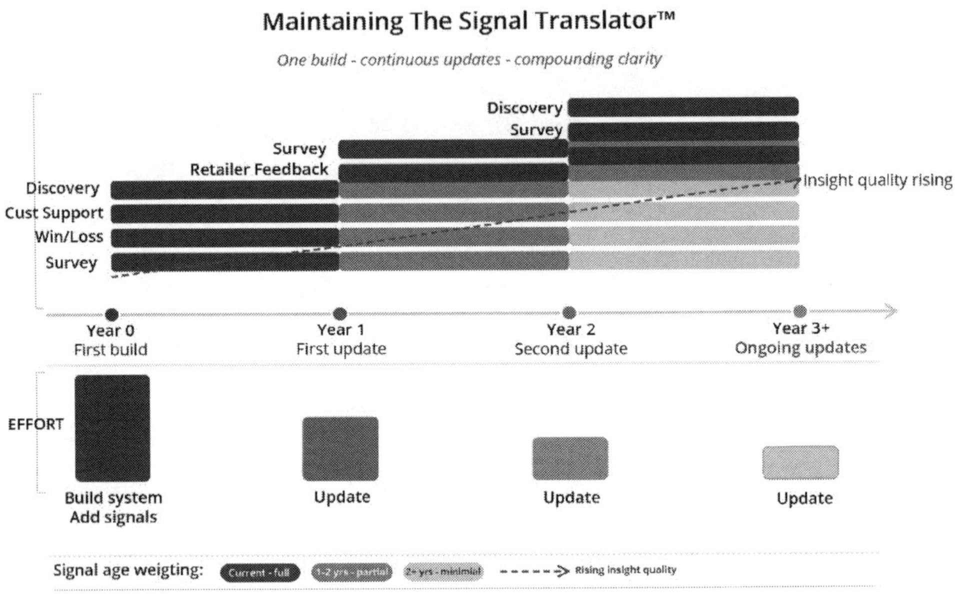

Building a Responsive Model

Evidence does not become wrong simply because it is old. A discovery interview from 18 months ago that revealed genuine customer friction is still evidence that the friction existed. A survey from two years ago that showed high importance and low satisfaction for a particular criterion is still evidence that the criterion mattered to the market at that time.

What changes is the evidence's relevance to the current moment. A market that was characterized by certain patterns two years ago may or may not be characterized by the same patterns today. Competitors have launched new products. Customer expectations have evolved in response to what is now available. Macro conditions, economic pressures, technological shifts, and category trends have influenced what customers prioritize. The older evidence is real, but it describes a past state of the market rather than the current one.

When continually updated, the Signal Translator can handle this by applying a decay principle to older evidence. The specific implementation can vary, but the logic is consistent: signals from the most recent period, such as the last quarter or the last six months, are weighted at full value. Signals from one to two years ago can be weighted at a lower value. Signals from more than two years ago are weighted at minimal value or retired from the active analysis entirely.

The practical effect of this weighting is that the Signal Translator reflects a view of the market that is anchored in current evidence while preserving the historical context that reveals which patterns are stable and which are shifting. A need that scores strongly in both recent and older signals is durable. It has persisted across market conditions and competitor responses. A need that scores strongly in recent signals but weakly in older ones may be emerging. A need that scored strongly in older signals but weakly in recent ones may be fading, which may indicate a problem that competitors have begun to address or that customer expectations have shifted away from.

This temporal dimension is one of the most strategically valuable things a continually updated Signal Translator produces. It converts a static snapshot into a dynamic view, one that reveals not just what the market needs now, but how those needs are changing over time. That is what allows product and strategy teams to get ahead of the market rather than simply reacting to it, and it is what allows the system to improve over time while staying anchored in durable customer challenges.

Making Synthesis Continuous

The transition from a one-time Signal Translator to a continuous Signal Translator requires building the organizational habits and structures that keep the system active.

A continuous Signal Translator has five practical components.

A Central Repository

A single, shared file or platform where the Signal Translator lives and where all team members can access, contribute to, and reference the current state of market understanding. The specific tool matters less than the discipline of using one tool consistently rather than fragmenting the synthesis across multiple systems and individual files.

A Defined Intake Process

A mechanism for capturing new insights as they arrive and routing them to the Signal Translator. Without an intake process, new evidence accumulates in email threads, meeting notes, and individual files and never makes it into the system. A simple shared form that captures the source, the date, the relevant criteria, and a signal strength assessment is sufficient for most organizations. What matters is that the process is habitual, so that when a support trend report arrives, or a retailer field note comes in from the sales team, the path to the Signal Translator is clear and easy.

A Recurring Review Cadence

A scheduled meeting, typically quarterly, where the team examines the Signal Translator together, updates scores based on new evidence, applies time-decay weighting to older signals, and identifies any significant shifts in the opportunity rankings. The quarterly review is where the Signal Translator does its most important work. It is the moment when accumulated new evidence is synthesized into an updated picture of the market. The team asks whether their current strategic direction is still well-grounded in what the market needs.

A Designated Steward

A specific person who owns the Signal Translator, maintains the intake process, facilitates the quarterly reviews, and ensures that the system does not quietly become stale between formal review cycles. The steward does not need to do all of the signal collection or analysis work themselves. Their role is to ensure that the system remains active and that someone is accountable for its currency. In most product organizations, this role naturally falls to a product manager or a customer insights lead.

The steward role carries a requirement that most organizations underestimate. **It requires genuine Jobs-to-be-Done expertise.** Maintaining the Signal Translator accurately is not just a data management task. It requires knowing how to map incoming insight to the correct Job Success Criteria, how to distinguish Product Jobs from Core Jobs, and how to recognize when a new signal is genuinely distinct from existing criteria versus an expression of something already in the system. These are Jobs-to-be-Done judgment calls, and they require someone who understands the framework deeply enough to make them correctly.

This expertise is uncommon in most organizations. Companies that want to maintain a living Signal Translator have two viable paths. The first is to build the expertise internally, which requires genuine investment in Jobs-to-be-Done training and, critically, organizational commitment to keeping Jobs-to-be-Done expert practitioners in the steward role for meaningful lengths of time. The most common way organizations destroy the integrity of their Signal Translator is by developing strong internal Jobs-to-be-Done practitioners and then promoting them into other roles, leaving the system in the hands of someone without the expertise to maintain it accurately. The system degrades slowly and invisibly until the picture it produces is no longer trustworthy.

The second path is to build an ongoing relationship with an external Jobs-to-be-Done practitioner who can serve as a periodic steward and calibration resource, someone who participates in the quarterly reviews, helps the internal team map new signals correctly, and ensures that the framework is being applied with the precision the system requires. This is not a sign of organizational weakness. It is an honest recognition that Jobs-to-be-Done expertise is a specialized capability that takes years to develop, and that the value of maintaining a high-integrity Signal Translator far exceeds the cost of the expertise required to do it well.

A Communication Rhythm

A regular cadence for sharing the updated Signal Translator outputs with the broader team and with relevant stakeholders. It only creates organizational value if the understanding it produces is accessible to the people making product, marketing, and strategy decisions. A quarterly synthesis summary, a brief document highlighting which opportunity patterns remain stable, which are emerging, and which are fading, keeps the broader organization connected to the current state of market understanding without requiring everyone to engage with the full Signal Translator directly.

For Big Sky, this might look like a shared file maintained by Shelton, updated quarterly with inputs from the support team, the field sales organization, and a rotating schedule of fresh customer conversations. The quarterly review takes two hours. The synthesis summary takes a page. The investment is modest. The strategic value, a continuously current view of where the market most needs improvement, is substantial.

What Continuous Synthesis Makes Possible

An updated Signal Translator produces a different kind of market understanding than any single study can generate.

A single well-executed study produces a snapshot, a precise and reliable picture of the market at a specific moment. A continuously updated Signal Translator produces a longitudinal view, a picture of how the market is moving over time. These are not the same thing, and the difference matters enormously for strategic decision making.

The longitudinal view enables five capabilities that the snapshot cannot.

Distinguishing durable needs from temporary noise

Markets are full of signals that appear important in a single study but fade as conditions change. A Signal Translator, by tracking signals across multiple time periods, separates patterns that persist from those that are momentary. The needs that score consistently high across multiple updates are genuinely durable. The needs that spike and fade are noise, and treating them as strategic priorities is an expensive mistake.

Detecting meaningful departures from established patterns

A continuously updated Signal Translator establishes a baseline of how needs behave over time. When a new signal departs sharply from that baseline, the system makes that deviation immediately visible. This can indicate that something in the market has changed in a meaningful way, such as a new constraint, a shift in customer expectations, or a competitive move that is altering behavior. It can also indicate that the signal itself is flawed, such as a poorly executed discovery effort, a biased sample, or inconsistent measurement. In either case, the deviation becomes a prompt for investigation. Instead of accepting new inputs at face value, the team can quickly determine whether the change reflects a real shift in the market or a problem with how the signal was generated.

Detecting emerging needs before they become dominant

Some of the most significant market shifts begin as weak signals, small increases in support ticket volume, subtle shifts in the language customers use in reviews, or early competitor moves that have not yet altered customer expectations but signal where the market is heading. A team that reviews its Signal Translator quarterly will notice these weak signals accumulating before they become loud enough to be undeniable. A team that conducts research every two years will notice them only after they have already reshaped the competitive landscape.

Tracking the effectiveness of strategic decisions

When a product or positioning change is made in response to a high-priority opportunity, the Signal Translator provides a structured way to monitor whether the change is having the intended effect. If satisfaction scores on the criteria the product was designed to address begin rising in subsequent surveys and support ticket volumes on those criteria begin falling, the system detects evidence that the strategy is working. If those scores remain flat or worsen, the system detects evidence that the strategy has not addressed the underlying need.

Reducing organizational dependence on opinion

In the absence of current market intelligence, product and strategy decisions tend to be made based on the opinions of the most senior or most persuasive voices in the room. A Signal Translator that is current, accessible, and trusted provides an alternative: a shared empirical reference point that grounds debates in evidence rather than opinion. It does not eliminate disagreement, but it changes its nature, from competing beliefs about what customers want to competing interpretations of what the evidence shows, which is a far more productive conversation.

What Comes Next

Discovery has done its work.

The Big Sky team has not simply uncovered customer needs. They have mapped them, measured them, prioritized them, cross-validated them across multiple independent sources, and built a system for keeping their understanding current. The market is no longer a collection of impressions and assumptions. It is a structured, evidence-based picture of where customers most need improvement and where existing solutions fall furthest short.

Now a different question emerges: What should we do about it? That question, how to turn market understanding into competitive strategy and winning products, is the work of the next phase of Prism, STRATEGIZE. The final chapter of this book examines that transition: what discovery has produced, what it makes possible, and where the journey from customer understanding to market-winning innovation goes next.

Key Takeaways

- Research clarity is perishable. A Signal Translator built once and never updated will accurately reflect the market as it was when the study was conducted, and become increasingly unreliable as the market moves forward. The cost of this is not just outdated data — it is the repeated cost of starting over.
- The first Signal Translator is the hardest build. Every update after that is leverage. The Market Lens, job map, and Job Success Criteria only need to be created once. Subsequent cycles add evidence to an existing structure rather than rebuilding the foundation.
- Evidence ages at different rates. A Signal Translator applies time-decay weighting to older signals, giving recent evidence more influence on the current picture while preserving historical context that reveals which patterns are stable and which are shifting.
- A system for maintaining the Signal Translator as a living insight system has five components: a central repository, a defined intake process, a recurring quarterly review cadence, a designated steward, and a communication rhythm for sharing updated outputs with the broader organization.
- The steward role requires genuine Jobs-to-be-Done expertise. Maintaining Signal Translator accuracy is not a data management task. It requires the ability to map signals correctly, distinguish job levels, and apply the framework with precision. This expertise is uncommon. Organizations must either build it internally with a genuine commitment to retaining it or maintain an ongoing relationship with an external Jobs-to-be-Done practitioner.
- Continuous synthesis produces strategic capabilities that no single study can generate, including the ability to distinguish

durable needs from temporary noise and to detect emerging needs before they become dominant.

- The Signal Translator has value far beyond product development. It informs marketing and messaging, website positioning, sales conversations, and M&A decisions. It is not a product tool. It is a market truth system.
- A well-maintained Signal Translator is an early warning system. It tells the organization what the market is becoming, not just what it was. Over time, that foresight compounds into one of the few genuinely sustainable sources of competitive advantage.
- DISCOVER is a practice. A disciplined, repeatable way of building and maintaining structured market understanding that becomes more valuable over time as evidence accumulates and patterns become clearer.

V. EPILOGUE: From Needs to Product Strategy — A Preview of STRATEGIZE

What You Now Have

You began this book the way most product teams begin: with a mandate, a set of assumptions, and a strong instinct to start generating ideas. You end it with something more valuable than ideas. You have a method: a repeatable, structured system for turning customer conversations into market intelligence that is precise enough to act on and robust enough to trust.

You know how to define a Market Lens that anchors discovery to the right customer in the right context. You know how to map the job, not just the obvious central action, but the full sequence of work from beginning to end, including the steps where friction hides quietly and unexamined. You know how to plan and execute a customer interview, probing for breadth and depth. You know how to translate vague customer language into precise Job Success Criteria, how to measure those criteria across a market, how to rank them by the size of the opportunity they represent, and how to cross-validate what the data shows against the full body of evidence your organization already possesses.

You know, perhaps most importantly, that discovery is not a project. *It is a practice.* A Signal Translator, maintained and updated over time, becomes more valuable with each passing quarter, a continuously current view of where your market most needs improvement and where strategy should focus.

That capability, once built, is tremendously difficult for competitors to replicate. It results in a moat, wide and deep. It is not a framework they can copy or a tool they can purchase. It is an organizational habit, a way of seeing the market that produces better decisions across every function and every stage of the product lifecycle.

What Comes Next

The Discovery Engine has done its job. The team knows what job customers are trying to accomplish, how they judge whether it was done well, and where existing solutions are falling short. That is genuinely hard-won clarity. But there is more to do.

Knowing where the opportunity lies is not the same as knowing what to do about it. That is where STRATEGIZE begins.

Before getting there, it is worth stepping back for a moment. Early in this book, we described the innovation process as two cycles of diverge-then-converge. DISCOVER was the first: exploring the full landscape of customer needs, then narrowing to the opportunities worth pursuing. STRATEGIZE and EXECUTE together form the second: expanding outward to consider what the product could be, then converging on what it should be. The work in this book was always the first half of something larger. STRATEGIZE is where the second half starts.

STRATEGIZE covers Steps 4 through 6 of the Prismatic Product System. In Step 4, Develop Adjacency Strategy, we introduce a model for growth that starts from safe, occupied ground and moves deliberately toward attractive opportunities just beyond it. Not reckless bets. Intelligent ones, with a real understanding of where the risk lies and why the move is worth making.

In Step 5, Target a Winning Position, we work through the discipline of positioning. This is the process by which a company decides what it wants to be known for, carves out a distinctive space in the customer's mind, and makes that position credible enough to hold.

In Step 6, Build the Product Strategy, we translate that targeted position into something concrete: a strategic blueprint that becomes the foundation for product design. Designing the actual product is the work of the third book, EXECUTE.

EXECUTE is where strategy meets reality. It addresses how organizations take everything DISCOVER uncovered, and STRATEGIZE planned, and turn it into something a customer can actually buy, with the same rigor the first two phases demanded. A market-winning strategy that gets compromised during development will not create a competitive advantage.

Together, the three phases form a complete path from customer understanding to market-winning innovation. Each one sharpens the next. Discovery makes the strategy clearer. Strategy makes execution more focused. And when the work is done with discipline at every stage, the results compound in ways that intuition-driven product development simply cannot match.

Author's Note

Honest confession: the framework in this book is not difficult to understand. Applying it for the first time is a different story.

Most teams hit friction in three places. Running discovery interviews well requires trained moderators and enough awareness of confirmation bias to catch it before it shapes the findings. Designing a quantitative survey that produces results worth acting on is harder than it looks, even for teams that have done research before. And building and maintaining the Signal Translator requires Jobs-to-be-Done expertise that is rarely available in-house, and the gap tends to be invisible until the first mapping decision needs to be made and nobody in the room is quite sure how to make it.

Here is something worth being direct about: most companies will ultimately bring in outside help for at least part of this work. That is not a failure. It is a reasonable response to the reality that Jobs-to-be-Done expertise takes time to develop, and that the cost of getting the foundational research wrong is high.

But here is what makes the difference between companies that get amazing results from that partnership and companies that do not. The best results come when the people inside the company understand the process well enough to be genuine partners in it. A product leader who can use their domain expertise to evaluate and improve Job Success Criteria. A leadership team that appreciates the power of a Signal Translator and enforces the discipline to maintain it. Understanding the process, even when someone else is executing key steps, puts you in a position to get far more from it.

If you want to talk through where your team is and what would actually help, I would enjoy that conversation. Here is how to do that:

To connect with me directly:
www.wscottburleson.com

For free resources, including templates, book summaries, and thought-pieces on jobs-to-be-done and product management:
www.LearnPM.pro

To learn more about the Prismatic Product System™:
www.Prismatics.pro

The work of innovation is genuinely worth doing well. It's not just about building better products. It's about seeing your market more clearly than your competitors do, and acting on that clarity with confidence.

Once you begin working this way, it becomes difficult to go back. Assumptions feel incomplete. Opinions feel ungrounded. You start to expect evidence, structure, and precision in how decisions are made.

I hope this book made that shift a little more accessible. The voyage of discovery has many rewards.

See you in STRATEGIZE.

About the Author

W. SCOTT BURLESON is the creator of the Prismatic Product System™, a structured approach for turning customer understanding into clear product direction. DISCOVER is the first of three books in the series, followed by STRATEGIZE and EXECUTE.

He is also the creator of the Jobs-to-be-Done Pyramid™, a framework for understanding customer motivation across functional, identity, and emotional dimensions. His work focuses on helping teams move beyond surface-level insights to uncover what customers are truly trying to accomplish and to translate that understanding into confident product decisions.

Scott brings systems-level thinking to the practices of product management and innovation, a perspective shaped early in his career as a manufacturing engineer at Converse.

He has led customer insight and product development efforts across a wide range of markets, working with organizations to build discovery systems that produce decision-ready insight. As a former Director of the Strategyn Institute, he trained under Tony Ulwick and applies the principles of Jobs-to-be-Done in a practical, system-oriented way, helping teams navigate the complexity of real customer environments.

Earlier in his career, Scott developed the product strategy behind one of John Deere's most successful offerings, the 1-Series tractors, grounding the work in deep customer understanding and measurable success criteria. That experience shaped his belief that great products are not the result of better ideas, but of better insight. That insight must be built, maintained, and continuously refined through a disciplined system, executed by an engaged, cross-functional team.

In addition to *DISCOVER: From Customer Noise to Product Signal*, he is the author of *The Jobs-to-be-Done Pyramid*™ and *The Statue in the Stone: Decoding Customer Motivation with the 48 Laws of Jobs-to-be-Done.* He also writes about product discovery, customer insight, and innovation strategy. His work reflects a consistent focus on clarity, structure, and practical application.

As Chief Product Officer of The AIM Institute, Scott leads product strategy for a portfolio of software products serving industrial B2B manufacturers.

Made in the USA
Monee, IL
16 September 2026

63296733R00236